Sport Facility Management

Organizing Events and Mitigating Risks

— SECOND EDITION —

Robin Ammon, Jr., EdD
Slippery Rock University

Richard M. Southall, EdD
University of North Carolina at Chapel Hill

Mark S. Nagel, EdD
University of South Carolina

Fitness Information Technology

A Division of the International Center
for Performance Excellence
West Virginia University
262 Coliseum, WVU-CPASS
PO Box 6116
Morgantown, WV 26506-6116

Library of Congress Card Catalog Number: 2009943328

ISBN: 978-1-935412-07-6

Cover Design: Bellerophon Productions
Cover Photo: Lucas Oil Stadium opening night (Photo © MediaWright
    Photography, used with permission)
Typesetter: Bellerophon Productions
Production Editor: Val Gittings
Copyeditor: Maria denBoer
Printed by Thomson-Shore, Inc.

10 9 8 7 6 5 4 3 2

Fitness Information Technology
A Division of the International Center for Performance Excellence
West Virginia University
262 Coliseum, WVU-CPASS
PO Box 6116
Morgantown, WV 26506-6116
800.477.4348 (toll free)
304.293.6888 (phone)
304.293.6658 (fax)
Email: fitcustomerservice@mail.wvu.edu
Website: www.fitinfotech.com

Sport Facility Management

Titles in the Sport Management Library

Contents

Acknowledgments

I'd like to acknowledge Jason Fleming, Todd Seidler, and the Fresno Grizzlies for their assistance with photos, and my graduate assistant, Mike Ruffing, for developing the Power Point slides.

—RA

To Robin Ammon and Mark Nagel, thanks for allowing me to work with you on this text. To my current and former students, thanks for wanting to learn and grow. And, most importantly, to my family, thanks for all your support and love.

—RS

Special thanks for the continued support from my family and from my colleagues in the Department of Sport and Entertainment Management at the University of South Carolina.

—MN

1

Introduction

Preliminary Thoughts

The intention of this textbook is to provide you with a vast amount of information while increasing your awareness of the sport facility and event management industry. In addition, the information in this textbook is organized and presented in a clear, concise, and easy to comprehend manner. Finally, much of the material presented is practical and easy to apply to real-world experiences.

Many of you may not be considering a career in sport facility or event management. Hopefully, once you have read this textbook you will see the benefits and opportunities in this growing and exciting industry. Even if you never work in facility operations, it is imperative that you understand the issues and concerns event and facility managers face every day.

Some basic information needs to be briefly discussed before any specifics are explored. Sport and entertainment *events* occur in many shapes and sizes. The Olympics, the Fédération Internationale de Football Association's (FIFA) World Cup, a Rolling Stones concert, a Six Nations Championship Rugby match, the X-Games, the Ringling Brothers and Barnum and Bailey Circus, a local 5K road race, and a high school field hockey game are just a few examples of the thousands that take place. The *facilities* where these events occur also come in a variety of shapes and sizes: stadiums, arenas, ice rinks, ski areas, golf courses, tennis courts, football fields, and high school gymnasiums. Finally, each event and facility has specific *risks* associated with it: slips and falls, inadequate insurance, defective equipment, poor planning, foul balls and broken bats, poor supervision, lack of adequately trained staff, and intoxicated spectators exhibiting inappropriate behavior. And certainly one of the most amazing aspects of facility management has been the truly massive construction costs for some of the monolithic structures. For example, in the United States alone, $3.34 billion was spent on new sport facilities during 2008 (Muret, 2008). You may be asking yourselves, "Why not just renovate existing sport/entertainment facilities rather than build new ones?" Interestingly enough, it has been estimated that upgrading most facilities to meet modern-day expectations would cost 25% more than building new ones (Fox, 2007).

Sport facilities are not new concepts; in fact, they have been in existence since medieval times. Some current sport facilities, like the Los Angeles Memorial Coliseum, have names of ancient facilities (Beauchamp Newman, Graney, & Barrett 2005). However, the first university sport management program wasn't established until 1966 at Ohio University (Parks, Quarterman, & Thibault, 2007). While sport facilities and managing the events held in them have been around for centuries, the components of sport management curriculums, including event, facility, and risk management, have been around for less than 50 years.

Anyone with an interest in pursuing a career in the event or facility management industry needs to understand the connection and synergy between the events themselves, the facilities they occur in, and the events' accompanying risks. Some authorities in the field maintain that if sport managers understand the various aspects of event and risk management pertaining to a large facility, then they will have a relatively easy transition to events in a smaller venue (Ammon, Southall, & Blair, 2004; Farmer, Mulrooney, & Ammon, 1996). Therefore, understanding the management techniques for dealing with smaller sport facilities and events, such as community golf courses and high school volleyball tournaments as well as multisport entertainment facilities and large events such as Lucas Oil Stadium and the National Basketball Association (NBA) All-Star Game, is imperative for anyone interested in pursuing a career in this area. Even though the sport and entertainment facility industry has experienced substantial growth in recent years, the amount of information and published materials available is far from extensive. This textbook will attempt to provide sport management students with the answers to a variety of questions surrounding sport and entertainment events, their risks, and the facilities they take place in.

The variety of sports requires a diversity of venues.

Topics for Further Investigation

The chapters in this text will discuss a variety of specific topics that impact facilities and events, such as facility financing, alcohol management, crowd management, and box office management. The authors would be remiss, however, not to mention a variety of trends in the facility and event management industry that merit continued analysis. Many facility management experts agree that regardless of what else takes place in facility design and other related new concepts, the two largest trends facing facility managers are *green facilities* and *security-related concerns* (Deckard, 2007; Henricks, 2007). These two topics will continue to grow in importance, provide opportunities for creative implementation of fresh ideas, and generate innovative and improved industry standards, as well as produce challenges to provide increasingly safe and secure experiences for all associated stakeholders. These stakeholders, or individuals most impacted by these topic areas, include players, artists, employees, and spectators.

Green Facilities

Recycling is an easy way to promote sustainability. (BigStock Photo)

Sustainability is a comprehensive philosophy in which a variety of environmentally friendly materials and procedures are utilized to help reduce energy expenditures. Even though conservation, litter removal, and recycling have been extensively discussed and practiced in many areas of the United States since the first Earth Day in 1970, the tremendous increase in the Earth's population over the past 20 years and a better understanding of the Earth's finite resources have caused the sport industry to alter facility design and operating practices.

As well they should, within the past decade many individuals and organizations in the sport and entertainment industry have begun to focus on sustainability. Whenever thousands of individuals gather in a confined space, such as a stadium or arena, vast quantities of garbage are produced. Aluminum beer cans, plastic beverage cups, popcorn containers, food wrappers, peanut shells, partially eaten food, and discarded game programs all contribute to the tons of waste produced at sporting events. In addition, sport facilities produce millions of gallons of waste water associated with concessions, irrigating playing fields, and sewage disposal. The extensive kilowatt hours required for lighting, heating, ventilating, and air conditioning facilities also impacts the environment and natural resources. Understanding the effect that sustainability has on the proverbial bottom line, architects and facility planners are aware that "the focus on energy depletion, energy costs, the costs of operation and the impact on the environment that buildings bring is going to shape building design for quite a while" (Henricks, 2007, p. 37).

Thus, one trend in facility construction definitely involves building green facilities. Dick (2007) defined a green facility as "a structure that is designed, built, renovated, operated, or reused in an ecological and resource-efficient manner" (para. 1). This concept has begun to receive a great deal of publicity and will continue to be a growth industry for many years.

Standards have been established by the U.S. Green Building Council (USGBC) that measure and certify buildings that have met some or all of the council's criteria. This certification is termed Leadership in Energy and Environmental Design (LEED). Being LEED-certified qualifies a facility to be designated as a green facility and provides measurable criteria by which the stadium's level of green-ness can be quantified (Lamberth, 2008).

Nationals Park, home of Major League Baseball's (MLB) Washington Nationals, cost more than $611 million to construct. The facility, which opened in 2008, was the first LEED-certified professional sport stadium. The stadium saves 21% in energy costs by employing high-efficiency lighting, utilizing special parking for fuel-efficient automobiles, and incorporating low-flow plumbing fixtures that should save 10 million gallons of water per year (Fall, 2007).

Other sport facilities have begun utilizing alternative energy sources and environmentally friendly operational standards. The Olympic Village at the 2008 Summer Olympics employed a solar power system. The athletics stadium in Kaohsiung, Taiwan (site of the 2009 World Games), utilized such features as recycled construction materials, solar panels, rainwater retention technology, and an underground trash-sorting treatment facility (Carlson, 2008).

Finally, a multitude of campus recreation centers, including those at the University of Maine, San Diego State University, Washington State University, the University of

Nationals Park in Washington, D.C., is a LEED-certified facility. (BigStockPhoto)

California-Berkeley, the University of Nebraska, and Southern Illinois University, have embraced environmentally beneficial practices. These include using environmentally friendly cleaning supplies, scheduling custodial work during regular business hours to reduce lighting needs at night, communicating via text and email messages instead of paper, providing paper and magazine recycling receptacles, composting organic waste, and selling beverages in refillable bottles.

For almost 40 years the conservation of natural resources, the proper disposal of waste, and the reduction of carbon emissions have gradually become accepted worldwide practices. Although an organization's or facility's failure to devise methods to conserve energy, water, and other natural resources can clearly be viewed as unethical behavior, it may also potentially be seen as semi-negligent conduct since such conservation methods, while initially expensive to implement, typically—over time—save an organization or franchise money. As many facility managers will attest, sustainability is not only the right thing to do; it makes good business sense.

Violence in Sport and Entertainment

The terrorist attacks on September 11, 2001, had an immediate and wide-ranging global impact. Neither event and facility management nor risk management will ever be the same after that tragic September morning. Post-9/11 the most immediate challenge facing event and facility managers was to address jittery guests' safety concerns. Many individuals who planned to attend sport and entertainment events had second thoughts about their personal safety, since large crowds were viewed as potential terrorist targets. Such apprehension, coupled with a slowing economy, produced a residual drop in ticket sales. As a result, many managers were forced to find new ways to decrease costs (Barbieri, 2001). Industry representatives were concerned about the difficult juggling acts that event and facility managers were forced to undertake. Faced with decreasing operating budgets, sport facility and event managers still had to implement new (and costly) strategies to ensure spectator safety. These new strategies involved the introduction of metal detectors (magnetometers), constructing permanent barricades (bollards), instituting no fly zones over stadiums, and training security and crowd management personnel in biological agent and explosive device detection techniques.

Bollards prevent vehicles from getting too close to a facility.

The ongoing threat of future terrorist attacks has had long-term effects on the event management industry. Sporting events such as the Olympics, FIFA's World Cup, and the Super Bowl are examples of mega global sporting events. Unfortunately, these events also provide attractive targets for any terrorist group wishing to make a statement. Experts estimate that a major stadium attack could result in 10 to 15 times the number of fatalities at the World Trade Center (Abernethy, 2004). Event managers recognize the threat posed by terrorists. However, for a variety of reasons (many of which are beyond an event or facility manager's control) implementing totally fail-safe solutions to such threats may not be possible.

While the events of September 11, 2001, had nothing to do with sport events or facilities, violence has often occurred during sport events. A Palestinian terrorist attack on Israeli Olympians during the 1972 Munich Summer Olympics left 12 dead. Two individuals died and more than 100 people were injured after a bomb went off during the 1996 Summer Olympics in Atlanta. During the past several years, Major League Baseball fans have witnessed two separate incidents in which fans came onto the playing surface and assaulted a first base coach and a home plate umpire. During the summer of 2003, 20 people were killed and dozens wounded when two bombs detonated at a rock festival outside Moscow, Russia. Another tragic incident occurred outside Memorial Stadium while more than 84,000 spectators were watching a University of Oklahoma versus Kansas State University football game. Shortly before halftime on October 1, 2005, a University of Oklahoma student, Joel Hinrichs, detonated an explosive-filled backpack 175 yards from the stadium. While the event was officially listed as a suicide, rumors persisted Hinrichs had attempted to enter the stadium, but because of his carrying a backpack he was denied entry. Whether or not he attempted to enter the stadium, this incident highlights the numerous threats faced by facility and event managers.

Concerned that National Football League (NFL) stadiums were attractive terrorist targets, NFL officials implemented pat-down searches during the 2005 football season. However, as a result of a lawsuit the searches were stopped at Raymond James Stadium (home to the Tampa Bay Buccaneers) in November 2005. Tampa was the only NFL city where the pat-downs were successfully challenged in court, though suits were also filed in Chicago, Seattle, and San Francisco.

In today's threat-conscious environment, facility and event managers throughout the world attempt to provide effective security measures to prevent violence and terrorism. Pat-downs, limits on bag size, and vehicle barriers are all important, but facility managers have to adopt the pragmatic attitude that incidents *will* occur. While discussing security needs at sport facilities after the 2005 London transit bombings a United Kingdom (UK) stadium manager commented that his American counterparts may be too focused on the "preventative" element of crisis management at the expense of developing "reactive" procedures. While prevention is critical, facility managers have to accept that incidents *will* occur. As part of this worldview, managing a crisis should involve every facility staff member: full-time, part-time, and volunteer. It is crucial to remember staff decisions (especially those made within the first two minutes following an incident) will save lives and mitigate facility damage.

Innovative Stadia Designs and Events

So now that we have discussed some broad concepts that will affect many sport/entertainment facilities and events, let's spend a few moments discussing the facilities themselves. As previously noted, the growth of new facilities and the need for managers to staff such venues are continuing on an exponential level. In fact, worldwide 34 new arenas (costing a total of $4.4 billion [USD]) are expected to be completed between 2007 and 2010 (Deckard, 2007). What will these new complexes look like? Will they employ radical new designs, like that of Allianz Arena in Munich, Germany, home to both FC Bayern Munchen as well as TSV 1860 Munchen? The material on the outside of Allianz Arena is transparent and allows the colors of the building's exterior to change to match the home team's colors (from blue and white for Bayern, to red and white when TSV 1860 plays). New stadia might have retractable roofs similar to that of the University of Phoenix Stadium, home to the Arizona Cardinals, and Lucas Oil Stadium, home to the Indianapolis Colts. Or perhaps existing stadiums will promote unique events similar to those of the Stade de France, an 80,000-seat stadium outside of Paris, France. The Stade has played host to a variety of sport/entertainment events, such as FIFA's World Cup Final in 1998, a Rolling Stones concert, and international rugby championships. The Stade's highest-attended event, however, was called "Ben Hur" and consisted of a variety of acts, including chariot races that drew more 300,000 spectators over a 5-night engagement (Dejardin, 2007).

Another unique use of sport facilities that may occur more often includes hockey games being played in football stadiums. For example on New Year's Day 2008 the Pittsburgh Penguins played the Buffalo Sabres in Ralph Wilson Stadium, home to the NFL's Buffalo Bills, in the National Hockey Leagues (NHL) Winter Classic. The game attracted more than 71,000 fans—an NHL record at the time. The following year the Detroit Red Wings faced the Chicago Blackhawks at Wrigley Field. A similar event occurred in Bern, Switzerland, drawing a sell-out crowd of more than 30,000 (James, 2007).

Skiing in Dubai is now a possibility.

The renovations at Wembley stadium have rejuvenated a historic British facility.

The Globalization of Sport

Though individual facilities and events operate in a local community, the world has become much smaller due to *globalization*. It is has been estimated that during 1990–2005 more than $22 billion (USD) was spent on the construction and renovation of major professional sport facilities in the United States (Baade & Matheson, 2002). Students, however, should not be naive enough to believe that this is just a U.S. phenomenon; international sport has also reached epic proportions. The National Hockey League opened its 2007–2008 season in London at the newly remodeled 02 Arena. Also in 2007, the NFL elected to play a regular season game in Great Britain after historic Wembley Stadium had undergone a £800 million 8-year renovation. Other noteworthy examples of international sport facilities and events include the following:

- 2003—A European sport marketing company brought seven of the best global soccer teams to the United States to play a series of eight matches. The renowned teams included soccer giants such as Manchester United, Juventus, Barcelona, AC Milan, and Celtic.
- 2003—Major League Baseball opened a Tokyo office in order to increase promotional activity and sponsorship opportunities.
- 2006—A partnership agreement was signed by Chelsea F. C., the England Premier League Champion, and AEG (Anschutz Entertainment Group) that marketed the Chelsea team during its U.S. tour.

- 2006—The World Baseball Classic (WBC) took place. Japan won the initial championship.
- 2007—The NBA created NBA China and established several offices in China as well as numerous marketing deals.
- 2007—A professional soccer team from Spain, Real Madrid, signed a multiyear contract with SCP Worldwide to market the soccer club's U.S. broadcast rights, tours, and soccer academies (Mickle, 2007).
- 2008—The Masters Golf Tournament was won by a South African.
- 2008—AEG finalized an agreement to operate and book the Beijing Olympic Basketball Arena (Manica, 2008).

If the previous items are viewed independently they may appear to be isolated events, but two common threads connect all of them. First, these developments demonstrate the international fascination with sport. Second, some type of sport facility was impacted by each of these events. Due to sport's global popularity, no matter where they are held, sport events are highly publicized, revenue producing, and potentially dangerous entertainment extravaganzas.

Summary

The multitude of new sport facilities around the world will undoubtedly generate impressive television and sponsorship fees. In addition to increased revenue streams, the increased public and media exposure accompanying *events* held at these facilities has emphasized the need for sport and recreation managers to have a clear understanding of what it takes to *manage* sport facilities and events, while attempting to diminish accompanying *risks* and liability.

In order for event and facility management to continue to grow, visionaries within the field must understand both the history and current practices in the industry and apply such knowledge to address future challenges. Even in tough economic times, the need for sport facility and event managers remains strong and there are tremendous opportunities for students to actively pursue (Li, Ammon, & Kanters, 2002). This textbook will provide you, as a potential sport facility manager, with the basic fundamentals to comprehend the field of facility and event management. Ideally, you will complement your reading of this textbook with practical experiences, including a good internship. From there you will be able to enter this exciting industry as a full-time professional. Good luck!

2

Sport Event Operations: The Nexus of Sport Event and Facility Management

Application Exercise

As part of a practicum experience, you and another sport management student have been hired by your university's student government association (SGA) to manage an upcoming professional wheelchair basketball game between two NWBA (National Wheelchair Basketball Association) teams to be held on your campus. You are responsible for planning, organizing, and managing the event. Your staff will consist of sport management student volunteers. Some of the volunteers may have taken a facility or event management class, but many may not have taken such a course.

This is the first such event ever held on your campus. You are the event manager.

The SGA president has told you she expects the event to draw a capacity crowd and generate good press coverage and university-wide recognition for SGA. The planning and production of the event is up to you. If the event is a success,

A successful event, from local to Olympics, requires planning.

you will receive the praise. If the event is not a success, your reputation and the reputation of your university's sport management program will be negatively impacted. Develop a workable event management plan. Information to be included may come from interviews or observations of event managers of local high school, collegiate, or professional sport organizations. Additional information may be obtained from a variety of sources, including your class notes, the Internet, this textbook, and your professors.

What Is Event Management?

Faced with planning and producing an event, figuring out what it is you have been hired to do—in other words, defining event management—is a necessary first step. Successful event management involves many elements. While this chapter cannot possibly cover all facets of sport event management, there are certain elements we will discuss in the following pages. Before considering any focus areas, it is critical for a prospective facility/event manager to recognize the importance of having a thorough familiarity with a facility's philosophy and mission. A facility's organizational philosophy and mission affects not only the facility's management and marketing, but also shapes the selection, marketing, and management of any sport event, as well as the activities surrounding any chosen event. Given this context, this chapter will focus on the following areas: (1) suggestions for recruiting and training professional event management staff and volunteers; (2) developing good relations with various community and corporate partners; (3) conducting event risk assessment and developing an event risk management plan; and (4) implementing an adequate guest management system.

During the event planning and production process, facility and event managers are continually asking and answering questions: This chapter introduces you to this questioning modus operandi. By the end of this chapter, you should be able to answer the following questions:

- Has the facility/event management team completed a thorough SWOT (Strengths, Weaknesses, Opportunities, Threats) analysis of past events, as part of the upcoming event?
- What is the facility's (and event's') primary objective? Simply put, Why is the facility hosting this event? How will the facility or organization determine if any specific event is a success?
- How will this event assist the facility and/or organization in developing or maintaining good relations with community and/or corporate partners?
- What are the crucial event planning and production managerial steps of which the facility and event management staffs need to be aware?
- What are the necessary steps in recruiting and training staff and volunteers for this event? For which duties and responsibilities will full-time staff be responsible? How will the facility/event handle volunteer recruitment and training?
- What are the necessary steps to ensure proper crowd management?
- What programs, policies, and procedures have been developed to ensure a high level of customer satisfaction for participants, spectators, and sponsors?

• Does the facility/event management team have a comprehensive risk management plan, including a medical emergency and evacuation plan, in place?

You will find answers to these and many other facility management and governance questions throughout this textbook. As you read, and during your in-class discussions, this questioning process should become second nature. Facility and event management is a combination of science and art: things change and a sport facility/event manager must adapt to this constant state of change. Answers to any of the questions posed above are situational, based on the unique fact pattern of each situation. While there is no cookie cutter recipe for success, there are industry best practices that can be of great use to new sport facility/event managers.

Despite the need to continually adapt and improve management strategies as times change and things evolve, a commitment to utilizing a best practice philosophy commits a facility and/or organization to the process of developing and following a standard way of doing things that all levels within that facility or organization can use in managing an event. As a sport facility/event manager, it is a good idea to develop and maintain professional connections with as many other well-respected professional colleagues as possible, identify what they consider to be best practice approaches, and assess emerging trends by learning how these managers and their best-in-class organizations are excelling. In short, you need to aspire to do things the way the best do things! If they can do it, you know you can too.

Be aware the answers provided in this textbook are not the only possible answers. Don't just think outside the proverbial management box; recognize that both the box and what's inside or outside the box may constantly change: *today's* answers may be *tomorrow's* questions.

The Nexus of Sport Event and Sport Facility Management

While it may seem a minor and self-evident point, it is vitally important for you to remember that almost all sport events are held at a permanent sport facility. As a result, event management occurs within a sport facility setting. The management of a specific event is impacted by the facility in which it is held. Fundamentally, planning and producing a sports event, like any event planning and production, involves elements of *management* occurring within an organizational setting or framework. A commonsense definition of management is getting things done (accomplishing goals) through people. In the context of a sport facility, sport event management is a social and technical process that utilizes a facility's resources and influences human behavior (of staff and volunteers) to produce an event consistent with a facility and event's philosophy, mission, and goals. Bolman and Deal (1997) describe organizations as complex, surprising, deceptive, and ambiguous. With this in mind, planning and producing a sport event will be a complex process, full of unforeseen circumstances and constrained by a specific facility's limitations. However, even though such complexity is a given, a sport event manager must deal with this complexity and uncertainty and develop a plan capable of bringing a semblance of order out of this uncertainty. The bottom line is: while events come and go, facilities are much more permanent. Even if your facility is a multiuse venue, its limitations are its limitations. These physical limitations, and the facility's philosophy and mission, will serve as major limitations on an event's marketing and management.

Two Conceptual Devices:
The Event Triangle and Festival Frames

Within this context, two helpful conceptual devices for the event manager have been developed. One allows us to visualize important event stakeholders, while the other allows us to envision a trip through an event's frames. The first event management theoretical tool provides us with a view of an event triangle (see Figure 2-1). Each side of the triangle represents important stakeholders (parties who have a stake in the event's success) who must be satisfied for the event to be a success: participants, sponsors, and spectators. Part of your job as a sport facility/event manager is to (1) accurately identify various stakeholders' expressed or unexpressed needs, wants, and desires; (2) recognize if and when stakeholders' needs, wants, and desires conflict; and (3) successfully negotiate contested areas of conflict to (as much as possible) satisfy each group's needs, wants, and desires. (We might think of this as stakeholder service management.). Since such conflicts are, most likely, inevitable, one surefire sport facility/event management admonition is to be ready to "adapt, improvise, and overcome."

Conceptualizing each individual sport event as a series of concentric frames or rings, through which spectators migrate on their way to the actual sport contest, allows us to break the event down into its constituent parts and differentiate one frame from another (see Figure 2-2). The festival frame consists of a series of rings, including the parking lots outside the stadia entrances, and venue entrances and concourses. This frame consists of parking and tailgating areas, concourses, and atriums where vendors or concessionaires are located. Some sport venues delineate the festival frame from the specta-

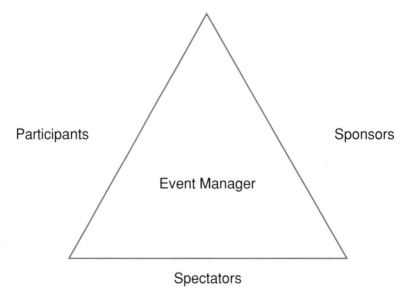

Figure 2-1. Event Triangle

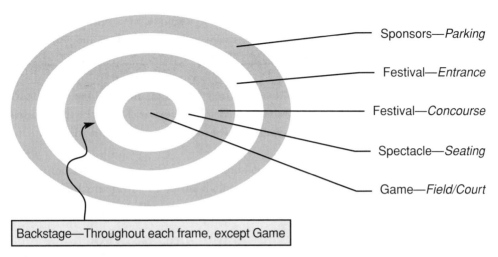

Sponsors—*Parking*

Festival—*Entrance*

Festival—*Concourse*

Spectacle—*Seating*

Game—*Field/Court*

Backstage—Throughout each frame, except Game

Figure 2-2. Sport Facility/Event Festival Frames

cle frame through the use of tunnels or walkways (known as "vomitoriums") that prevent fans from having direct sight lines into the spectator bowl.

The spectacle frame includes seating or spectator areas. The spectacle frame is the layer from which spectators view the actual sport event. This frame consists of seating and/or viewing areas, including general or reserved seating areas, club or box seating, and luxury suites and even restaurants. The spectacle area is separated from the game by wood, stone, concrete, steel, glass, or vegetation. The merging of festival and spectacle frames is a more recent development and one that differentiates modern sport facilities from more traditional stadia.

Festival frames include more than just the playing field or court.

The final facility/event frame is one that exists throughout each of the other frames and consists of behind-the-scenes or backstage areas of a sport facility/event. Backstage areas include loading docks, commissaries, player locker rooms, staff offices, security command centers, emergency medical stations, and electrical, heating, and air-conditioning rooms. These areas are often invisible to, or ostensibly hidden from, spectators and are not meant to be part of sport fans' festival experience. However, this hidden frame is the infrastructure that actually allows for facility/event management to occur within the visible frames.

It is important to recognize that festival frames are the elements that are not within the playing field or court. These are the areas in which sport management, specifically facility and event management, takes place.

Steps in Planning and Producing an Event

Planning and producing an event can be defined as the (1) achievement of identified goals/objectives, by (2) coordinating the actions of people/organizations, while still (3) recognizing the constraints of limited resources (Chelladurai, 2001). Shaw (2003) developed an event planning model comprised of four planning phases and three testing and readiness phases. Fundamentally, planning involves deciding what to do prior to beginning to do it. Planning is paying attention to details before they occur. Sounds easy, doesn't it? As a sport event manager waits for her volunteers to arrive for their first briefing, she must know what needs to be accomplished during this initial meeting; she must have planned for the meeting. Let's take a look at the planning phase in more detail.

Within the event planning model adopted for this chapter there are four identified phases: (1) strategic planning, (2) conceptual planning, (3) operational planning, and (4) contingency planning (Shaw, 2003). Each of these planning phases is critical to a successful event. They are not distinct and separate. Here are some steps in planning and producing a sports event. (*Note:* Steps may not always occur in the described sequence.)

Different events may reflect different organizational goals.

Strategic Planning: Agree upon Event Goals

One of the most important elements of strategic planning is agreeing upon an event's goals. Is the event intended to make money for the organization? How much money? Is the event designed to generate publicity for the organization? Is the event unique, unlike anything else ever done? Asking these types of questions enables the event management staff to conceptualize the event's purpose and focus. In addition, searching for answers to these questions helps frame the event planning structure. Before spending time dealing with specific logistical concerns, a sport manager needs to define the event and its associated goals. Reaching a consensus about an event's goals focuses the event planning process toward achieving agreed-upon goals.

Strategic Planning: Identify Strengths, Weaknesses, Opportunities, and Threats

As this questioning process takes place, both the organization's and event's strengths and weaknesses can be identified. While event planners, even in ancient times, probably asked these questions, one of the first documented examples of this process was developed and used in the 1950s by U.S. military planners and was referred to as a Strengths, Weaknesses, Opportunities, and Threats (SWOT) analysis (Chelladurai, 2001; Graham, Neirotti, & Goldblatt, 2001; Slack & Parent, 2005). Many types of managerial functions call for a SWOT analysis but performing a SWOT analysis is extremely important in event planning. Initially, a SWOT analysis involves identifying an organization's and/or event's strengths and weaknesses. What is the organization good at doing? Do members have experience in planning and producing the event? Such event management experience will likely be an organization's strength. However, if no one in the organization has ever organized and produced a similar event, such inexperience is probably, at least initially, a weakness. Referring back to the wheelchair basketball game scenario at the beginning of this chapter, even if none of the sport management students have produced a wheelchair basketball game, perhaps some students have produced or worked at other sport events. Perhaps some students have experience as student-managers or trainers. Maybe some students have worked as security staff or concession stand employees at a game.

When performing a SWOT analysis, managers need to move beyond just looking at an organization's strengths and weaknesses. The next two steps (identifying opportunities and identifying threats) involves looking outside the organization at the surrounding social, cultural, economic, and political environments.

While it is important to identify weaknesses and threats, it is just as important to recognize that identified weaknesses and threats can often be transformed into organizational strengths and opportunities if managers can learn to effectively utilize the environments that surround an event. For example, even though a fledgling student-run organization may not have specific expertise in managing a wheelchair basketball game (a weakness), the event still provides the organization excellent opportunities for media exposure and sponsorship opportunities not available from many other events. These

Managing large-scale sports events is challenging.

opportunities arise from economic, social, cultural, and political situations that surround this type of event.

Threats may come in many shapes and sizes. A threat may be a similar event scheduled at the same time, or it may be the fact that many students commute and are not on campus at night. A threat may be economic in nature, such as a lack of funding for the event. Whatever the results of the SWOT analysis, it is important that the event planning staff move on to the next step, generating alternative courses of action based on the SWOT analysis. In addition, plans of action must be measurable. A manager has to be able to evaluate the efficacy or success of any plan.

To help make a SWOT analysis more effective, it is a good idea to develop checklists that list and evaluate the organization's strengths, weaknesses, opportunities, and threats. Constructing these checklists should involve as many of the central members of the organization as possible. After the checklists have been developed, it's a good idea to have someone who was not involved in this process perform an evaluation and provide comments and suggestions.

Conceptual Planning: Event Staff Planning Process

One element of managing a sport event involves making sure the field, arena, or stadium is ready for the game. Another important component is doing everything possible to ensure the fans' event experience is memorable. The sport industry's customer service nature makes conceptual planning (i.e., applying strategic planning to the process of identifying staff and volunteer needs, and recruiting and training necessary staff) vitally important. In managing large-scale sport events this becomes more challenging. Properly staffing a sport event is a process that requires a great deal of planning.

In addition to coordinating activities within and between various functional areas (also known as departments), a sport event/facility manager will be working with a variety of staff types or categories:

- Paid (full-time, temporary, loaned, seconded)
- Volunteer
- Contractor

In order to achieve the goal of a memorable fan experience, it is important for sport event managers to grasp the basic elements of the event staff planning process. Staff planning is just *one part* of the overall event staffing process. It is important to remember that staffing is—aside from new venue construction—the single most difficult aspect of producing a major sporting event.

Over the past decade, as the scale and scope of sport events has increased, the staff planning process has become more centralized. The larger the scale (size) of an event the more critical the need to use a centralized method of planning staff. Such centralization provides for several advantages, including the ability to utilize multiple economies of scale, increase organizational efficiency, more quickly discover staffing gaps and overlaps, obtain consistent headcount data, standardize communication strategies, and more likely ensure staff members stay on the same page throughout the event.

The first step in the staff planning process involves determining the scope of the event and your organization's responsibilities within the event. Specifically, what are your and your staff's duties before, during, and after the event? Once you understand the event's scope, you can develop functional areas, operational titles, and an organizational structure that reflects these areas. Fulfilling these functional area responsibilities necessitates developing job descriptions and identifying staffing demand. If staffing demand is optimized (i.e., not too many, not too few), downstream processes (e.g., recruiting, in-processing, training) can be more efficient and less waste (of time, space, and money) occurs.

Once job descriptions and needs have been determined, managers can begin the recruiting process. How many paid staff members, volunteers, or independent contractors must be found? Recruiting adequate staff members involves developing bona fide occupational qualifications (BFOQ) and finding enough staff members who possess the identified qualifications. In essence, what are the necessary knowledge, skills, and attitudes you will want in your staff members? After screening of potential staff members to ensure they possess necessary job qualifications and skills has occurred, and required background checks have been performed (see Chapter 7), the next step in the process is setting up and conducting interviews of potential staff members.

At the completion of an interview, the new staff person needs to be assigned to an appropriate functional area. In addition, the new staff member must be in-processed, a process that includes being *rostered* (all appropriate human resource information collected and forwarded), *uniformed*, and *credentialed*.

After the new staff member has been in-processed by the human resource staff, the event manager's job really begins. Training paid staff or volunteers, as well as ensuring that independent contractors fulfill their contractual obligations, is a crucial part of a facility/event manager's job. We will discuss specific training elements later in this chapter. Since it takes a great deal of time, money, and effort to identify, recruit, and train new staff members, another important part of the staff planning process is doing everything possible to retain staff. It makes little sense to go through the trouble of hiring qualified staff and then not do everything to keep them around.

How often a sport event takes place impacts staffing needs, training demands, and retention requirements. In addition, an event's frequency affects the out-processing of staff members. Since many events occur more than once, whether annually, monthly, or weekly, managers may want to determine a staff member's availability for a future event. In addition to tracking staff members, out-processing involves determining staff member satisfaction. Are they likely to want to be part of a future event? Since future managers may want to know how well staff members performed their duties, it is crucial that a systematic and objective evaluation is included in each staff member's personnel file.

Operational Planning: Training Staff Members

As anyone who has ever been part of an athletic event knows, coaches and players always meet before a game. Players may meet with individual position coaches. Players may meet among themselves. Then, the entire team meets just before kickoff, tip-off, or when the gun sounds. Why do teams meet just before athletic events? If a coach hasn't already prepared the team for the game, isn't just before game time too late to solve any problems? If the players have practiced and developed the skills necessary for success, is a rousing pre-game pep talk going to magically make them run faster or jump higher? If they aren't already motivated to do their best, are clichés going to suddenly instill a sense of purpose? The answer to each of these questions is, "No!" But most coaches would never consider not meeting with their team just prior to a game. Most event planners also recognize the need to meet with their event staff prior to an event.

Why conduct pre-event briefings? More than anything, such briefings allow all event team members to make sure that pre-event checklists have been completed, upcoming logistics are coordinated, and the event's planning is on schedule. They also increase the likelihood that any last-minute glaring oversights are caught and corrected. Each pre-event briefing involves going over the highlights of the specific event plan one final time before the event begins. It serves to refocus the attention of event staff members on their duties and assigned responsibilities.

Pre-event briefings may be developed for a wide variety of events and activities. Figure 2-3 is an example of a pre-event briefing checklist for a specific specialized recreational activity/event—a self-contained underwater breathing apparatus (SCUBA) dive from a boat. This example can be helpful to future sport event managers; it breaks down a five-minute event (the briefing) that takes place before a SCUBA dive into a series of items that must be completed. Once the staff member and the participants jump off the boat and go underwater, it is hard to communicate. You cannot easily change a SCUBA-diving plan once it has begun. Just as dive guides shouldn't surprise their SCUBA-diving customers with changes in plans while they are underwater, good event

Underwater or at the Water Cube, pre-event briefings are crucial.

managers will not surprise their staff members with new plans or schedule changes unless it is absolutely necessary. A pre-event briefing is not the time to make drastic changes in an event's schedule or reassign staff duties. It is a time to make sure all of the staff is on the same page. Remember, if staff members don't know what to do by now, they never will!

Continual and ongoing pre-event briefings are opportunities to cement a culture of professionalism within an organization. From the moment the upper-level event management staff holds its first conceptual event brainstorming session to functional area briefings involving team or department managers, to individual team briefings, each pre-event briefing needs to build on the previous briefing. The number of pre-event briefings for various functional areas needs to be determined by the overall event manager well in advance. An event's complexity determines how many briefings are needed. Each pre-event briefing needs to be concise and clear. Regardless of an event's complexity, there should be at least three pre-event briefings: (1) one overall briefing for all event staff members, (2) one briefing with the overall event manager and all supervisors, and (3) at least one briefing conducted by all supervisors with their individual staff members.

In-class Exercise

Using a pre-event briefing checklist utilized by trained professional SCUBA personnel to conduct a SCUBA dive from a dive boat (Figure 2-3) as a template, develop a pre-event briefing for a sport or recreational event *of your choosing*. While most of you will be totally unfamiliar with SCUBA terminology, developing a pre-event briefing for any recreational or sport event follows a logical progression regardless of the specific event. Don't be intimidated by the fact the supplied checklist is a SCUBA checklist. Look at the commonalities between the provided briefing and one for a sport event with which you are familiar. To help you make the connection, we have left you some helpful hints in parentheses throughout the checklist.

Dive Briefing Checklist	Yes	No
Site (_____)		
Topography, points of interest, hazards, depth (overview of the facility)		
Divemaster's (supervisor's) role		
Entry and exit considerations (identify facility entry and exits)		
Dive procedures (brief event timeline)		
Course to follow, safety stops, air reserves		
Course to follow, safety stops, air reserves		
Course to follow, safety stops, air reserves		
Protocols		
Buddy separation		
Low-air/out-of-air		
Diver recall procedures		
Signal review (review communication procedures)		
Roster/Buddy check (introduce team members)		
Environmental & aquatic life (customer service policies, any legal considerations, etc.)		
Hazards		
Diver responsibilities		
Discourage feeding		
Take only memories . . .		
Pre-dive safety check (daily functional-area checklist)		
"Divers are responsible for their own profiles" (necessary documentation procedures)		

Figure 2-3. Sample Scuba Diving Briefing Checklist

Make sure to think about as many possibilities as you can in developing the briefing. Break your briefing down into a manageable 5- to 10-minute block of time. Be prepared to justify your choices of what you have included and/or deleted from your briefing.

Contingency Planning: Track the Event in Real Time

One common event planning error is losing track of the event as it unfolds. Checklists are linear, and managers have a tendency to want to work down a list from the top to the bottom. On the other hand, events sometimes unfold in a nonlinear fashion that requires adaptability and improvisation by event staff and/or managers. However, just because something unexpected happens, event checklists and plans should not be abandoned. Doing so makes as little sense as throwing a road map out the window because of an unexpected detour around some road construction. If an event's planning is solid, the event itself will most likely unfold according to plan. If nothing goes according to plan, then perhaps the plan was deficient. Keep that in mind during post-event evaluations.

When possible, it is a good idea to set benchmarks within an event to allow staff supervisors to assess the event's status. It is critical for supervisors to periodically communicate with managers to allow ongoing event assessment. While it is imperative for event managers to monitor their supervisors, an efficient manager will refrain from micromanaging his or her supervisor and event management staff. Since an overall event manager cannot be everywhere at once, she or he must trust staff members to do their jobs. If the event's plan is sound, including the training and motivation of staff members, it is likely that the event will be successful.

To help ensure an event's success, managers should train supervisors to track the success and failure of each phase of the event, and let supervisors and staff members know that while perfection is not expected, they must prevent the same problem from continually reoccurring. By encouraging supervisors to freely share both event failures and successes, future event supervisors can better avoid similar problems at future events. Staff members should be encouraged to log event successes and failures as soon after they occur as possible. This will help ensure that important items are not forgotten. It is not essential that *everything* is written down, but if *nothing* is written down, too much is forgotten. In addition, something that seemed catastrophic during the event may not seem so bad afterward. Through a judicious real-time tracking of the event, the post-event evaluation process will be more meaningful.

Operational Planning: Manage Event Logistics

After developing the event checklist, the next questions that face a sports event manager are, "How do I check off checklist items?" and "Whom do I get to help get things done?" These questions involve managing an event's logistics. The phrase "The devil is in the details" sums up the challenge of managing event logistics. Assign specific duties to specific persons. Demand accountability for accomplishing the assigned tasks on time. Also, recognize people when they complete their tasks. If you are going to demand, then reward, too!

Develop a timetable and methods for effective communication. Make sure everyone involved in the event knows who to contact for information and answers. However, as part of the training process of staff and volunteers, empower event staff members to solve problems on their own. Make it clear to both staff and volunteers that they are expected and encouraged to be problem solvers within their job description parameters. Point out that not all situations require contacting a supervisor. Let them know you expect them to recognize the difference between a situation they are qualified to handle and one that requires a supervisor's intervention. Throughout the training process, allow staff and volunteers to be active participants in the event planning process. Encourage analysis and utilize, where appropriate, their suggestions. This process helps develop critical thinking on the part of event staff and volunteers. If you, as the manager of the event, fail to practice this technique, you will become nothing but a firefighter, saddled with the responsibility of constantly putting out problem fires, thereby decreasing your effectiveness and the overall likelihood of your event's success.

Train event staff to perform their jobs. Never assume any level of knowledge or skill. If staff members have not been trained, a manager does not know if they have the ability or motivation to perform their assigned tasks. With this in mind, developing checklists to train staff members on their individual duties and responsibilities is critical.

Figures 2-4 to 2-6 are examples of orientation/training completion checklists for staff members. Complete the checklists as staff members perform the tasks. It is important the managers do more than simply ask staff, "Do you understand?" Staff members must actually *show* a trainer they can perform their duties.

Most often event staff members possess the physical and mental abilities to perform their jobs. When they don't perform their jobs correctly, it is because they have not internalized the importance of doing so. In other words, they were not motivated to do their job! Since there are numerous types of motivation, including extrinsic and intrinsic motivations, one of the biggest challenges facing an event manager is discovering how to motivate and influence staff members.

It is important to note that volunteer orientation/training will often not include all of the elements contained in the staff examples in this chapter. Volunteer training, while often limited, should not be overlooked. Since volunteers have varied schedules, trainers must make the most efficient use of the limited time available for training. It is criti-

---

PHASE 1—GENERAL ORIENTATION

Estimated Time to Complete: _____		[✔ = Done]
1. Explain the kind of organization we are.		[ ]
2. Describe who our customers are.		[ ]
3. Review our company/organization's history, traditions, and values.		[ ]
4. Describe our most recent changes: past, present, and future.		[ ]
5. Describe who our competition is, and how we differentiate ourselves.		[ ]
6. Explain how we are organized (i.e., levels of management).		[ ]
7. Explain how our company/organization is unique or special.		[ ]
8. Review products and services.		[ ]
9. Familiarize employee/staff with vendors and suppliers.		[ ]
10. Tour the facility/event area.		[ ]
11. Introduce employee to people he or she will work with.		[ ]
12. Give employee copy of Employee/Staff Handbook.		[ ]
13. Allow employee time to review Handbook.		[ ]
14. Answer questions.		[ ]
Supervisor: _____	Employee/Staff: _____	

Figure 2-4. Sample General Orientation Checklist

PHASE 2—GENERAL ORIENTATION		
Estimated Time to Complete: _____		[✔ = Done]
1. Summarize job description.	[	]
2. Define major job responsibilities.	[	]
3. Communicate job expectations and standards of performance.	[	]
4. Explain Introductory Period.	[	]
• Length of time	[	]
• Define *conditional employee*	[	]
5. Discuss employee benefits and eligibility requirements.	[	]
• Insurance*	[	]
• Vacations*	[	]
• Holidays*	[	]
• Sick leave*	[	]
6. Discuss pay periods, rates of pay, and how figured.*	[	]
7. Discuss payroll deductions (voluntary and involuntary)*	[	]
8. Discuss overtime.*	[	]
• Approvals required	[	]
• How calculated	[	]
9. Explain purpose of this Orientation and Training Program.	[	]
10. Emphasize company as Equal Employment Opportunity employer.*	[	]
11. Explain the performance evaluation system.	[	]
12. Summarize company/organization rules.	[	]
• Ethics	[	]
• Sexual Harassment guidelines	[	]
• Alcohol and drugs	[	]
• Personal appearance and name badges	[	]
• Safety	[	]
• Cell phone/text messaging use	[	]
• Smoking	[	]
• Parking	[	]
• Visitors	[	]
13. Respond to questions.	[	]
Supervisor: _____ Employee: _____		
* (*Note:* These elements may not be appropriate for certain events or organizations.)		

Figure 2-5. Sample Job Orientation Checklist

cal that volunteer training is hands on. Keep volunteer responsibilities to a minimum. Trainers must ensure that volunteers perform the critical tasks required. In addition, leave any checklists with volunteers as reference tools. Volunteers do not want to appear stupid or unable to perform. Their primary motivation for volunteering is contributing to a cause or from a feeling of altruism. If they are asked whether they understand what their duties and responsibilities are, almost every volunteer will say, "Yes." Meanwhile, they often have no idea what is expected of them, or they assume they can figure it out on their own.

PHASE 3—OPERATIONS ORIENTATION AND TRAINING

Estimated Time to Complete: _____   [✔ = Done]

1. Review with the employee how to _____ .   [   ]
2. Review with employee all emergency procedures.   [   ]
3. Review with employee _____ approval levels.   [   ]
4. Review with employee all _____ response codes.   [   ]
5. First review and demonstrate each procedure listed below.
   Determine if employee has acquired the ability to perform
   each action by asking him or her to demonstrate it for you.

   • _____   [   ]
   • _____   [   ]
   • _____   [   ]
   • _____   [   ]
   • _____   [   ]
   • _____   [   ]

6. Demonstrate _____ procedures. Ask employee   [   ]
   to demonstrate.
7. Explain _____ procedures. Ask employee to review   [   ]
   the procedures with you.
8. Review all _____ procedures. (Refer to Event Manual.)   [   ]
9. Explain how to deal with _____ . Familiarize   [   ]
   employee with proper forms.
10. Discuss _____ , its causes and preventive measures.   [   ]
11. Define and review _____ procedures.   [   ]
12. Answer questions.   [   ]

Supervisor: _____   Employee/Volunteer: _____

Note: Successful completion of this ORIENTATION DOCUMENT verifies that on (Date _____) (employee/staff member) _____ demonstrated the ability to perform the tasks listed above.

Figure 2-6. Sample Operations Orientation and Training Checklist

Contingency Planning: Develop and Conduct Post-event Debriefings

Just as coaches meet with their teams prior to the game, they also meet with their teams after the contest is over. This post-game meeting allows a coach to go over the positive and negative incidents that occurred during the game. If the team achieved its goals, the coach congratulates the players. If the team didn't achieve all of its goals, a good coach still discusses the many positive aspects of the game. In addition, the coach often uses this post-game talk to address methods of correcting the deficiencies in the team's performance and working to maintain the team's cohesion. Similarly, a good event manager will conduct post-event briefings.

If one of the organization's goals is to conduct the event more than once, perhaps on an annual basis, then discussing the positive and negative incidents that occurred during an event will help in the planning for future events. As the saying goes, "Those who do not learn from the mistakes of the past are doomed to repeat them." By going over event checklists and supervisor logs, a manager can begin to evaluate an event. Managers should look for event positives and negatives, think of ways to improve and streamline all phases of the planning and production of the event, make amendments or changes to the checklists as soon as possible, and engage in thorough discussions of the benefits and drawbacks of making a change in event protocol.

Before changes are made in an event's future plans, managers should determine whether the failure occurred because of faulty planning or because the external environment was different than anticipated. Will the change allow for adaptation to the external environment? Will the external environment be the same or different at the next event? The problem should be discussed with the staff members who actually encountered the problem. These staff members should be involved in plans to ensure the problem does not occur again. Staff members who adapted and improvised to deal with the problem during the event are a great resource for developing possible long-term, permanent solutions.

Once a sport event manager has decided that a change needs to be made, he should not put off making changes to his checklist or procedures. If he does not make necessary changes immediately, changes are often forgotten and the same problems may reoccur during future events. Once the change has been made, care must be taken to begin the process of ensuring that the solution or change becomes part of the organization's culture—the way the organization does things.

Operational Planning: Event Cleanup, Closeout, and Reconciliation

As any college student knows, hosting a party is often not as fun as attending someone else's. Why? Because, the host of the party always has to clean up. One of the hardest parts of any event is the cleaning up, closing out, and/or shutting down of the event site. The fans have gone home, the teams or participants have received their rewards, and the press has left to file their stories. All that is left is the mess! The adrenaline of the event has dissipated; the glamour is gone. Just as actors must go back to their dressing room and slowly remove their makeup, designated event staff members must pack up the event.

An event manager needs to plan this event cleanup process so it is as efficient and painless as possible. This process of post-event wrap-up must be planned as carefully as the rest of the event. If this process is too long, too taxing, or too dreary, the event manager risks alienating volunteers, damaging equipment, and ending the event on a sour note. Managers must remember that the motivation and adrenaline that the event generated are over; so ensuring that staff members and volunteers are still doing things correctly depends on maintaining staff motivation and professionalism. Shoddy cleanup procedures cannot be tolerated. Shortcuts in event cleanup can negatively impact an event's profitability and the prospects for future events.

Managers should develop checklists that cover this entire process. All event planning should include a thorough discussion of the post-event cleanup and closeout process.

An event's staff must truly believe that the event is not over until the cleanup is completed. It is critical that a sport event manager stay upbeat during the cleanup process. An event's staff will follow their supervisor's lead, so a manager must ensure that supervisors also stay upbeat during this process. Conducting a complete and thorough event cleanup and closeout allows for a seamless transition to the accounting and reconciliation process.

The process of accounting and reconciliation actually begins during the event cleanup. Accounting and reconciliation includes dealing with equipment used during the event that must be properly inventoried and ensuring that procedures for returning any rented equipment or warehousing equipment the organization owns are followed. The event settlement process begins during the immediate post-event cleanup, but includes much more than just monetary reconciliation.

Settlement involves more than just balancing the books. Although it's critical that the event budget is reconciled, there is much more to the settlement process. Some questions that a sport event manager needs to answer during this process include:

- Did the event make money? How much money? Have all the bills been paid?
- If event participants were given prizes or some sort of mementos, have all the prizes been distributed?
- Have all volunteers been publicly and personally thanked for helping? Have all participants been thanked for participating?
- Have all the results been communicated to the media?
- Have any sponsors been thanked publicly and personally? Have these sponsors been encouraged to be sponsors for the next event?

The settlement process really begins before the event starts. Again, develop checklists to ensure that planning is well conceived and the accounting process is completed according to the plan. Since this process occurs long after the event's conclusion, it is more likely that there will be fewer volunteers available and that more of the workload will fall on a few organization members. With this in mind, prioritize the items and work steadily, but quickly, to complete the checklists.

The accounting and reconciliation process can be invaluable as a final evaluation of the entire event. As an event manager deals with an event's final loose ends, he can think back through the entire event. By going over the entire event again an event manager can increase future event planning efficiency. As both psychic and physical distance from the event increases, an event manager can gain useful insights into his personal performance and the event staff's performance during all phases of the event. Taking part in accounting and reconciliation allows an event manager to better plan future events.

Additional Event Planning and Production Suggestions

A useful technique is to plan from after your event is completed, including cleanup and post-event evaluation, back through your event to the first event planning session. Then, assign a completion date for each task/item item. Practicing event planning in reverse forces you to think in greater detail about the nuts and bolts of the event. Think about how much concentration and attention to detail it takes to drive a car in reverse. Planning this way is another example of thinking outside the box. Managers are less likely to forget things when they are forced to look at things from this type of reverse perspective.

Some additional suggestions for monitoring the development and management of an event include the following:

- Event checklists need to be developed to reflect the event's budget. Do not plan things the budget cannot support.
- Make sure to check items off the lists, but check back with the person(s) responsible for that item to confirm and reconfirm completion of the task(s).
- Design specific checklists for each facet of the event. Splitting the master checklist into smaller checklists for specific areas of the event helps each person in charge of that specific area keep tabs on her individual area(s) of responsibility.
- Make each checklist as specific as need be. It's better to be more specific than too general, but also keep in mind the nature of the event, and possible threats and their consequences.
- Recognize that Murphy's Law exists! (Anything that can go wrong will go wrong!) Recognition of this law should guide the development of event checklists. You need to plan for unusual and unlikely occurrences. Build flexibility and adaptability into the event checklist. Use *branch-chain thinking* (developing alternative outcomes based on changes in the external environment) in construction of the checklist. As you build your event checklist, continually ask yourself, "What if . . . ?"

Summary

1. Event planning and production is getting things done (accomplishing goals) through people.
2. Event management involves satisfying the needs of event participants, sponsors, and spectators.
3. The planning process includes achievement of identified goals by coordinating the actions of people/organizations, while still recognizing the constraints of limited resources.
4. The event planning model adopted for this chapter includes four identified phases: (1) strategic planning, (2) conceptual planning, (3) operational planning, and (4) contingency planning.
5. An event SWOT analysis consists of identifying the Strengths, Weaknesses, Opportunities, and Threats associated with a particular event.
6. The use of event checklists is an excellent event management strategy.
7. Most event staff members possess the ability to perform their assigned tasks. When they don't perform their tasks correctly, it is most often due to a lack of motivation.
8. Pre-event briefings allow all event team members to make sure that pre-event checklists have been completed, upcoming logistics are coordinated, and the event's planning is on schedule.

9. Training a staff member involves not only showing a trainee how to perform a specific task, but also ensuring the trainee's ability to perform the task by having the person demonstrate the task correctly.

10. Regardless of an event's complexity, there should be at least three pre-event briefings and three post-event debriefings. All the event staff members should attend organization-wide briefings and debriefings. There should be pre- and post-event meetings attended by the overall event manager and all supervisors. And each individual supervisor should conduct a briefing and debriefing with individual staff members whom he or she directly supervises.

11. It is important to develop and complete checklists that cover the entire cleanup process following the actual event.

12. Settlement of an event involves not only monetary accounting and reconciliation procedures but also conducting a thorough post-event evaluation of all facets of an event's management.

Questions

1. What are the steps in event planning and production?
2. Why is it important to agree upon an event's goals at the beginning of the event planning and production process?
3. What is a SWOT analysis?
4. What is an important element of staff training that's often overlooked?
5. Identify and give an example of each of the rules of influence discussed.
6. Why is it important to conduct pre-event briefings and post-event debriefings?
7. Why is it critical that event managers develop shut down checklists and ensure that they are completed?
8. Identify the critical elements in event accounting and reconciliation.

3

Construction and Finance

Application Exercise

Laura Smith, a sport management student at a public university, has volunteered to serve on a committee that will investigate the financial viability of building a new campus event and recreation center. The current on-campus facility has aged and will soon no longer be able to service the needs of the campus community. In addition, the building will likely require extensive and costly remodeling and maintenance expenses to remain viable in the near future—meaning that building a new facility is the most cost-effective way to satisfy the needs of the campus. Although there is strong initial campus and community support for the construction of a new center, the committee will investigate the financial resources needed to build. After determining the overall construction costs of the facility, the committee must then evaluate the viability of different methods available to procure the needed funds. In addition to the initial construction costs, the committee must also determine how much revenue will be needed to offset yearly operating expenses. Of particular concern are the rapid growth of the campus population and the increasing popularity of some of the intercollegiate athletic teams. The campus currently has 12,000 full-time students, but the master plan projects more than 18,000 full-time students within the next 10 years. With the additional anticipated expansion of the intercollegiate athletic programs, the center must be constructed and financed in a manner that permits the recreation portion of the building to accommodate a growing student population, while the athletic department can expand the competition and office space areas of the events center. The committee must fully understand the potential funding mechanisms and select the one that makes sense for all of the campus stakeholders.

Introduction

The situation facing Laura Smith's committee is not unusual in sport, recreation, and entertainment. Proper facilities are needed to operate events. Even an event held outdoors, such as a beach volleyball tournament, will likely require some sort of physical

Campus recreation centers are significant student recruitment tools.

structure—even if it is temporary—to be operated effectively. Though sport and entertainment venues have historically occupied a position on campuses and in local communities, over the past 10 years their importance has grown. For some campuses, the athletic and recreation facilities are among the most significant aspects for student recruitment and retention. Many municipalities have noted the effect a recreation center or entertainment venue can have on overall quality-of-life perception of local citizens. Over the past 10 years, such facilities' perceived and realized importance has resulted in a dramatic increase in sport facilities' construction and renovation.

Before any sport or entertainment facility can be constructed, input from important constituents must be solicited. Certainly, anyone who will likely use a facility should have the opportunity to have input regarding its construction. However, other stakeholders, many who may never set foot in the new facility, may positively or negatively impact the project's success or failure. Ms. Smith's committee will undoubtedly include university faculty and staff representatives, as well as the recreation and athletic department personnel who will eventually operate the building. However, though it will be a campus facility, local community members will be impacted by its construction and eventual operation. Therefore, the committee should include key community representatives, including local government and business leaders. While each facility construction project will have a different size and scope, requiring differing numbers and types of representatives, any such facility committee should never become too large so as to be operationally unwieldy.

Facility finance committee members should not be drawn randomly from relevant stakeholder groups. To maximize the committee's effectiveness, its members should possess financial analysis expertise, particularly in the building of sport and entertainment facilities. Ideally, committee members should not only represent specific constituencies, but also possess varied experience, including:

- Accounting
- Legal aspects

- Underwriting/debt financing
- Architecture
- Construction
- Government affairs
- Zoning requirements

Once the financing team is determined, then the facility's financing and construction plans can be researched and evaluated. For Ms. Smith's committee, a few important considerations must be addressed prior to soliciting construction bids.

Researching and Evaluating Financing and Construction Plans

Facility Use

Prior to commencing construction, a facility's short- *and* long-term purposes must be determined. Unfortunately, buildings often become partially obsolete soon after they are constructed. Though such obsolescence is unavoidable, to mitigate this reality, future expansion and renovation should be integrated into all facility designs. However, it may be difficult to envision a facility's many potential uses. In 1992, when U.S. Airways Center (originally named America West Arena) was built in Phoenix, Arizona, few stakeholders envisioned a National Hockey League (NHL) team being interested in relocating to the desert Southwest. However, during the 1990s, numerous Canadian-based teams moved to the United States. The Winnipeg Jets decided to move to Arizona in 1996 to become the Phoenix Coyotes. The U.S. Airways Center, one of the National Basketball Association's (NBA) premier venues, had terrible sightlines for hockey—primarily because its designers never envisioned that hockey would ever consistently be played in the venue. Although the hockey team attempted to make the best of a difficult situation, in 2003 it relocated to a new facility in nearby Glendale.

Land Acquisition

Once a facility's short- and long-term needs are identified, a number of areas must be investigated and/or approved before a building plan can be developed and implemented. Certainly, the probable building site must be identified and potentially purchased. This can pose a variety of problems, particularly for facilities requiring multiple acres for construction. In metropolitan areas, multiple acres of land may have to be purchased from disparate parcels. Once one parcel is identified and purchased, the adjacent parcels instantly become more valuable, causing those landowners to likely increase their reluctance to sell unless potential compensation is increased—sometimes drastically. Since negotiating with a series of separate land owners at one time can be cumbersome, many facility managers needing to purchase land will obtain a series of *options* to purchase a property. An option will have a set time period in which the potential purchaser may exercise the option to purchase the land at an agreed-upon price. If the potential purchaser cannot acquire enough options for the land needed for the project, the options can be allowed to expire.

In some cases, land purchases are made by representatives of the purchasing party to attempt to shield the identity and primary intention for purchasing. Some public and private developers have utilized intermediaries to hide their identity and long-term intentions and to suppress potential prices. In the Atlanta metropolitan area, some school districts encountered controversy when they began purchasing land for new school sites in secret. Since the government is supposed to represent the taxpayers, secret land negotiations were not approved at open meetings. Taxpayers complained that purchases of this magnitude should definitely be reviewed and discussed in a public forum before the school boards took action. The school boards countered that a public discussion would disclose their intention to purchase land to build new schools and the resulting increase in land costs would add to the potential expenses for taxpayers and also decrease the likelihood the project could be completed ("In Atlanta, unrest over secret school deals," 2007).

Eminent Domain

Government agencies have a unique ability to compel private citizens to sell land. This process is called *eminent domain*. The U.S. Constitution permits the government to forcibly take land from private citizens, but it must provide adequate compensation (Fifth Amendment). The land secured from private citizens must be used for the public good. Traditionally, this has meant seized land must be utilized to build roads, canals, bridges, or other structures that are utilized by a variety of constituents. It could also be used as a site for a publicly owned building, such as a community recreation center. There have been a variety of lawsuits regarding eminent domain. Most have involved private citizens attempting to keep their land in the face of government seizure or have involved a dispute regarding the fair compensation the landholder would receive after the government forced him to vacate.

However, the recent decision in *Kelo v. New London* (2005) has potentially changed the scope of eminent domain in the United States. In *Kelo* nine homeowners refused to allow their land to be taken through eminent domain because they felt it violated the U.S. Constitution. The land in question was to be given to another *private* party that was going to redevelop the land. The local government argued, and by a 5-4 margin the U.S. Supreme Court ultimately agreed, the local government could compel private citizens to sell their land to another private citizen for a fair market value if the new landowner would provide a public good in the form of a greater tax base. In many areas the *Kelo* decision created a public outcry among citizens (Nagel & Southall, 2007). Some state and local governments, under pressure from constituents, have passed anti-eminent domain statutes that restrict government takings if the land will be utilized by another private entity.

The state of Texas passed one of the more restrictive anti-eminent-domain-for-private-use statutes, but allowed the Dallas Cowboys' new $1.1 billion facility to be exempt from the law (Lucas, 2006). The city of Arlington initially announced in 2005 that it would utilize eminent domain to acquire land for the Cowboys only as a last resort. However, dozens of landowners refused to sell or agree to the terms the city proposed.

The Dallas Cowboys' stadium was exempt from anti-eminent domain laws. (Photo courtesy of Ryan Kirkpatrick.)

When the city utilized eminent domain, numerous landowners sued. Although property owners were restricted from retaining their real estate, they felt the city had not provided adequate compensation for taking their houses. As of 2008, the city of Arlington had successfully increased their payments to some affected landowners, but numerous other lawsuits were still unresolved (Mosier, 2008).

Preparation

Once the building site has been identified and purchased, it must then be prepared for construction. Preparing a building site involves a variety of factors potentially including, but not limited to, the following:

1. Securing proper zoning. A building can only be constructed in an area that conforms to its use (i.e., areas zoned residential are suitable for single-family dwellings). Zoning is typically approved at the local municipal level, but often concerned citizens may complain that a new facility may increase traffic congestion, noise, lights at night, and the like.
2. Meeting environmental concerns. These may involve ensuring that new construction will not have an adverse effect on the surrounding air, water, and soil. There often must be an investigation of the impact construction may have upon endangered species.
3. Creating the physical characteristics necessary to build. This may include grading the soil so that it is stable, removing trees and other impediments, and establishing the infrastructure for utilities (power, water, phone, etc.). Cost overruns can easily occur in these areas.

Preparing to build a sport or entertainment facility requires more planning and potential government approval in these areas than was involved 20 years ago. Intensive investigations and building delays due to zoning and environmental analyses are positive because they should help ensure that the new facility does not have an unusually negative impact. However, some government officials may abuse their power and intentionally delay projects in order to grandstand in front of their constituents. In extreme cases, concerned citizens may attempt to override the decisions of land owners and the government even after the initial investigation and debate has concluded. The University of California-Berkeley encountered some strong local resistance to their efforts to remodel their football field and other athletic department facilities for many years. Some of the facility upgrades were not only delayed almost two years by court order, but also by citizens actually *living* in a grove of trees near the stadium (Brenneman, 2008).

In cases where a current facility is being remodeled or a new facility is being built near or adjacent to an existing facility, a variety of issues immediately present themselves. If construction will impact the operation of the current facility, then contingency plans for continued operations must be put in place. In the case of the Oakland-Alameda County Coliseum, the 1995 return of the National Football League's Raiders necessitated extensive renovations to build new seating areas. Some of the construction occurred during games involving Major League Baseball's Oakland Athletics, creating situations in which drills, hammers, and saws were being used while baseball action on the field unfolded. When Yankee Stadium was completely remodeled, the Yankees played their 1974–1975 home games in Shea Stadium, home of the New York Mets. When these situations occur, an attempt should be made to mitigate the potential hassle the construction will create.

Soliciting Bids

Since Ms. Smith's university has already identified and procured sufficient vacant acreage for the new facility and has completed the initial building preparation requirements, her committee will not need to concern itself with contingency plans for the current facility (though a new committee that would determine the fate [remodel, demolition, etc.] of the outgoing facility may need to be established at a later date). The committee can proceed to a solicitation for assistance for facility design and construction. For a project of this magnitude, there will certainly be an extensive investigation of architects and potential contractors. The initial process will likely involve a request for qualifications (RFQ), which asks for interested architectural companies to submit their qualifications to be evaluated. The RFQ is often followed by a request for proposal (RFP) or a request for bids (RFB), asking the potential architects what they would do in their design of the project. Though each of the requests has a slight difference, the ultimate idea of each is the same. The facility-finance committee is asking potential architects to submit the reasons why they should be chosen for the project and if they are chosen, what specifically they will do to complete the project and at what price. It is important to note that in many cases, RFPs will be sent to a variety of different organizations as the building of a campus recreation and event center will require architects, contractors, subcontractors, environmental impact studies, soil studies, and numerous other areas to consider. The committee will likely find some qualified architects who have successfully worked with specific contractors and subcontractors in the past; this could certainly be beneficial, as using architects and contractors who work well together can result in lower costs and a higher likelihood the facility will be completed on schedule. In some cases, full-service construction companies may have their own architects and other personnel to provide most, if not all, of the necessary steps to take a project from design to completion.

The selection of an architect and building contractor (as well as additional vendors) will involve a variety of factors. The total cost of the project is certainly an important consideration. Unfortunately, for many people or organizations, it may become the *only* consideration. Construction costs obviously impact the bottom-line projections regarding the facility's financial viability. However, facility-finance committee members must not simply look at the total price when making their evaluations. Often, the lowest bid may not provide the quality of building materials, equipment, and human resources needed. Too often, poorly designed or constructed facilities end up costing more in the immediate years after the building is completed because radical alterations must be made to keep the facility viable. In addition, the time it takes to complete the project is an important factor. Time is money, so the longer it takes to complete the project, the longer the organization has to wait to begin collecting certain revenues (see Chapter 5). The evaluation of bidders should also investigate their expertise and experience completing this type of project, as design flaws can cause short- and long-term financial losses. Table 3-1 highlights key questions to ask facility bidders.

Table 3-1. Key Bidder Questions

What sport- or entertainment-related facilities have you completed? Are there people on your staff with expertise in this area?
Unfortunately, there have been many sport and entertainment facilities designed and built by highly effective architects and contractors who have little-to-no understanding of the unique aspects of sport and entertainment. For instance, an architect or contractor who is not familiar with tennis may design tennis courts that face east-west. Tennis players would obviously know that courts should face north-south to prevent the sun from interfering with a player's vision during a serve. Similarly, baseball/softball fields should be built to have the sun set in a direction that does not interfere with the batter's vision.
May we see some examples of your work and contact past clients?
This will provide a better indication of the quality of the vendor. Prior clients, especially ones who have been in facilities for an extended period of time, can help determine how well the potential vendor's work will withstand and adapt to time.
What types of building materials will you use? What is your rationale?
Though it may seem obvious to people who have participated in numerous sporting events, some architects and contractors have little understanding of the nuances of sport facilities. One particular case at a university in the state of Colorado resulted in a contractor delivering pea gravel for a warning track on an outfield. The contractor had failed to understand the purpose of the warning track and the university did not notice until after the gravel had been delivered.

(continued on next page.)

Table 3-1. —Continued

How easily can the building be remodeled or expanded after it is built?
The building should be designed for potential internal and external expansion. Most facility managers will discover that more square footage is needed—sometimes immediately after they have moved into the new facility. Facilities should always be designed and constructed with some consideration for future uses.
Where will you place storage rooms?
Storage is always a concern in any facility, but in sport and entertainment facilities *proximity* to storage is as critical as overall available square footage, since related activities typically involve frequent changeovers. Even something as simple as having to get volleyball nets and a scorer's table from a room not adjacent to the gymnasium can waste time and diminish employee morale.
How will technology impact the facility's present and future operation?
The ease of access for the installation of new wiring, cable, data ports, and the like can have a dramatic impact upon future costs for upgrades. Many current sport and entertainment facilities have crawl spaces and other hidden areas that have had to be dramatically remodeled to be able to accommodate new wiring.
Do you understand how the American with Disabilities Act (ADA) impacts sport and entertainment events? (See Chapter 6.)
Architects and contractors certainly understand rules regarding the number of required handicapped parking spaces. Most also know that a certain number of seats must be handicapped accessible. However, sport facilities are different from structures such as movie theaters. Many facilities have been designed with flaws, as people in wheelchairs must be able to see the performance area at all times, not just when other customers are seated.
How will you incorporate an energy-efficient design?
Facilities can be designed in a variety of ways. Since sport and entertainment activities may be different from those in other buildings, architects must understand the proposed activities in the designed areas. Some design characteristics will maximize the environment to lower energy costs, while others may dramatically increase the facility's overall utility costs. For instance, extensive use of skylights and windows facing south (in the Northern Hemisphere) can provide sunlight throughout the day. This would be beneficial if the area needs heat (such as in an entry foyer), but could be detrimental if allowing such excess light requires additional cooling (such as in a weight room or cardio-fitness area).

Outdoor sport facilities must incorporate the direction of the sun in their designs. (Big Stock Photo)

Additional Cost-related Considerations

Outdoor stadiums in particular have to be designed and built with weather as a significant consideration. Candlestick Park in San Francisco was built in an area that has pleasant weather during most fall and spring days. However, during summer evenings, wind gusts can become unbearable. Fans attending a San Francisco Forty-Niners' National Football League game on a fall afternoon may enjoy the weather, but the majority of the San Francisco Giants' Major League Baseball games are played at night, causing many fans to bring thermal blankets to watch summer games at Candlestick Park. When the Giants moved eight miles north, planning for their new stadium (AT&T Park) incorporated numerous wind studies to determine the best location and positioning of the facility to minimize potential wind concerns.

Acoustics can also have a dramatic impact upon an event's viability and are therefore much more important at an entertainment event than they might be otherwise. Outdoor facilities that host concerts can generate significant noise—and noise complaints. Generated noise may be transmitted differently over various topographical features (water, hills, flat ground, etc). Significant noise tests should be conducted before construction begins.

AT&T Park was designed to minimize winds from the San Francisco Bay.

Candlestick Park was built in an area where high winds and cold temperatures impacted nighttime baseball games. (Photo courtesy of Jon Rahoi.)

Once an architect's and a contractor's understanding and ability to build the required sport or entertainment facility are established, the financial solvency of the contracted organization should be evaluated. Contractors who are experiencing financial difficulty may underbid a contract in a last-ditch attempt to remain in business. Too often, such companies are merely one small setback from financial ruin. Contractors should also be familiar with the local community, as there are unique aspects to construction in every market (weather concerns, labor laws, availability of materials, etc.). This is particularly important when government agencies become involved in potential noise complaints, zoning issues, inspections, code violations, and the like. The key to evaluation is to determine exactly what each bid entails and to then proceed with the bid that meets the organization's expectations of performance and budget.

Project Budget

Before making the final choice of vendors, it is important to consider the total project budget. Project costs involve preliminary costs, architectural fees, infrastructure improvements, construction costs, furniture/fixtures/equipment costs, insurance costs, and contingencies. Too often, finance committees forget that opening the facility will require considerable funds *after* the construction has been completed. This is especially important if revenue sources may need time to be developed in the new facility. It is critical that potential contingency fees be overestimated to maintain the project's financial solvency.

Once the architect, contractors, and other vendors have been identified and a compensation package consummated, there are still some financial considerations to be addressed. A valid contract (see Chapter 8) is obviously a requirement for any business arrangement, but in this case some specific areas need to be addressed beyond the financial remuneration. Timing of payments to contractors is important. The contract should note the dates and times of any preliminary payments and should also specify inspections necessary prior to final payment. Contractors often do not appreciate inspection of their work or work areas prior to completion, nor do they want to have any encumbrances moving materials to and from the worksite. Since charting the progress of a new facility may be part of a greater public relations campaign, it is critical that the contract specifically states when visits may occur and under what conditions. To ensure the project will be completed in the event of contractor financial insolvency, contractors should furnish insurance that covers the facility owners in the event the contractor is unable to complete the work (due to bankruptcy, etc.). Contracts should also detail what happens if a tragedy occurs and work is delayed. The construction of Miller Park in Milwaukee was delayed when a crane accident killed three workers in 1999. The delay cost MLB's Milwaukee Brewers millions of dollars in lost revenue (Stavropoulos, 1999).

When the work is completed and final payment is expected, the contractor and facility committee (and other important personnel) should complete a walkthrough of every area of the facility. Under no circumstances should a contractor's final compensation be provided until all systems are operational. In addition, some facilities require contractors to ensure their work so that defects that are discovered after the facility is completed can be rectified. The final walkthrough of a facility is certainly an exciting time, and some facilities have found creative ways to involve their constituents in the opening of a new facility. One particular marketing opportunity is to have a "Final Flush" to test the building's water system. Since a large facility will have multiple bathrooms and sinks, some organizations have invited students, fans, and staff to attend an opening party where all the toilets are flushed at the same time. This type of event not only allows the facility to test its water capacity, but it also lets future event attendees see the new facility.

Laura Smith's committee determined that the sport and recreation facility they want to build can be completed for $30 million. After spending considerable time interviewing and evaluating potential contractors, they identified a series of companies that should be able to complete the project on time and within budget. Ms. Smith's committee now must determine exactly how to pay for the facility. The least expensive method to pay for a facility is to utilize cash and to pay contractors and other vendors as they complete various tasks. If a facility is constructed in this manner, few problems occur. Most organizations have an *operational budget* that covers the costs of yearly activities. However, operational budgets typically do not account for major *capital projects* such as constructing or remodeling a facility.

To assemble $30 million would likely require a commitment from a variety of sources. Since it is a public university, the state government could fund the entire facility. If it were a local public high school, the school district could elect to provide the money. However, in most cases, governments are unable and/or unwilling to simply write an *immediate* check for an athletic facility. To acquire an extra $30 million above the normal yearly budget, Ms. Smith's committee would likely need to solicit the state legislature for funding. That would likely take considerable time—potentially many years before the government would provide any money for a capital project of this magnitude. The committee may have eventual success procuring a commitment for the $30 million, but if considerable time elapses before the money is secured, the cost of construction will likely increase due to *inflation*—a gradual increase in prices. The longer a project takes to complete, the more likely that prices for construction materials and labor will also increase.

Though a direct contribution from the legislature is unlikely to occur quickly, there are certain government grants potentially available for sport and entertainment facilities and events. Various government agencies and other nonprofit organizations offer grants to further educational programming. Despite the availability of these potential funds, it is unlikely that any one funding source would provide $30 million for a project of this magnitude, but potential grants could be solicited for specific programming in the new facility.

The committee could also solicit donations from alumni or other supporters of the university or its athletic department. The advantage of this method is potential donors receive a *tax deduction* for contributing to the advancement of a nonprofit organization. However, it is unlikely enough donors could be identified in a short period of time. More than likely, utilizing donations will require an ongoing process to raise such a large sum of money. Similar to the issues presented with a direct solicitation from the state legislature, time becomes a problem as costs increase. Although it is unlikely that sufficient donations could be solicited in a short period of time, they should certainly be a part of the overall funding activities.

Despite the difficulty due to cost, size, and scope, there have been prominent sport and recreation facilities built solely through donations. In 2006 the University of Southern California (USC) opened its $147 million on-campus athletic facility, the Galen Center. Since USC was prohibited from using educational funds for the construction, they were forced to solicit donations (Tokito, 2008). Fortunately for USC, Lou Galen donated $50 million in 2002—two years before construction began. Galen's donation was utilized as the foundation for other fundraising activities. His large contribution enabled USC to find other benefactors and then pay for the facility without using any debt (Tokito, 2008).

Though the most inexpensive method to pay for a facility is to utilize cash, in the majority of cases it is simply impractical. Most public organizations do not have vast financial reserves and time becomes a problem, as costs can increase more rapidly than donations and other financial resources can be secured. For this reason, the vast majority of public facilities are built by utilizing some form of *debt financing*. Whenever an individual or an organization goes into debt, it is taking a risk by *leveraging*. Debt increases the cost of purchasing an item because *interest* is paid for the privilege of borrowing money. However, debt can enable an expensive item to be purchased immediately with the cost spread over an extended period of time. There are some key things to remember whenever debt financing is utilized:

1. Any deferred financial obligation should be contemplated with benefits and potential detriments clearly understood.
2. Items purchased via debt financing should be long-lasting and unlikely to quickly lose their value. Ideally, debt financing will be used only when there is a likelihood that the item purchased may actually increase in value (such as for buying real estate).
3. The repayment of debt obligations should occur *before* the item purchased loses its useful life. Unfortunately, the city of Seattle was still paying interest for the construction of the Kingdome *after* it had been demolished.

Stadia Financing

For most public institutions, borrowing money is a necessary component to building facilities. However, some of the typical methods to borrow money used by individuals or private businesses may not be available for public entities. Typical *mortgage loans* that individuals may procure when buying houses are not usually available for public institutions like a city, county, college, or university. A lending institution will usually not want to become involved in a standard mortgage loan with a university because the ultimate recourse for mortgage loan default is repossession. It would be difficult for a bank to take possession and operate or resell an on-campus facility!

There are a variety of debt instruments that public institutions may utilize, but the main method involves the issuing of promissory notes known as *bonds*. When many people think of bonds, they might remember receiving a savings bond for a birthday or Christmas present. More than likely those bonds were issued by the U.S. government. Even though many think of bonds solely in that context, bonds may be issued by a variety of entities. Governments from around the world issue bonds when they seek investment capital in their country. State and local governments issue bonds when they are attempting to generate money for buildings or other improvement projects. Large corporations often issue bonds to raise capital for new buildings or to expand production or service offerings. Even individuals have issued bonds. In 1997, musician David Bowie issued $55 million in bonds. The Prudential Insurance Company purchased the 10-year notes, which were backed by royalties from more than 200 of Bowie's previously recorded songs.

Any bond that is issued will be evaluated by potential investors. Bonds will be sold when investors determine there is a balance between risk and potential reward. Since bonds are merely a promise and do not convey any ownership rights or potential collateral, investors must evaluate the likelihood that the bond issuer will remain financially solvent. Typically, governments or institutions that are financially stable can sell bonds at a low interest rate because investors will deem them highly likely to repay. *Junk bonds* are promises issued by institutions that are *unlikely* to repay. Since junk bonds carry much larger risks, they are often issued at considerably higher interest rates—sometimes as much as 6 to 10% higher than bonds issued by more financially stable institutions. Even though most junk bonds are not repaid, in the cases that the organization backing the junk bonds is financially successful, the bond investors will be well compensated.

A variety of institutions will evaluate the financial worthiness of bonds. Entities such as Standard & Poors (S&P), Moody's, Fitch, and A. M. Best are well-known credit evaluators. When bonds are evaluated, they are typically given a letter grade or series of letter grades that signifies their credit-worthiness. A bond issuer's credit rating can change for a variety of reasons. If a bond issuer is downgraded, it becomes more difficult for that entity to sell additional bonds that it issues. Conversely, companies that improve their financial performance can be upgraded, which makes it easier to sell future bond offerings. Bond ratings, though informative, are merely a guide. Bonds that are highly rated might still encounter financial difficulty. The Washington Public Power Supply

HOW TO FINANCE A HOUSE

Purchasing a home is typically the largest financial purchase an individual will make. Most often individuals do not have enough money to pay cash, so they will utilize debt financing and apply for a mortgage from a lender. If approved, the homebuyer promises to pay the lender the purchase price of the home plus interest over a period of time. There are a variety of factors lenders consider in making such loans. Most lenders are primarily concerned with a borrower's ability to repay the obligation. Lenders will examine an applicant's *credit score* to examine his or her past history repaying other debts. In addition, lenders will usually expect verification of employment to ensure the applicant is likely to have future income. Other considerations include, but are not limited to, the amount of money the applicant can put down, how much money the applicant owes to other creditors, and the number and types of people who may co-sign the loan with the applicant.

Lenders tend to offer lower rates to the borrowers who are likely to repay their debts. For this reason it is critical that *all* individuals monitor what they purchase and how they utilize credit. Unfortunately, many students misuse credit while in college and are then forced to take higher rates on home or car loans when they graduate. In some cases, poor credit management can result in borrowers needing to wait months or even years to clean up their credit before a lender will offer them a home loan.

If the mortgage application is accepted, the borrower pledges the purchased home to the lender in the event of *default*. Technically, the lender owns the home until the mortgage is paid, but most people who purchase a home say they are the owners. There are a variety of available mortgages and applicants should understand each type before signing any documents. The typical home mortgage involves paying principal and interest each month over the life of the loan. Most home loans are for 30 years, but some are offered at 15, 20, 40, and, in some cases in extremely expensive areas, 50 years. When an applicant takes a principal and interest loan, the loan amount is *amortized*. Though amortization can be a difficult concept to understand, the most important aspect that all borrowers should remember is that the majority of interest on the loan is paid in the early stages of the mortgage and the majority of principal is paid in the later stages of the loan. The following example will provide details.

A borrower is offered a 30-year, 7.00% interest mortgage on a new home costing $150,000. The borrower has the lender compute an amortization table for the monthly payment and portion of the monthly payment applied to principal and the portion applied to interest. Each year the borrower will pay the lender $11,975.40 ($997.95 × 12 months). However, as Table 3-2 displays, the first year's payments will allocate $1,523.71 to principal and $10,451.73 to interest. Each year the amount applied to principal slowly increases and the amount applied to interest slowly decreases. But the borrower must understand that after 5 years $141,197 of the original $150,000 still remains as unpaid balance on the loan!

By utilizing an amortization table, borrowers can determine exactly how much money they still owe on their mortgage. In some cases when little or no down payment is made, borrowers may have difficulty in recouping their initial investment when selling the home since early payments are applied primarily to interest. Most real estate professionals advise only purchasing a home if there is a high likelihood of owning the home for an extended period of time. Even though the lender takes the much larger share of the mortgage payment as interest in the early stages of the loan, most borrowers who can remain in a home for at least five years will benefit from purchasing a home.

System was highly rated but still became the largest bond failure in U.S. history when it defaulted on $2.25 billion worth of bonds in 1983 (Crompton, 1999). Recently, Jefferson County, Alabama (Birmingham), has contemplated defaulting on $3 billion in bonds, which would become the largest bond default in U.S. history (Bissonnette, 2008). Some have warned that the U.S. bond rating could be lowered due to excessive debts from current and future deficit spending (Gokhale, 2008).

Monthly payment: $997.95			
Year	Interest	Principal	Balance
2010	$10,451.73	$1,523.71	$148,476.29
2011	$10,341.58	$1,633.86	$146,842.42
2012	$10,223.47	$1,751.98	$145,090.44
2013	$10,096.82	$1,878.63	$143,211.82
2014	$9,961.01	$2,014.43	$141,197.38
2015	$9,815.39	$2,160.06	$139,037.33
2016	$9,659.24	$2,316.21	$136,721.12
2017	$9,491.80	$2,483.65	$134,237.48
2018	$9,312.26	$2,663.19	$131,574.29
2019	$9,119.73	$2,855.71	$128,718.58
2020	$8,913.29	$3,062.15	$125,656.42
2021	$8,691.93	$3,283.51	$122,372.91
2022	$8,454.57	$3,520.88	$118,852.03
2023	$8,200.04	$3,775.40	$115,076.63
2024	$7,927.12	$4,048.33	$111,028.30
2025	$7,634.46	$4,340.98	$106,687.32
2026	$7,320.65	$4,654.79	$102,032.53
2027	$6,984.16	$4,991.29	$97,041.24
2028	$6,623.34	$5,352.11	$91,689.13
2029	$6,236.43	$5,739.01	$85,950.12
2030	$5,821.56	$6,153.89	$79,796.23
2031	$5,376.69	$6,598.75	$73,197.48
2032	$4,899.67	$7,075.78	$66,121.71
2033	$4,388.16	$7,587.28	$58,534.42
2034	$3,839.68	$8,135.77	$50,398.65
2035	$3,251.54	$8,723.90	$41,674.75
2036	$2,620.89	$9,354.56	$32,320.19
2037	$1,944.65	$10,030.80	$22,289.40
2038	$1,219.52	$10,755.92	$11,533.47
2039	$441.97	$11,533.47	$0.00

Total of 360 payments: $359,263.35
Total interest paid: $209,263.35

Figure 3-2. Amortization table for 30-year loan on $150,000 at 7% interest.

There are two main types of bonds utilized by public entities wishing to build a sport or recreation facility. *General obligation bonds* are issued with the full financial backing of the issuer. When a general obligation bond is issued, the purchaser is entitled to receive repayment with assigned interest regardless of the financial solvency of the project for which the bonds were issued. In the case of a city or county wishing to issue bonds to build a new baseball complex or some other recreational facility, general obligation bonds would likely be backed by *ad valorem*, or property, taxes. Property taxes are assessed to property owners based on the individual parcel's value. For a city or county, there are typically limits regarding the issuing of debt in relation to the overall property tax base. Since general obligation bonds dictate that purchasers are entitled to receive their money from the general tax revenues even if the project is a financial failure, taxpayers typically have the right to vote on referendums seeking to issue additional guaranteed debt instruments.

General obligation bonds issued by a college or university to build a recreation facility would be backed by the university and, therefore, by extension, the students. In most cases, general obligation bonds issued by a campus entity are backed by student fees. If Ms. Smith's committee were to recommend general obligation bonds as part of its financial plan, the students would need to be consulted and, in most cases, permitted to vote for the student fee increase. Since general obligation bonds are backed by resources beyond the money generated from the project financed by the bond revenue, the bond rating tends to be higher and therefore the interest that needs to be charged can be lower.

Revenue bonds are issued with only the potential financial support of the proposed project. When a revenue bond is issued, potential purchasers must evaluate how likely it is that the project will generate sufficient revenue to repay the bond's interest. If the project is a financial failure, the bond holders have no recourse against the other assets of the issuer. For this reason, revenue bonds tend to be offered at higher interest rates than general obligation bonds in order to attract investors. For example, if a university issued revenue bonds to build a recreation facility, investors would likely want to ensure that the facility would generate sufficient revenue to cover the financial obligations. Often, entities issuing revenue bonds must pay particular attention to activities that generate revenue rather than focusing solely on providing a wide range of program offerings.

Entities wishing to issue bonds will likely need to solicit significant legal and financial assistance. The language of the bond offering must detail a variety of specific information that is more complex than simply stating how and when interest payments are to be made. Small technical or legal errors can result in bond issues being invalidated. Many potential issuers solicit advice from a *bond counsel*—typically someone specifically trained to understand the legal and financial aspects of issuing bonds. A bond counsel can also advise the issuer regarding the bond's overall viability and assist in setting an interest rate that will attract investors (Crompton, 1999).

There are other types of financing mechanism for public entities, including *tax increment financing* (TIF) and *certificates of participation* (COPs). Tax increment financing typically involves areas that have recently experienced a loss of value. The government agency may deem an area a potential redevelopment zone. Once the area is identified, the government agency then issues tax increment bonds and uses the proceeds to purchase land, sometimes through eminent domain, in the redevelopment area. The government then begins to build, repair, or remodel facilities in the acquired land. The bonds are repaid with the increase in tax revenue that the parcels immediately surrounding the redevelopment zone generate. Though not an often utilized funding mechanism, tax increment financing has been utilized by governments to build park and recreation facilities (Crompton, 1999).

Certificates of participation are formed when the government first creates a corporation to buy land and/or build the facility. Next, this corporation issues COPs to raise money for the facility. The government then leases back the land and/or building. The lease payments then help to pay back the interest due to investors (Regan, 1997). Typically, COPs are issued over an extended period of time (20 years or more) (Crompton, 1999). Since the project is not backed fully by the constituents, the aforementioned scenario takes place without a vote from the public. The COP typically will be rated slightly lower than a general obligation bond. This type of arrangement is usually popular during times of recession as real estate values and property taxes are waning (Regan, 1997).

Summary

Though this textbook primarily covers facility and event operations, it is critical to understand the basic elements of financing a public facility. Governments, schools, park districts, and other entities are constantly acquiring land and building or remodeling facilities. An understanding of finance will help anyone working in the facility industry. Ms. Smith's team must investigate every potential funding mechanism. In most cases, a combination of a variety of options will be utilized. Each member of the teams should understand the long-term ramifications of their decisions. If mistakes are made, future projects by the university could be hampered.

Questions

1. What types of constituents should be included on a facility financing team?
2. Why do real estate investors often need to utilize options when purchasing land?
3. Why do governments utilize zoning requirements? How might these requirements potentially impact construction of a sport or entertainment facility?
4. Explain the concept of eminent domain. What are some of the controversies concerning its use for acquiring land for sport and entertainment facilities?
5. What are some important criteria to investigate when selecting potential vendors for a facility construction project?
6. How does inflation impact facility financing sources?
7. If debt financing is to be utilized to finance a facility, what are some key questions that should be answered before proceeding? Why is utilizing debt a potentially risky proposition?
8. What are the differences between general obligation bonds and revenue bonds?

4

Public
Subsidies

Application Exercise

Lynette Jones is the owner of a minor league baseball franchise. She and her staff face a critical dilemma. The team currently plays in a 35-year-old facility that requires extensive maintenance to operate. Five years ago the team's attendance and sponsorship revenues began to decrease, resulting in a diminishing profit level. Three years ago the team's expenses equaled its revenues for the first time in franchise history. During the past two seasons, the team has been unable to generate sufficient revenues to offset expenses, resulting in a financial loss for Ms. Jones. The upcoming season is likely to generate significant financial losses for Ms. Jones, as ticket and sponsorship sales have decreased from last year's levels.

Many of the potential problems are due to the current facility. Ms. Jones and her marketing staff have worked tirelessly to promote the players and the entertainment aspect of the team. However, despite their best efforts, it has been difficult to attract an adequate number of customers because the stadium has a variety of problems. The concourses, concessions stands, and restrooms in the facility are small and cramped. Though the team has updated 20% of the wooden bleachers with new seats, the remaining 80% of the seating is not appealing to most customers. In addition, there are only two luxury suites. Regrettably, the facility has outlived its usefulness, and since it was not designed for expansion, any major remodeling that would make the facility attractive enough to reenergize the fan base will not be cost feasible.

During the past five years, Ms. Jones has been attempting to convince the city and county that the team cannot stay in the current facility due to the financial situation. Though the city has responded by lowering the team's yearly rent, it has balked at providing assistance with maintenance expenses or with sharing some of the parking revenue the city generates from a parking lot it controls across the street from the stadium. Ms. Jones cannot continue to lose money, but she also does not necessarily want to leave the city. Two other cities in the region have offered to build the team a new state-of-the-art facility if the team will agree to move and then commit to staying in their new location for at least 15 years. Ms. Jones is preparing to make a last-ditch plea to the city to build a new facility before she completes her analysis regarding her other two options. Though she hopes to stay, she realizes this is likely the last year for the team in its current location.

History of Professional Sport Facility Financing

For most of the first half of the 20th century, professional sport owners did not receive significant public subsidies from their local municipalities. Though popular, sport was usually not seen as a necessity for the public good. Franchises certainly worked with their local governments on a variety of issues, but cities, counties, and states did not usually view a professional sport franchise as a high priority. In the late 1940s the relationship between governments and teams began to change. After World War II, the United States began to see rapid population growth in a variety of areas such as the West and the South. Technological innovations such as air conditioning allowed previously inhospitable cities not only to grow, but to rapidly increase their population density. The new interstate highway system and air travel connected the United States much more effectively than slower-moving railroads. The entire country became more mobile and no longer did many people live their entire lives in proximity to the area where they were born.

As cities began to attract transplanted residents, the need for structured forms of live entertainment increased. Many rapidly growing cities desired to have professional sports as an entertainment option. In 1946 the Cleveland Rams of the National Football League moved to Los Angeles, becoming the first major professional sport team to move from the Midwest or northeastern section of the United States to the West Coast. The Rams played their home games in the Los Angeles Memorial Coliseum, site of the 1932 Summer Olympic Games. The Rams' move created a problem for visiting teams as it was certainly more expensive and time consuming to travel to Los Angeles from New York, Philadelphia, Boston, and Chicago than it was to travel to Cleveland. The Rams provided an additional $5,000 above the normal revenue sharing for visiting teams during their first years in Los Angeles for this inconvenience (Gietschier, 1995). The Rams experienced many successful years in Los Angeles and received strong fan support throughout much of the team's history.

The city of Milwaukee noted the Rams' move westward and desired to provide its growing population with a major professional sports franchise. For many years Milwaukee had hosted a minor league baseball team (which at one point was owned by legendary baseball maverick Bill Veeck), but city officials felt that attracting a Major League Baseball (MLB) team would provide the city with a "Big League" image. In 1953 the city convinced the Boston Braves to relocate to Milwaukee by offering a newly constructed publicly owned stadium and other financial support. The financially struggling Braves attracted huge crowds and large profits after they moved to Milwaukee, which certainly made every other MLB team take notice.

While the Braves were experiencing tremendous profits in Milwaukee, another MLB team was trying to avoid having to make a move from its longtime home. The Brooklyn Dodgers, a team that had a passionate local fan base, had played for many years in Ebbets Field. By the 1940s, Ebbets Field clearly needed to be replaced. Though Dodger owner Walter O'Malley has long been perceived by many Brooklynites as a mercenary, concerned only with maximizing his profits, he worked tirelessly to build a new facility in Brooklyn. O'Malley did not ask for any direct financial support for construction, but he did ask the city of New York to help with land acquisition, infrastructure improvements involving parking and a subway terminal, and potential zoning changes. Despite O'Malley's efforts, Robert Moses, the New York city parks commissioner and (likely) most powerful man in New York, repeatedly rejected O'Malley's pleas. Moses had deemed that any new stadium would be constructed in Queens (where Shea Stadium would eventually be built for the New York Mets in 1964) rather than in Brooklyn (D'Antonio, 2009).

Once the city of Los Angeles realized that the Dodgers were experiencing potential obstacles to their stadium plans in Brooklyn, government officials began to recruit O'Malley. Eventually, the city offered the Dodgers 352 acres (acquired through eminent domain) located strategically near three Los Angeles freeways in an area known as Chavez Ravine in exchange for a less valuable Los Angeles parcel O'Malley had acquired earlier. O'Malley could eventually build the stadium of his dreams on the land without any concern that the local government would interfere. Despite his love for Brooklyn, O'Malley realized that Los Angeles afforded a new beginning—one where the team could not help but make tremendous financial profits by playing in the rapidly growing Southern California market. O'Malley convinced New York Giants owner Horace Stoneham, who had for years been talking about leaving New York due its dwindling fan base and aging stadium, to move his team to San Francisco, where they

Dodger Stadium is located near three major freeways. (Photo courtesy of Dan Brewster.)

would also eventually receive public financial support for a new facility. With the Giants and the Dodgers moving in 1958, National League teams could travel to California to play both teams over a week rather than just the Dodgers for a few days.

Every professional sport franchise paid close attention to the Dodgers' move. Teams realized that potential profits could be enhanced by receiving direct and indirect financial support from a local municipality. Emerging cities realized that if they wanted to become "Big League" they could entice an established team—even one as locally popular as the Dodgers—to move with the promise of a better financial situation. Cities with professional teams also realized that other cities might attempt to steal their teams, so more public money needed to be made available to retain existing franchises.

During the 1960s and 1970s, numerous American cities began to build or renovate facilities to attract or retain professional sport franchises. In most cases, stadiums were designed to maximize seating capacity since ticket sales were typically one of the most important revenue sources. Large, multiuse facilities became the norm as the local football and baseball teams could share the publicly financed facility. Since most Americans traveled primarily by automobile in the 1960s, the vast majority of sport facilities were constructed in suburban areas where enough land was present to host not only a facility but also thousands of parking spaces. Facilities such as Riverfront Stadium in Cincinnati, Three Rivers Stadium in Pittsburgh, and Veterans Stadium in Philadelphia became known as "cookie-cutter" facilities because they had features similar to most of the rest of the multipurpose facilities built in this timeframe.

In the late 1980s and early 1990s a new facility construction boom began. Two facilities spurred a change in the type of facilities that would be built. In 1988 the National Basketball Association's Detroit Pistons opened The Palace at Auburn Hills, a 22,000-seat facility that included 180 luxury suites. Though most existing facilities had some

Numerous bars and restaurants have opened in the vicinity of Coors Field. (Photo courtesy of Jason Fleming.)

luxury suites, the Pistons' ability to sell all 180 suites generated millions of dollars in revenue that was quickly noticed by every other professional sport franchise as well as most Division I athletic departments. In 1992 Major League Baseball's Baltimore Orioles began playing games at Oriole Park at Camden Yards, a new baseball-only facility with a distinctive design that was unique because it provided fans modern amenities packaged in a retro style. The tremendous financial success of the Detroit Pistons and the Baltimore Orioles caused many other teams to demand new or significantly remodeled facilities. Unfortunately, for some cities such as Miami and Charlotte, The Palace and Camden Yards caused some newer facilities to become instantly financially obsolete though they were structurally sound. In Miami, the NBA's Heat left Miami Arena after only 11 years for the American Airlines Center in 1999. When the Charlotte Hornets played in the 24,000-seat Charlotte Coliseum they set NBA attendance records, but the building had few luxury suites, which partially precipitated a move by the team to New Orleans in 2002. When the expansion Bobcats joined the NBA in 2004, the city quickly built them a new facility that opened in 2005.

Professional Sport Franchises: Economic Boon or Boondoggle?

Though there was a tremendous sport construction boom in the 1990s and early 2000s that was financed often by government resources, not every municipality elected to provide direct financial subsidies to professional sport franchises. Though public support for a private professional sport franchise certainly enhances a professional sport franchise, the potential benefits for the supporting municipality are not as clear. Professional sport franchises certainly have argued that their presence creates tremendous financial benefits for the surrounding community. Much like a manufacturing plant, distribution center, or other organization, a professional sport franchise will generate economic activity. However, recent research indicates that the potential return on investment for the municipality is typically quite low. Unfortunately, proving the true economic impact is quite difficult due to the need to utilize economic impact studies. These studies involve the gathering of data concerning the spending habits of visitors who have come to the local community *specifically* because of the sporting event. Once the initial data is collected and the *direct spending* is determined, the application of *multipliers* is utilized to determine the total *indirect* and *induced spending* that occurs. The selection of applicable multipliers is often subject to interpretation or even potential bias, making it difficult to trust many of the numbers that are reported. Perhaps one of the most indicative problems regarding economic impact studies involved the Baltimore Colts leaving for Indianapolis in 1984. City of Baltimore officials, trying to appease constituents upset about the team's departure, contended that their economic impact analysis showed the Colts generated minimal economic impact for the city of Baltimore and the state of Maryland. However, the Colts' economic impact study (cited as one of the reasons the city should have provided a greater subsidy) indicated that the local community would lose millions of dollars once the Colts vacated. Each faction retained highly qualified economists to conduct its study, making it difficult for citizens to understand the team's true economic value to the region.

Though there is often confusion regarding sport franchises' and facilities' exact economic impact, numerous sport economists have recently raised several commonsense questions about their economic effect. Though major North American professional sport franchises do hire highly paid players, many of these players do not live in the local community throughout the year. The majority of the remaining full-time employees (normally around 100) typically do not make high salaries. In addition, many team employees are part-time workers who usually work at the facility only on game days. The overall economic impact numbers for minor league sports are typically worse (though the initial government investments are considerably lower), as not only will the small number of staff members be hourly employees, but the players also usually do not earn salaries that are much higher than the national average.

Proponents of extensive sport subsidies have argued that constructing new facilities can lead to a revitalization of the area surrounding the facility. Prominent examples such as the lower Denver area surrounding Coors Field are often cited as the reason why a new facility should be subsidized. Though anyone who has visited the area surrounding Coors Field can appreciate the large number of bars and restaurants that did not exist prior to the facility's construction, many economists warn that these revitalized areas are simply displacing other businesses in the local marketplace. The only money that is truly providing an economic impact is the new money that is entering the marketplace from visitors. If there are citizens who have chosen to eat at a restaurant near the stadium rather than at one three miles away, then economic activity has merely been shifted from one vendor to another. In addition, if customers are attending games in a new facility, it must be determined what their entertainment purchases would have been if the facility did not exist. If fans have merely attended the game instead of going to the movies or a concert that evening, then those individual's spending has merely shifted. The overall tax revenues accrued from consumer spending has not changed, as the same amount of money is being spent by customers; it is just being paid to new vendors.

In addition to the potential minimal return on investment, economists also note that many sport and entertainment facilities that cost a city, county, or state hundreds of millions of dollars hurt the government's *opportunity costs*—the other options that were potentially available at the time the team's subsidy was provided. For instance, if a municipality invests $100 million in direct support of a team's new facility, that is $100 million that cannot be returned to the citizens as tax refunds, used to build new roads, bridges, or canals, or provided as a subsidy to other businesses that might hire many more employees resulting in a higher net economic impact. In some cases, the newly constructed facility actually may act as a financial detriment to the city.

Though the research regarding the economic impact of professional sport facilities typically argues against extensive direct financial support, sport organizations do provide *psychic benefits* not easily mimicked by other businesses. The presence of a major professional sport team can signal to the rest of the country that a metropolitan area is "Big League," rather than merely another mid-sized city. Unlike a supermarket, automobile dealership, or dentist's office, a sport team can capture a city's, a county's, or an entire state's attention. A sport franchise's performance, as well as its star players' exploits, are tracked daily in the media. Teams are marketed to fans as belonging to the community, and fans will often embrace a team's success and failures as their own, basking in the reflected glory (BIRGing) of a championship season. Though the emotional benefits of hosting a professional team may be felt by local citizens, measuring and quantifying the specific psychic benefits of an individual franchise is difficult. Most people would recognize that sport generates passion and excitement among the local community, but further research regarding the value of this income to the community (and hence the potential subsidy that an individual municipality should provide) should be investigated. For some communities, the loss of a team would devastate a majority of the citizenry, but for other sport franchises, minimal psychic impact would occur.

Ultimately, if a municipality wishes to subsidize a sport facility or event, it should thoroughly understand the potential benefits and detriments. There are certainly examples where the economic and psychic benefits accruing from the team may be worth a public investment. For instance, because the town of Green Bay, Wisconsin, is much smaller than most other NFL cities, the Packers' presence has a huge impact on the local economy and upon the citizens' mood. When the Packers played in the Super Bowl in 1997, every hotel room in Green Bay was sold out for two weeks after the National Football Conference (NFC) Championship Game. Since Green Bay does not typically attract thousands of tourists in late January, the Super Bowl appearance generated significant economic activity. The presence of tourists and media members in the city hotels was particularly interesting because the Super Bowl, and therefore, the Packers, were in New Orleans, Louisiana, rather than Wisconsin for the final week prior to the game. While the Packers may be an example of a large economic and psychic benefit to a local community, the city of Los Angeles provides an interesting contrast. The city's economy has certainly not been greatly affected by the Rams' and Raiders' 1995 moves to St. Louis and Oakland respectively. In addition, numerous pundits have noted that the community really does not miss having a professional football team in town.

The Oakland Raiders were lured back to Oakland in 1995 with a subsidy for improvements to the Oakland-Alameda County Coliseum.

Forms of Public Subsidies for Private Sport Franchises

Municipalities can provide a variety of direct and indirect forms of subsidies to attract or retain a professional sport franchise. This section is designed to introduce some of the more popular subsidies that are utilized. Table 4-1 provides a list of selected facilities and the form of government support that was provided for their new facility.

As with any business, a direct financial subsidy in the form of a yearly government check is certainly beneficial to a professional sport franchise. As part of their 2001 lease agreement with the city to remain in the Superdome, the New Orleans Saints were to receive $186.5 million in direct subsides over a 10-year period. In 2009, the Saints renegotiated their arrangement. Though the new agreement diminishes the city's direct cash subsidization, it made other concessions, including $85 million in Superdome improvements. Critics of such an arrangement allege that corrupt or incompetent government officials are willing to provide the Saints, a for-profit business, with public subsidies while the city of New Orleans suffers from severe financial and social problems due to a stagnant economy and devastation from Hurricane Katrina. The Saints have defended these payments as a necessary component of maintaining the Saints in Louisiana. In addition, the Saints have noted their first home game after Hurricane Katrina, in the newly rebuilt Superdome, provided a truly unique opportunity for the city and state to come together, heal, and celebrate. The team and it supporters argue that the Saints provide a common interest that would be lost if the team were to leave the region ("Saints Agree to New," 2009).

Most professional sport franchises do not receive a yearly check from a government source. Due to potential political backlash, it is usually much more beneficial to provide

The City of San Francisco provided no direct financial subsidy to the Giants, but it did improve roads and public transportation when AT&T Park was built.

the subsidy through another mechanism rather than a direct payment. One of the most politically viable methods to provide support for a professional sport franchise is to approve zoning changes and to enhance the infrastructure surrounding the proposed new facility. Most constituents do not deem zoning changes to have a direct financial cost for the citizenry. Infrastructure improvements, though certainly beneficial to the professional team, can also be beneficial to the surrounding community. The San Francisco Giants played for many years in Candlestick Park. The facility, built in an area where wind gusts caused fans attending summertime games to often wear heavy jackets to stay warm, had begun to show its age in the 1980s. Four times, the team tried unsuccessfully to convince taxpayers to help directly fund a new facility. Eventually, the team realized that if they were going to build a new facility that it would have to be almost exclusively privately financed. However, despite the city and county refusing to provide any direct financial support for the project's construction, the government did assist the Giants by building a new freeway off-ramp and by widening roads near the facility at a cost of $80 million (Gordon, 2004). Many citizens who opposed direct subsidies to the Giants are happy with the infrastructure improvements, since they enhance traffic flow.

Taxes

The most common method that governments have to raise money for professional sport facilities is to change the tax code. As discussed in Chapter 3, governments often will issue bonds that are backed by various revenue sources to raise money to build a facility. Municipalities may also offer *tax abatements* to professional sport franchises. Though tax abatements essentially result in a financial loss for the government since tax revenues are reduced, many citizens and politicians do not understand the financial ramifications since abatements are often not seen as a direct subsidy. In 1982, the city of New York agreed to eliminate the yearly property tax owed by Madison Square Garden, the home of the NBA's New York Knicks and the NHL's New York Rangers. The abatement was provided to help pay for facility remodeling and to prevent the teams from seeking another potential home. Though for many years few people complained, recently pundits have noted that the Dolan family, which also owns Cablevision and other profitable businesses, is receiving a $14 million subsidy and has accumulated over $300 million in total forgiven taxes since 1982 (Katz, 2009). Ed Koch, the mayor of New York City in 1982, thought the subsidy would be eliminated after 10 years, but the legislation authorizing the tax forgiveness is to be enforced as long as the teams continue to play in Madison Square Garden ("NYC Council: Enough," 2009). Critics of the agreement note the tremendous financial subsidy to the teams is occurring at a time when the city has numerous financial needs. In addition, the subsidy was probably unnecessary when first proposed because the teams are unlikely to leave Manhattan.

There is a growing trend against the subsidy of professional sport franchises, particularly when a direct tax increase is utilized as the subsidy mechanism. The increase in an existing tax or the creation of a new tax will likely be met with political resistance. Many citizens feel that they are overtaxed and that additional tax money generated by the government is likely to be wasted. When a new tax goes directly to subsidize a

Table 4-1.

League	Team	Sales Tax	Hotel Tax	Rental Car Tax	Food & Beverage Tax	Long Term Loan	Entertainment Tax	Sin Tax	
MLB	Astros		X	X					
	Brewers	X						X	
	Cardinals					X			
	Diamondbacks	X							
	Giants								
	Indians							X	
	Mariners	X		X	X				
	Mets								
	Nationals				X				
	Orioles								
	Padres		X						
	Phillies			X					
	Pirates	X	X						
	Rangers	X							
	Reds	X							
	Rockies	X							
	Tigers		X	X					
	White Sox		X						
	Yankees								
NBA	Cavaliers							X	
	Hawks			X					
	Heat		X						
	Magic		X	X					
	Mavericks		X	X					
	Pacers	X	X	X	X			X	
	Rockets		X	X					
	Spurs	X	X	X					
	Suns	X							
	Thunder	X							
	Timberwolves						X		

	Parking Tax	Property Tax	Wage Tax	Admission Tax	Lottery Revenues	Excise Tax	Sewer & Water Revenues	Gas Tax	Project Generated redevelopment fund	General Fund
										X
		X								
				X	X					
		X								
				X						
					X					
		X							X	
				X						X
	X		X							X
										X
										X
										X
	X	X								
								X		
				X						
	X	X								

(continued on next page.)

Table 4-1. — Continued

League	Team	Sales Tax	Hotel Tax	Rental Car Tax	Food & Beverage Tax	Long Term Loan	Entertainment Tax	Sin Tax	
NFL	Bengals	X							
	Broncos	X							
	Browns			X					
	Buccaneers	X							
	Cardinals	X							
	Colts				X				
	Cowboys	X	X	X					
	Eagles			X					
	Falcons		X						
	Jaguars	X	X						
	Lions		X	X					
	Packers	X							
	Rams		X						
	Ravens								
	Seahawks	X	X	X					
	Steelers	X	X						
	Texans		X	X					
	Titans								
NHL	Coyotes	X							
	Hurricanes		X						
	Lightning	X	X	X	X				
	Panthers	X	X						
	Predators								
	Sabres								
	Sharks								
	Stars		X	X					
	Thrashers			X					
	Wild	X							
Future Stadium									
MLB	Twins (2012)	X							

	Parking Tax	Property Tax	Wage Tax	Admission Tax	Lottery Revenues	Excise Tax	Sewer & Water Revenues	Gas Tax	Project Generated redevelopment fund	General Fund
										X
	X			X						
			X							
				X						
					X					
					X					
							X			
						X				
	X			X						

professional sport franchise, a high level of resistance is likely. In some cases, proposed taxes are voted on by the citizens through direct referendum; in other cases, the city, county, or state legislature may vote for the tax increase. In Wisconsin, State Senator George Petak had consistently noted his reluctance to vote for a tax to subsidize the new Miller Park for the Milwaukee Brewers. When Petak changed his mind and voted in favor of the subsidy in 1996, he was recalled by his constituents and voted out of office. Petak's experience was minor compared to what happened to Maricopa County Supervisor Mary Rose Wilcox. After voting to subsidize the Arizona Diamondbacks' new facility with a quarter-cent sales tax increase, Wilcox was shot by Larry Naman. Wilcox fortunately survived the incident.

Taxes issued to help subsidize professional sports can be paid by all citizens or by those affected by the new area of taxation. For instance, imposed *sales taxes* will usually be charged on all purchases made within the designated area. Every citizen who makes a purchase, regardless of his or her desire to ever attend a professional sporting event, will be funding the facility. For example, citizens in the counties in and surrounding the city of Denver agreed to a sales tax increase in 1998 to fund the Broncos' new stadium—Invesco Field at Mile High. The Broncos' sales tax proposal received an added boost since the team had won the Super Bowl over the Green Bay Packers earlier that year.

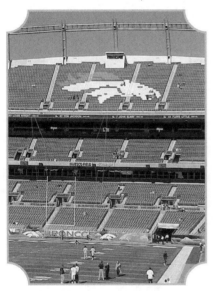

Invesco Field at Mile High was funded by a sales tax increase.

When a sales tax is passed, there is always a concern that the tax will have a *regressive* aspect that disproportionately impacts the poor and lower-middle class. To prevent this, sometimes *property taxes* are utilized. Property taxes are paid only by those citizens who own property—typically real estate. Since real estate renters usually do not make as much income as real estate owners, a property tax will tend to be paid by the upper-middle class and the rich rather than the lower-middle class and the poor. However, in a quest to capture any potential revenue source, some municipalities have begun to issue personal property taxes on items such as automobiles. This type of property tax will usually affect more residents than taxes on real estate and are therefore sometimes more difficult to pass.

Since local residents usually pay a higher percentage of sales and property taxes than visitors, these types of taxes can experience significant political backlash when proposed. However, other forms of taxation can be more easily passed since the people who will pay the majority of the taxes have no direct influence on the passage of the tax. *Tourism taxes* such as *hotel* and *rental-car taxes* are paid by the people who utilize these services. When a person stays at a hotel or rents a car, a tax is added to the final bill. The Seattle Mariners' Safeco Field was partially funded by a variety of tourism taxes. Though tourism taxes tend to be popular in areas where tourism is a central component of the economy, they have recently received closer examination. Though the majority of hotel rooms and car rental transactions are made by out-of-town visitors, the numbers of locals paying these taxes is higher than many had initially believed. Many local businesses pay hotel taxes to house incoming visitors. In addition, the percentage of cars rented by local citizens and businesses has recently been increasing. Tourism taxes are also subject to rapid shifts due to emergencies or dramatic changes in the economy. When a major hurricane destroys parts of a city, tourism is limited and tourism tax revenue decreases. During an economic slowdown, people are often reluctant to spend considerable sums of money to take a vacation, resulting in a decrease in tourism tax revenues.

Within the past 25 years, numerous government entities have passed taxes on the consumption of products and services that are not deemed to be beneficial to consumers. *Sin taxes* on items such as alcohol and tobacco can generate significant revenues—as long as citizens continue to consume those products. Cuyahoga County in Ohio has utilized cigarette and liquor taxes to fund Quicken Loans Arena and Jacobs Field, the homes of the NBA's Cavaliers and MLB's Indians, respectively. There is always a potential problem for governments utilizing sin taxes as consumers who decide to limit or eliminate their consumption of these products will no longer contribute to tax revenues.

In addition to alcohol and tobacco taxes, numerous states have sponsored lotteries to raise money for a variety of sources, including professional sport facilities. The state of Maryland utilized lottery funds to assist in the financing of Oriole Park at Camden Yards and M&T Bank Stadium (home of the Baltimore Ravens). Proponents of lotteries note that anyone can avoid subsidizing the lottery's beneficiaries because lottery participation is voluntary. However, lottery opponents note the poor—those least able to afford Orioles or Ravens' tickets—tend to participate in lotteries at a disproportionate rate. In addition to taxes on alcohol, tobacco, and gambling, some state and local governments have began to propose taxes on items such as red meat and carbonated beverages because they are "harmful" to consumers ("Cooking the Books," 2009). Though these types of taxes have not yet been passed in most areas, it is likely that once they are implemented, professional sport franchises will ask the government to receive a portion of these proceeds.

Though not utilized often, perhaps the best method of taxation to construct a professional sports' facility is to implement *entertainment taxes*. Typically, an entertainment tax is placed upon a ticket purchased for an event. These taxes are therefore paid only by the end users of the product—in this case the attendee at a professional sporting event. For many critics, entertainment taxes are the absolute best way to fund a sport facility because anyone who does not visit the facility can avoid paying the tax. Ticket taxes for sporting events have typically not been supported because in most cases additional sources of tax revenue must be procured to fund sport facilities. However, the theory behind entertainment taxes may be helping to spur the reluctance of municipalities to directly subsidize professional sport franchises. Ultimately, if a professional team finances and builds its own facility, the attending customers will pay for the facility. If there is not a sufficient number of ticket buyers, the team will lose money and may eventually go bankrupt. For many sport owners, the San Francisco Giants' decision to build a privately financed facility was concerning because it signaled a continuing trend away from public subsidies toward a system where the teams, and their customers, finance new facilities.

Summary

During the past 30 years, privately owned professional sport franchises have sought government support for their operations—typically in the form of funding for new or significantly remodeled facilities. Government subsidies for professional sports franchises can be provided in many different forms. Regardless of the type of subsidy, the potential backlash from citizens is always present. For some, professional sport is seen as an important economic and emotional component of a metropolitan area, while for others, professional sport is a private enterprise that provides little benefit to anyone beyond the owners, participants, and attendees. As governments continue to address numerous budgetary issues, the debate regarding potentially funding professional sport organizations will continue.

Questions

1. Why did cities begin to subsidize professional sport franchises in the 1950s?
2. How do you feel about the Dodgers leaving Brooklyn for Los Angeles in 1958? What were the main issues regarding the move?
3. How did Oriole Park at Camden Yards and the Palace at Auburn Hills change professional sport? What do you think may be the new amenities that customers may want in future facilities?
4. Explain the concept of economic impact analysis. How can these studies be misinterpreted or potentially abused?
5. Define "psychic income." How much psychic income does your school's basketball team provide to the campus and the surrounding community?
6. List and explain the various forms of typical public subsidies of professional sport franchises. What are the positives and negatives of each form?

5

Revenues and Expenses

Application Exercise

Laura Smith's committee, which analyzed and selected financing options for a
new campus event and recreation center (Chapter 3), has a second task it must
undertake. Before the facility is financed and built, the committee must project
revenue and expenses from yearly operations. Smith's committee cannot recommend
that the facility be built unless the facility can remain financially viable after it has been
constructed and opened. Therefore, the committee must analyze and project financial
operations for the first five years of the facility. In order to make an informed decision,
the committee will need to seek information regarding the operation of similar facilities
at other schools. In addition, it must determine any factors that are unique to its campus before completing the final projections. Failure to properly project revenues and expenses will result in the university raising additional emergency revenue from other
campus sources or diverting funds budgeted for other projects to fund the potential
shortfall. For this reason the committee must ensure that its projections are accurate before proceeding with financing and construction.

Introduction

Projecting revenue and expenses is one of the most important aspects of managing a
sport or entertainment facility. If yearly revenues do not at least match yearly expenses,
then a financial loss will occur. Consistent financial losses for private businesses lead to
bankruptcy and potential closure. The goal of any facility manager will be to generate
revenues that exceed expenses by a targeted percentage so that the facility can remain
open and investors can earn profits. If a business cannot generate profits, investors are
likely to seek opportunities to divest and put their money in more successful ventures.

The financial goals in a publicly owned facility may be different from those of a private individual or corporation. In many cases, managers of publicly owned facilities are
asked only to match revenues with expenses. In some cases, a government agency may
actually be willing to subsidize yearly financial losses in order to provide services for local constituents. For instance, some city or county governments may allow venues to
host live entertainment events at a financial loss so that they can tell their constituents
that the facility is bringing an entertainment option to the citizens and recognition to

the metropolitan area. Operating in a financial situation where a profit does not have to be realized certainly permits the facility manager to participate in potential activities that might otherwise be unattainable.

Regardless of the ownership status of a facility, every facility manager wants to increase revenues and limit expenses. Higher revenues present opportunities for the facility and its staff, whether they are utilized to increase salaries, host more events, remodel the venue, or participate in other activities. In order for this to occur, facility managers must have a detailed understanding of their current revenues and expenses. In addition, it is critical that managers research and project the likely availability of revenue sources and potential expenses in the future. The sport and entertainment industry is constantly evolving, and significant revenue sources from the past and present are not necessarily going to be available in the future. The informed facility manager must have the foresight to adapt facility operations in anticipation of industry shifts.

The following section details some of the typical potential sources of revenues and expenses for a facility. In many cases, certain revenue sources have been briefly introduced in this chapter but are explained in greater detail in later chapters.

Selected Facility Revenue Sources

Tickets

The first revenue source that is typically associated with sport and entertainment facilities and events is ticket sales (sometimes called gate receipts). For most live events, an admission fee will be charged. For this reason, most facility managers will consistently tell their staff, "Tickets are the life-blood of our business." One of the most important marketing concepts that any business should remember is that the most difficult and expensive thing to do is to make the first sale. Overcoming the initial resistance typically requires a considerable investment in time and money. Once the initial sale has been completed, if customers have a positive experience during their first visit they are much more likely to be repeat purchasers. Marketers often discuss acquiring new customers and then attempting to spur those existing customers to consistently purchase more products or services. It is critical that existing customers are not taken for granted. Far too often, businesses rely on their regular patrons for much of their overall revenue. Though it is easier to retain current customers, it is certainly not guaranteed.

These marketing concepts certainly apply to tickets for live events. Sport and entertainment organizations invest a tremendous amount of time trying to convince customers to purchase their first ticket. Often, this convincing is done through special promotions or on-site giveaways. Once a customer has attended an event, the organization will work to increase his or her consumption by attempting to sell him or her additional tickets to future events. As a person shows an interest in purchasing more tickets, the organization may offer *mini-plans*, which are a series of ticketed events during the season. There may be a theme that is attached to the mini-plan. For instance, in Major League Baseball (MLB) a team may sell a Sunday game mini-plan that provides tickets to every game on Sundays throughout the season. In the National Basketball Association (NBA), a team may offer a mini-plan that revolves around a specific set of visiting players, such as a package of games against selected all-stars or rising rookies. Symphony orchestras or other live entertainment events may also offer mini-plans. A symphony may offer a mini-plan revolving around German or Austrian composers. The goal with mini-plans is to increase the consumption of previous individual event ticket buyers.

Ultimately, the sport or entertainment organization should be working to motivate regular customers to purchase *season tickets*. A season ticket plan provides tickets to every game on the schedule (and typically permits the purchaser to have rights to purchase potential playoff game tickets). A season ticket is beneficial to the organization for a variety of reasons. Season tickets are usually purchased prior to the commencement of the season, so the organization receives all of the money for those ticket sales prior to allocating and paying any expenses for game operations (security, ushers, etc.). Some teams have begun to offer season ticket-holders the option to pay a portion of their season ticket money over extended periods of time. Though the team may prefer to have the money in one lump sum, certain factors, such as poor economic conditions, may influence the team to have a more flexible collection policy. It is certainly better to receive all the owed money over a period of time rather than not make a season ticket sale. Since a ticket has been sold for the entire season, the sales staff will not need to worry about that seat when it is selling single-game tickets or mini-plans. Season ticket sales also assist the game operations staff to prepare for anticipated crowds for each event.

Though tickets are and will continue to remain an important revenue source in the future, numerous other revenue sources have slowly diminished the importance of tickets. The percentage of overall generated revenues from ticket sales has been steadily decreasing over the past 30 years for most sport organizations.

Luxury Suites and Club Seating

While general admission tickets have recently decreased in importance, revenues from *luxury suites* and *club seating* have increased dramatically over the past 15 years. A luxury suite (sometimes called a luxury box) provides a sequestered-seating area as well as other comforts, such a private kitchen, bathroom, and eating area. Most luxury suite-holders are able to decorate their suites to their specific tastes. Usually, separate tickets for every event in the facility will be offered for sale to the luxury suite-holder. Much of the emphasis in recent facility construction has revolved around the plan to create more luxury suites to offer to individuals and businesses capable of paying much higher prices than those typically charged for tickets. In many cases, customers do not even care if the luxury suite has a direct view of the event. The Palace at Auburn Hills introduced five underground luxury suites leasing for $450,000 each in 2005. The suites were well received and the following year eight more suites were added at a leasing cost of $350,000 each per year ("The Palace of Auburn Hills," n.d.). Though the suites lack a direct view of the basketball floor, they have a variety of other special amenities, such as VIP parking and a separate facility entrance that make the attendees feel like they are visiting an exclusive club. Numerous other sport and entertainment facilities have also created no-view luxury seating.

All seats do not generate the same amount of revenue, but all are important to a sport facility's success.

Club seats are typically more comfortable than other seat options.

Club seats are another fairly new offering for facility patrons. Club seats afford a patron the opportunity to sit in the main seating sections of the facility, but in a more expensive seat. Club seats are usually wider and more comfortable than other seats in a facility and offer additional amenities, such as waiter service or separate concession areas. Some club seats may also offer video screens to watch individualized replays of prior game action. Many affluent patrons prefer the experience of sitting in a club seat rather than a luxury box because it is typically closer to the field and usually provides the customer the opportunity to better experience the feelings and emotions of the crowd.

Though the club seat experience is typically associated with professional sport and National Collegiate Athletic Association (NCAA) Division I athletics, a variety of sporting events have incorporated club seat concepts into their revenue plans. Numerous high schools have created club seats by cordoning off specific seating areas and providing those ticket-holders special privileges, such as access to a coach's pre-game talk or the players' post-game press conference. Though the special area may not be as nice as a club seat at a professional sporting event, the concept supporting the sale of club seats is similar regardless of the venue. By providing special amenities, facilities can potentially increase revenues.

Concessions

Concession sales can often be the most important revenue source for many facilities. Typically, the markup on concession items is quite large and attending customers do not have any options outside the available facility vendors. Every facility should conduct a *per cap analysis* at the conclusion of each event. A per cap analysis divides the total concession sales by the number of attendees in order to determine the average attendee purchase. Per cap analyses enable the facility to chart the changes in concessions sales from event to event. If the per cap is increasing or decreasing, the facility can investigate the potential reasons for the changes. Sometimes, the changes occur for reasons outside the control of the facility, such as when beverage sales increase due to extremely hot weather or decrease due to cooler weather. In other instances, the increase or decrease may be due to a change in the performance of the employees providing the customer service. Once the reason for the per cap change has been identified, appropriate action can be taken to either accentuate the per cap increases or diminish the per cap decreases. Some facilities have begun to chart per caps for individual sections of the facility. In addition, *fan affinity cards* may enable a facility to chart the specific purchasing behavior of individual patrons.

Facilities must determine specific policies that may impact concession sales. For instance, some facilities do not allow patrons to bring any outside food or beverages into the facility. Other facilities may permit outside food on a limited basis. Nearly every facility will prohibit patrons from entering the facility with containers, such as a bottle or unopened aluminum can, which can be potentially used as a projectile.

Every facility must analyze anticipated crowds to determine how many concession stands will be open for that event. If the facility opens too many stands, then employee costs will increase without a corresponding increase in revenues. However, if too few stands are open, long lines may develop, which could lead to disgruntled customers and a potential loss of sales. The facility should also examine what the crowd will likely consume from the concession stands. For some events, certain food and beverage items may not be appealing and therefore time and resources should not be invested in providing a large amount of those products. For instance, the sale of concession items may vary tremendously between a family show and a heavy-metal concert.

Parking

Revenues from parking have become important for many facilities. Some teams are now not only charging a fee when a car enters the lot, but customers who tailgate in additional spaces will be identified by facility personnel and charged an additional parking fee. When customers are to be charged for parking, their expectations regarding the service in the parking lot will increase. Adequate signage should direct approaching vehicles to their appropriate entry-point. Parking staff should be friendly

Well-organized and supervised parking lots can enhance facility revenue.

and knowledgeable not only about the parking lot, but also regarding other general facility policies. The facility should ensure that cars are able to quickly and efficiently enter and exit the parking area. Spaces should be clearly marked and specific areas for compact cars, larger vehicles, and buses should be provided. In addition, security monitors should regularly inspect the parking lot activities before, during, and after the event. Some facilities are now offering additional parking services, such as escorts to their cars after games or free battery charges for cars that will not start. Providing exceptional service helps to ensure that parking fees are not seen as a significant detriment to attending future events.

Licensed Merchandise

One of the most important revenue sources for most facilities is licensed merchandise. Players, teams, and leagues as well as musical acts and other performers often will desire to sell officially licensed products to attending spectators. Twenty years ago licensed merchandise typically involved hats, T-shirts, and some other souvenir items. However, most facilities now offer a variety of items, ranging from bobble heads to seat cushions to yo-yos. Some sport teams have even begun to offer officially licensed coffins and urns that can be ordered to continue following the team after death ("Red Sox Fans Can Get," 2008).

To maximize potential revenues, the facility should provide sufficient space to ensure that customers have room to comfortably stand in line. Signage that clearly displays product offerings and prices can quicken transactions, resulting in more potential sales. Providing properly trained employees in sufficient numbers to meet demand also helps keep customer lines moving efficiently. One of the critical components of maximizing licensed merchandise sales is to police the facility for illegal sales of *bootlegged merchandise* (see Chapter 14). Venues that host concerts must be particularly concerned about rogue salespeople attempting to sell T-shirts and other items before and after a concert. Each illegal sale decreases potential revenue for the facility and the performer and is a violation of intellectual property law.

Sponsorships

Perhaps one of the most dramatic changes over the past 30 years in the operation of sport and entertainment facilities has been the increased emphasis upon corporate *sponsorship*. Though signage at sport and entertainment events has always been present, facilities now better understand how to incorporate various additional sponsorship opportunities with existing signage to create a package that provides benefits to the investing sponsor. Sport and entertainment facilities can provide a sponsor access to patrons through signage, hospitality areas, public address announcements, on-site product giveaways, product coupons, and numerous other sources. Each of these sources has a potential value. Every facility will have at least one person dedicated to the identification, investigation, and solicitation of potential sponsors. In addition, facilities will usually retain staff members who provide service to existing corporate partners. Much like selling tickets, it is much more difficult to sell a sponsorship the first time than it is to retain and enhance the relationship with existing sponsors. Ensuring that sponsors are receiving more than what is contractually required is a critical component to providing quality service.

Though corporate signage has been a part of sport and entertainment facilities for many decades, the use of *naming rights* agreements is a fairly new business transaction. Though there had been corporate monikers attached to sport facilities due to the owners' relationship to the team or facility (Wrigley Field, Busch Stadium, etc.), the first time a company agreed to pay to have its name attached to a professional sport facility was the 1973 naming rights agreement between Rich Products Corporation and the County of Erie, New York, to name the home of the NFL's Buffalo Bills. Few naming rights agreements were signed during the rest of the 1970s and 1980s, but during the 1990s, the majority of professional sport facilities agreed to sell their name to a corporate partner. By securing the naming rights to a facility, a company could avoid potential *advertising clutter* from the numerous other signs in the venue.

Naming rights agreements typically generate millions of dollars per year to the facility. Though naming rights agreements have continued to be popular, some companies have begun to ask if the typical multimillion-dollar price for the naming rights is worth the investment. Some naming rights agreements have resulted in fan and media backlash. Though 3Com Corporation was successful in increasing its community recognition through its naming rights agreement with San Francisco's Candlestick Park, many local fans and members of the media refused to utilize the new moniker. Some also expressed their extreme disappointment and derision for the new corporate partner. Though the backlash to the Giants and their corporate partner was mostly due to the loss of a historical name, the New York Mets' naming rights deal with Citibank has encountered resistance from fans due to the role banks played in the economic meltdown and the subsequent federal bailout money that was provided to support the banks. Many critics were concerned that Citibank was funding its multimillion-sponsorship agreement with federal taxpayer dollars.

Confusion has also occurred when naming rights partners have been purchased by another company. One of the critical components of building *brand equity* is the consistency of the brand name. When a naming rights partner is purchased by another company, the new company must elect to retain the old corporate moniker or rename the facility. In Philadelphia, Pennsylvania, the home of the NBA's 76ers and the NHL's Flyers was first named the First Union Center, then the CoreStates Center, and then the Wachovia Center. Each time the facility is renamed, potential consumer confusion can decrease the value of the sponsorship (Nagel, 1999).

Though every sponsorship agreement retains some risks for both the sponsor and the facility, in extreme circumstances the relationship can become untenable due to one party's unsavory actions. A sponsor that offends a significant group of people in the community can have that anger and resentment reflected toward the facility. Starting in 1999 Enron was the naming rights sponsor of MLB's Houston Astros. When Enron's numerous financial scandals became public in 2001, anyone or anything associated with the company was portrayed negatively. Unfortunately for the Astros, despite the scandal, Enron continued to make its naming rights payments. The Astros were forced to pay Enron $2.1 million to end their naming rights partnership in 2002 so the team could eventually resell the name to Minute Maid ("Judge Ends," 2002).

Media

Though attracting media attention is a critical component of facility management, the vast majority of events will not result in a media outlet paying to have exclusive rights to broadcast. Certainly, major professional sport organizations such as the NFL, NBA, MLB, and NASCAR are able to negotiate multimillion-dollar rights agreements, but most sporting events will either receive no revenue from media contracts or will operate as a partner with the media by agreeing to cover some or all of the production costs while also retaining responsibility for advertising sales. Certainly, the goal of any facility should be to develop media revenues. Having staff people who are responsible for media negotiations is an important step when attempting to generate revenues in this area. If a media partner does pay to provide coverage, it is critical that the me-

Media coverage requires significant accommodation. (BigStock Photo)

dia outlet be provided the space and support necessary to perform its tasks effectively. Media partners who encounter difficulty when trying to broadcast an event are less likely to invest their time and money in the future.

Facility Rentals

Every facility should strive to have as many events throughout the year as possible. Traditionally, sport and entertainment facilities have focused upon the main event areas when investigating possible tenants. For instance, a baseball stadium would focus on its primary tenant, the baseball team, as well as seek concerts and other events. Since each of those tenants would likely require significant time before and after each event for set-up and take-down, the total number of possible events is likely limited to one per day or, in some cases, less than one per day. In the past 10 years, many facilities have begun to realize that other areas of their facility may be of interest to potential tenants. Many facilities have begun to rent some of their lounges and restaurant areas to individuals and businesses looking for a unique location to have a party. During these events, the changeovers that may be occurring on the playing surface are not an inhibitor to the tenant's enjoyment of the facility.

Facilities have also realized that some patrons may wish to tour the facility throughout the year—even when the primary tenant is not in season. Facility tours are now available at many professional sport facilities because they are an easy method to generate revenues. Professional sport facilities now also usually offer patrons the opportunity to "play like the pros" at fantasy camps. There are a significant number of fans who would like to step into the batter's box or shoot baskets at their favorite team's facility.

User Fees and Memberships

Some recreational facilities, particularly those on a college campus, do not operate live entertainment events. Though recreation facilities may not be as glamorous as a professional sport facility, there are typically many more recreational facilities and, hence, more employment opportunities. Much like selling tickets, a recreation facility may offer a *user fee* to patrons who wish to access the facility. Patrons may desire to purchase a membership that entitles them to use the facility as many times as they wish over an extended period of time. Selling memberships provides benefits similar to those from selling a season ticket. Revenues are collected prior to the patron using the facility over the allotted period of time. Unfortunately, many recreation facilities have taken many of their members for granted. Far too often, recreation centers will contract with a member for an extended period of time. During the time of the membership, the facility should ensure that the customer continues to have a positive experience. When a member does not use the facility, her likelihood of renewing her membership decreases and her likelihood of telling others of her experiences increases. Sadly, instead of focusing on generating long-term profits through enhanced customer retention, many facilities are content to have paid customers not use the facility and then subsequently not renew their memberships. The facility then has to work harder and spend more money to replace those non-renewing customers.

Student Fees

Though most people think that media and ticketing revenues are the largest source of college athletic department funding, student fees are actually the number one source of revenue for the vast majority of athletic departments. On some campuses, the allocation of student fees causes tension. Students are typically more likely to understand if semester student fees are charged to utilize a campus recreation center than they are if fees are used to fund intercollegiate athletics—particularly if students are also charged high prices for desirable games or if they are restricted in accessing athletic contests due to demand from other stakeholders. Proposing student fee increases is a political process. Athletic departments that rely extensively on student fees must be careful that they do not bite the hand that feeds them by simply taking students' money without demonstrating how the fees benefit the entire student body.

Donations and Grants

Nonprofit or government-owned or -operated facilities may be eligible to receive money for their good deeds. For instance, many colleges and universities seek donations for their athletic departments. The donors are given an opportunity to help the athletic department make improvements to athletic or recreation facilities while receiving a tax deduction. In some cases, donations are the facility's largest revenue source. Grants are often provided to facilities for their participation in activities that assist in the development of key constituents. For example, many college athletic facilities and community recreation centers apply for government grants to operate camps for low-income children who would otherwise not be able to participate in a paid-camp experience.

There are certainly numerous additional methods that facilities utilize to generate revenues. Each facility has a unique set of circumstances. Regardless of the situation, every facility should analyze and understand their current revenue mechanisms before attempting to procure additional sources.

Typical Facility Expenses

Before assessing any expense category, facility managers must understand that expenses potentially impact revenues. For instance, eliminating advertising expenses might provide a short-term cash flow increase, but it might also cause ticket sales to decrease. Facility managers also have to develop a philosophy regarding the provided level of customer service. Cutting expenses can easily be done if the quality of service is also decreased. For some facilities, it is better to have higher expenses by providing a better customer experience, as this will lead to greater retention of customers and higher sales. Ultimately, the most successful facility managers will look for opportunities to decrease costs without sacrificing necessary services and will recognize when certain expenses should not be eliminated.

Mortgage and Rent

The right to utilize a facility typically comes with an obligation to pay a predetermined amount of money. If a facility manager is acting as a representative of the owner of the facility, he or she may be responsible for paying the facility's monthly *mortgage* or for arranging for the scheduled *bond payments* to be paid. If the manager represents a facility's tenant, then a rental fee will likely need to be paid. Though a straight rent deal is simple and easy to understand, many facility rental negotiations may involve complex cost and revenue sharing components. In addition, the tenant may have the right to *sublease* some or all of the various areas of the facility during the rental agreement, making the agreement much more complicated. In those cases, the facility manager needs to retain an efficient accounting staff that can account for the various revenue sources that are generated throughout the rental period.

Maintenance and Repairs

Depending on the ownership or lease arrangement, the facility manager may be responsible for identifying and repairing potential problems with the facility. Large venues have a variety of areas that require regular inspection. Each year, the likelihood that a venue experiences a potential system failure increases. As a facility becomes older than 20 years, numerous areas of the facility may need to be replaced due to inefficiency or obsolescence. Rather than waiting until an area of the facility fails, facility managers should utilize preventative maintenance measures. Each area of the facility should be inspected at regular intervals to ensure that there are no signs of potential danger or failure.

Maintenance is a constant facility expense. (BigStock Photo)

Utilities

The operation of a facility requires the use of a variety of utilities, such as electricity, natural gas, and water. In addition, expenses accruing from sewer, garbage, and recycling must also be determined and paid. Collegiate and professional sport facilities utilize a tremendous amount of resources to operate effectively. If 70,000 people spend 4 hours at a venue, hundreds of thousands of gallons of water may be used and thousands of pounds of trash may be created. Most facilities are investigating methods to utilize more "green techniques" to not only decrease their costs but to also be more environmentally conscious.

Taxes

Every business or individual is responsible for knowing and paying their required taxes. There are a variety of applicable taxes that must be paid. For instance, an employer is not only required to pay taxes on company income, but must also pay a portion of an employee's Social Security and Medicare taxes. For businesses, adhering to the tax code is often a complex and frustrating endeavor. Since there are so many potentially applicable taxes, most business retain numerous people in their accounting departments to ensure that the business does not commit a tax violation. This causes costs associated with adhering to the various local, state, and federal (and in some cases international) codes to sometimes be as expensive as the actual taxes that are paid!

Marketing and Sales

Facilities will not attract any customers unless various target markets are aware of upcoming events. It is the responsibility of the marketing department to determine methods to drive sales. Though the marketing department officially supervises sales activities, in sport and entertainment employees should have the attitude that "everyone sells." In many cases, selling tickets and developing other revenue sources requires ongoing financial resources. Proficient facility managers will be able to not only determine the amount of overall dollars committed to marketing and sales, but they should also be able to provide insights regarding the specific benefits selected marketing activities may have for the organization.

Personnel Expenses

For most facilities, the largest expense category will concern personnel. A facility manager must hire and supervise employees in a variety of areas, including maintenance, sales, legal, accounting, operations, security, and many others. Facility managers must be aware of costs associated with personnel. For instance, not only is there a federal minimum wage but many states and cities have also established additional minimum wage rules. Additional policies may impact salaries or benefits that must be provided to employees.

Cost of Goods Sold (COGS)

If the facility is going to sell items such as food, beverages, and licensed merchandise, the facility manager must know each item's cost of goods sold (COGS). The facility can then determine an appropriate markup for each individual item that it purchases. The COGS is critical to understand, as it can impact the choice of products that a facility may select to then resell. COGS is also a key component in the analysis of the efficiency of concessions operations (see Chapter 14).

Insurance

Every facility needs to retain adequate insurance to cover potential facility damage or to pay off the losses accrued through a lawsuit. Though most facility managers know and appreciate the importance of liability insurance, there are additional forms of insurance that are unique to the sport and entertainment industry. For nearly any event where a prize may be awarded, insurance can be purchased to cover the facility if someone wins. In most cases, those insurance policies require proof that someone actually performed whatever was required to win the prize. For example, a facility may sponsor a "half court shot for a car" contest. If someone were to win, the insurance carrier would likely demand to see a videotape of the shot being made before it would cover the cost of the car.

Sport and entertainment facilities may seek various forms of insurance for the potential cancellation of events. Some venues may retain insurance in case an event is cancelled due to rain. In other cases, the venue may insure against an artist canceling a promoted show. When Michael Jackson died abruptly in 2009, AEG Live was forced to refund more than $85 million when it cancelled 50 shows that were scheduled to occur at The O2 Arena in London, England. Though AEG Live had insurance, it did not necessarily cover all of its marketing expenses for promoting the Jackson shows (Martens, 2009). Since there is a risk that professional sport players may not be able to productively negotiate a collective bargaining agreement with the owners, some facilities pay to retain labor stoppage insurance that covers some of a facility's losses from a player strike or owner lockout.

Outsourcing

One of the most important considerations for any facility manager is the need to maximize potential revenues and diminish related expenses. For most facilities, it will be difficult to maximize every revenue source *in-house* due to budget restraints, staffing considerations, or a potential lack of expertise in the specific area. For these reasons, many facility and event managers *outsource* certain aspects of their operations. Nearly any aspect of operating a facility or event can be potentially outsourced but some of the typical outsourced areas include parking services, ticketing, concessions, and crowd management (see Chapter 11). Recently, many sport organizations have also begun to utilize external companies for sponsorship sales and executive hiring decisions.

Companies that specialize in specific areas are typically able to provide a cheaper alternative to operating an activity in-house. In addition to a lower price, companies that specialize in specific areas can also sometimes provide a higher level of potential service to customers, leading to a greater number of potential sales or a diminished number of negative incidents.

The structure of the outsourcing arrangement is critical to investigate prior to signing a contractual agreement. When a company is contracted to provide a specific service, such as parking, concessions, or security, the facility or event must have contractual assurances that the function will be performed to a prescribed expectation level. In addition, the contract should explain what recourse the facility retains for a vendor who does not perform to established standards. Though the outsourced company will be responsible for the service, the facility will likely field any potential complaints that occur. For instance, a customer attending a football game will likely attribute a rude parking attendant or a cold hot dog to the home team rather than the contracted vendor.

The decision to outsource a potential area should be constantly evaluated. The legal and financial environment in which a facility or event operates may change—necessitating a potential reevaluation of the areas that are currently outsourced. For instance, sponsorship sales have dramatically increased in importance to a sport or entertainment facility's financial survival. This has caused many venues that used to sell their sponsorship inventory via in-house personnel to contract some or all of their sponsorship sales to outside companies. Though many athletic departments have recently outsourced their sponsorship sales responsibilities, Georgia Tech became the first university athletic department to outsource its ticketing operation in 2009 ("Georgia Tech Becomes," 2009). It is likely other schools may follow Georgia Tech's example—if it helps to increase revenues.

Privatization

When a publicly owned facility outsources some or all of its functions to an outside vendor, *privatization* has occurred. In many cases, privately owned organizations can provide services more efficiently than publicly owned entities. This idea has been investigated not only in facility management but in various other sectors of local, state, and federal government, such as in some hospitals and schools.

The recent increase in privatization is grounded in the fundamental belief that often government can, and should, do more with less and those government entities should increase their efficiency by operating in a competitive environment. Fundamentally, the goal of any form of privatization is increased efficiency and effectiveness of service production and/or delivery.

In the sport industry, management of publicly financed and constructed facilities has increasingly become privatized. Since 1977, when management of the Louisiana Superdome was contracted to SMG World, municipalities and stadium districts have overwhelmingly turned to private facility and event management companies to manage publicly constructed facilities, park maintenance, and recreational services.

Prominent Private Sport Facility and Event Management Companies

Though there are numerous private management companies that offer their services to sport and entertainment facilities, three organizations currently dominate the marketplace. SMG World is the leading provider of management for arenas, convention centers, stadiums, and theaters throughout the world. It currently manages 9 stadiums, 40+ theaters, 50+ convention centers, and 50+ arenas. SMG World currently manages more than 1.5 million seats and it is continuing to seek new opportunities ("SMG at a Glance," n.d.).

Global Spectrum, a division of the Philadelphia-based sports and entertainment company Comcast-Spectacor, calls itself the "fastest growing firm in the public assembly facility management field ("Welcome to Global Spectrum," n.d.). Founded in 1974, Global-Spectrum presently manages 5 ice facilities, 7 performing arts centers, 32 arenas, 25 convention centers, and 8 stadiums ("Venue List," n.d.). Global Spectrum is continuing to expand its presence globally, as it now has offices in the United States, Canada, the United Kingdom, and Singapore.

Perhaps the most interesting public assembly facility management company in the world is AEG Live. AEG Live has only recently begun soliciting facility management contracts, but their recent successes have been impressive. AEG Live has signed contracts with some of the top-grossing facilities in the world. In addition, it is overseeing the development of L.A. Live, a 4-million-square-foot, $2.5 billion sport, residential, and entertainment district ("About Us," n.d.). With the resources it has available and its commitment to the industry, it will be interesting to see how AEG continues to grow in the future.

Summary

Understanding revenue and expenses is critical to the operation of any business. Sport and entertainment facilities have a variety of unique revenue sources that require facility managers to understand in order to be effective at maximizing the facility's financial position. As revenue generation activities have become more complex, more private facility management companies have offered to provide their services to publicly and privately owned facilities. The choice to outsource some or all aspects of facility management should be done only after considerable contemplation of the potential benefits and risks.

Questions

1. Why might a publicly owned facility have a different philosophy regarding generating revenues than a privately owned facility?
2. What are the main sources of sport and entertainment facility revenues? Provide at least one important aspect regarding each area.
3. Describe the positives and negatives for naming rights partnerships (for both the sponsor and the facility).
4. What are the main expense areas in a sport and entertainment facility?
5. What are some of the unique insurance needs that a sport facility may require?
6. What are the important factors to consider before signing an agreement to outsource some or all of a facility's operations?
7. Who are the three dominant facility management companies?

6

Americans with Disability Act (ADA) Requirements

Application Exercise

You have finally landed your dream job: facility manager for a Football Bowl Subdivision (FBS) college football stadium. However, as is the case with many dream jobs, your new job has some minor issues that make it a challenge. First, your stadium—originally constructed in the 1960s at a cost of approximately $4 million (USD) and renovated and expanded in 1989 (cost: $20 million)—has severe deferred maintenance issues, does not meet industry standards, and is not in compliance with the Americans with Disabilities Act of 1990 (ADA). A recent study by a leading sport architectural firm found that between $120 million and $140 million would be required to renovate the stadium to current industry standards (excluding costs to bring the stadium into ADA compliance). You have been tasked with developing a facility evaluation checklist to be used to identify and develop recommendations for how to make *reasonable accommodations* to demonstrate a good faith effort to make the stadium as disability-friendly as possible.

Introduction

The Americans with Disabilities Act was signed into law by President George H. W. Bush in 1990 and was originally enacted by Congress to protect an estimated 43 million disabled persons in the United States who have been historically subjected to "purposeful unequal treatment" (ADA Act of 1990). The ADA specifies what employers, government agencies, and managers of public facilities (including sport facilities) must do to ensure people with disabilities are not unfairly excluded from social life. Specific to sport facilities, the statute states managers must provide "reasonable accommodations" for individuals with disabilities.

Sport facility and event managers, depending on whether their facility is public or private, should be aware of various ADA sections, or titles. Title II of ADA covers services, facilities, and programs operated by state, local, and federal governments. Complainants can make a complaint to the Justice Department, but may also bring a federal lawsuit to enjoin discriminatory conduct; limited monetary damages can also be awarded. Title III covers a vast array of private nongovernmental facilities and programs,

Throughout most of the world, granting persons with disabilities equal access to events is an accepted goal.

from bars and zoos to football stadiums and basketball arenas. An example of the type of ADA regulations of which a sport facility manager should be aware are provisions that wheelchair seating must comprise at least 1% of the stadium total, people in wheelchairs must have various options for seating and prices, accessible seating must be an integral part of any seating plan so people using wheelchairs are not isolated, and all accessible sight lines must be comparable to those of other areas and not obstructed by standing fans (www.ada.gov/stadium). Specifically, for newly constructed stadia with more than 300-seat capacity, dispersed accessible seating must be provided. This means that if more than 300 seats are provided, wheelchair seating must be in more than one location (U.S. Department of Justice, n.d.). In addition, building codes and state and local laws may determine guidelines for handicap accessibility. These may include provisions for a certain spacing between seats (usually 17 to 20 inches) or handrail necessity based on the number of steps.

The ADA mandates that reasonable accommodations be made toward those with disabilities. Examples of reasonable accommodations may be inclusion of ramps, railings, and certain types of listening systems in the facility. The philosophy behind such accommodations is that persons with disabilities must be granted equal access to a facility or event.

Americans with Disabilities Act History

As has already been stated, the overarching goal of the Americans with Disabilities Act was to mainstream and incorporate individuals into society as much as possible to ensure equal opportunity. From a historical perspective this incorporation philosophy can be seen in earlier specifications developed by the Occupational Safety and Health Administration (OSHA). In 1970, OSHA created specifications for equipment, maintenance, and safety in construction. Also in the 1970s, Congress began to enact legislation intended to expand opportunities for individuals with disabilities. The first such law was the Rehabilitation Act of 1973. Section 504 of the Act states, "No otherwise qualified handicapped individual in the United States . . . shall solely by reason of his handicap, be excluded from participation in, be denied the benefits of, or be subjected to discrimination under any program or activity receiving Federal financial assistance" (29 U.S.C. 794, [Supp. V 1993]). In addition, facilities receiving federal assistance had to meet strict accessibility standards. Public Law 94–142 also established appropriate *gratis* education for children in an environment that is least restrictive. Under Section 504 guidelines, "qualified handicapped persons" are protected from discrimination (Carpenter, 2000). According to Section 504, a "qualified handicapped person" is one who:

(i) has a physical or mental impairment which substantially limits one or more major life activities,

(ii) has a record of such an impairment, or

(iii) is regarded as having such impairment (Carpenter, 2000, p. 187).

Section 504 also details that major life activities include "caring for one's self, performing manual tasks, walking, seeing, hearing, speaking, breathing, learning, and working" (Carpenter, 2000, p. 187).

Another piece of legislation that addressed disability access specific to sport was the Amateur Sports Act of 1978, also referred to as Public Law 95-606. While broadly intended to coordinate and increase amateur athletic participation, the Act encouraged the development of amateur athletic programs for handicapped individuals.

Americans with Disabilities Act of 1990

As part of this historical move to integrate people with disabilities into society and recognizing that physical and mental disabilities in no way diminish a person's right to fully participate in all aspects of society, Congress passed the Americans with Disabilities Act of 1990. The ADA was intended to provide "provide a clear and comprehensive national mandate for the elimination of discrimination against individuals with disabilities" (ADA Act of 1990, Title 42, Chapter 126, section 12101, para. b). However, Congress recognized that as a result of various Supreme Court decisions (e.g., *Sutton v. United Air Lines, Inc.*, 527 U.S. 471 [1999] and *Toyota Motor Manufacturing, Kentucky, Inc. v. Williams*, 534 U.S. 184 [2002]) its expectation that the definition of disability under the ADA would be interpreted consistently with how courts had applied the definition of a handicapped individual under the Rehabilitation Act of 1973 had not been met. As a result, it passed the ADA Amendments Act of 2008 (P.L. 110-325), which sought to reestablish the clear and comprehensive national mandate for the elimination of discrimination against individuals with disabilities. In doing so Congress reaffirmed and expanded various definitions related to the ADA.

Accordingly, with respect to an individual, "disability" refers to:

- a physical or mental impairment that substantially limits one or more major life activities of such individual;
- a record of such an impairment; or
- being regarded as having such an impairment.

(ADA Act of 1990, Title 42, Chapter 126, section 12102)

As a result of the ADA Amendments Act, which went into effect January 1, 2009, Congress expects the Equal Employment Opportunity Commission (EEOC) to revise its regulations to conform to changes made by the Act. The Act emphasizes the definition of disability should be construed in favor of broad coverage of individuals to the maximum extent permitted by the terms of the ADA and generally will not require extensive analysis. The Act makes important changes to the definition of the term "disability" and rejects the holdings in several Supreme Court decisions. In effect, these changes make it easier for an individual seeking protection under the ADA to establish that he or she has a disability within the meaning of the ADA.

Additionally, the Amendment defines auxiliary aids and services to include:

(A) qualified interpreters or other effective methods of making aurally delivered materials available to individuals with hearing impairments;

(B) qualified readers, taped texts, or other effective methods of making visually delivered materials available to individuals with visual impairments;

(C) acquisition or modification of equipment or devices; and

(D) other similar services and actions.

(ADA Act of 1990, Title 42, Chapter 126, section 12103)

The first classification relates to conditions or diseases, such as AIDS, cancer, and mental disabilities, and is generally associated with the scope of ADA. The second classification prevents discrimination based on a person's history of such a disease or illness and the fact that that individual cannot be discriminated against. Third is the classification that represents and prohibits a stereotype or preconceived notion about someone with a disability. While physical impairments are easier to discern and provide accommodations for, mental conditions are more difficult to accommodate. A major factor of a disability covered under the ADA is that it "substantially limits one or more" of primary life activities, such as eating, breathing, learning, and walking. In total, the ADA has five components, which encompass (1) discrimination in employment, (2) state and local government concerns, (3) public accommodation, (4) telecommunications, and (5) a miscellaneous category (ADA Act of 1990).

Sport Frames and ADA Stadium Evaluation

In order to organize an analysis of how well a stadium complies with ADA regulations, it is useful to utilize MacAloon's (1984) classic notion of framing sport that was presented in Chapter 2 (see Figure 2-2.). Doing so helps organize a facility evaluation in the same manner as spectators experiences the facility on their way to the actual sport contest. Doing so allows us to segment the facility evaluation into logical parts and organize the requisite facility tour and develop a comprehensive facility evaluation checklist. Throughout this chapter the developed checklists utilize MacAloon's frames. By familiarizing yourself with this concept, you can frame any sport event facility and event.

Sport Facilities and the ADA

In addition to framing a sport facility, we also need to be familiar with both the underlying legislative philosophy and specific facets of the Americans with Disabilities Act. Specific to sport facilities, Title III of the ADA provides "no individual shall be discriminated against on the basis of disability in the full and equal enjoyment of the goods, services, facilities, privileges, advantages, or accommodations of any place of public accommodation by any person who owns, leases, or operates a place of public accommodation" (ADA Act of 1990, 42 U.S.C. §12182).

As a facility manager, you also need to be aware that anyone interested in pursuing a Title III claim must prove:

1. The individual is disabled;
2. The sport business represents a "private entity" operating a "place of public accommodation"; and
3. The person was denied the opportunity to "participate in or benefit from services or accommodations on the basis of his disability," and that reasonable accommodations could be made that do not fundamentally alter operations of the sport business. (ADA Act of 1990)

In plain language, as a future sport facility manager you need to be cognizant of making your facility available to everyone in a reasonable manner. It does not require separate facilities for those with disabilities; in fact, the intent is to grant access and interaction for all facility users. Since its inception, the ADA's mandate for "reasonable accommodation" to ensure availability to all has influenced the development of sport equipment, increased program diversity, and spurred innovative sport facility design.

Reasonable Accommodations

We have repeatedly used the term "reasonable accommodations" in referring to the ADA. Two other terms you need to understand are *public accommodations* and *commercial facilities*. According to the Americans with Disabilities Act Accessibility Guidelines (ADAAG) Checklist, which summarizes Department of Transportation (DOT) and the Department of Justice (DOJ) regulations implementing the ADA, public accommodations and commercial facilities are operated by private entities, their operations affect commerce, and they fall within at least one of the 12 categories listed in Table 6-1.

Under ADA requirements, all places of public accommodation must remove all architectural barriers, including structural communication barriers, as long as doing so is readily achievable (United States Access Board, n.d.). "Readily achievable" is somewhat difficult to define, but the ADA generally defines readily achievable as being easily accomplishable and able to be carried out without much difficulty or expense. If removal of architectural barriers cannot be readily achievable, other readily achievable measures that do not fully comply with ADAAG may be taken. However, the ADAAG guidelines stipulated that "no measure shall be taken that poses a significant risk to the health or safety of individuals with disabilities or others" (United States Access Board, para. 14).

Generally speaking, if barriers cannot be removed and access to services cannot be provided, new services need to be created. In addition, new construction must meet ADA standards unless it is impractical to do so. Furthermore, requirements of the ADA apply to facilities that are covered and can be owned by the government, nonprofit, or private sector.

Table 6-1. Public Accommodations and Commercial Facilities Categories

1. An inn, hotel, motel, or other place of lodging, except for an establishment located within a building that contains not more than five rooms for rent or hire and that is actually occupied by the proprietor of the establishment as the residence of the proprietor;
2. A restaurant, bar, or other establishment serving food or drink;
3. A motion picture house, theater, concert hall, stadium, or other place of exhibition or entertainment;
4. An auditorium, convention center, lecture hall, or other place of public gathering;
5. A bakery, grocery store, clothing store, hardware store, shopping center, or other sales or rental establishment;
6. A laundromat, dry cleaner, bank, barber shop, beauty shop, travel service, shoe repair service, funeral parlor, gas station, office of an accountant or lawyer, pharmacy, insurance office, professional office of a health care provider, hospital, or other service establishment;
7. A terminal, depot, or other station used for specified public transportation;
8. A museum, library, gallery, or other place of public display or collection;
9. A park, zoo, amusement park, or other place of recreation;
10. A nursery, elementary, secondary, undergraduate, or postgraduate private school, or other place of education;
11. A day care center, senior citizen center, homeless shelter, food bank, adoption agency, or other social service center establishment;
12. A gymnasium, health spa, bowling alley, golf course, or other place of exercise or recreation.
Source: United States Access Board, n.d.

Readily Achievable Guidelines

The regulations for existing stadiums differ from those for facilities undergoing significant renovation or that are newly constructed. In addition, while new facility ADA guidelines are clear, renovated standards may be more complicated. For example, removal of structural barriers to achieve readily achievable reasonable accommodation may be difficult to quantify. Determination of whether the ADA's readily achievable mandate has been met can be performed by applying a five-part test developed by the Department of Justice:

1. The nature and cost of the action;
2. The overall financial resources of the site or sites involved; the number of persons employed at the site; the effect on expenses and resources; legitimate safety requirements necessary for safe operation, including crime prevention measures; or any other impact of the action on the operation of the site;

3. The geographic separateness, and the administrative or fiscal relationship of the site or sites in question to any parent corporation or entity;

4. If applicable, the overall financial resources of any parent corporation or entity; the overall size of the parent corporation or entity with respect to the number or its employees; the number, type, and location of its facilities; and

5. If applicable, the type of operation or operations of any parent corporation or entity, including the composition, structure, and functions of the work force or the parent corporation or entity. (ADA Act of 1990)

Barriers

The Department of Justice has identified methods to satisfy readily achievable standards. Some of these methods involve undertaking renovations or other construction, while some involve simply moving or repositioning items. Table 6-2 highlights the Department of Justice's barrier laundry list.

Table 6-2. Department of Justice Barrier Laundry List

1. Installing ramps;
2. Making curb cuts in sidewalks and entrances;
3. Repositioning shelves;
4. Rearranging tables, chairs, vending machines, display racks, and other furniture;
5. Repositioning telephones;
6. Adding raised markings on elevator control buttons;
7. Installing flashing alarm lights;
8. Widening doors;
9. Installing offset hinges to widen doorways;
10. Eliminating a turnstile or providing an alternative accessible path;
11. Installing accessible door hardware;
12. Installing grab bars in toilet stalls;
13. Rearranging toilet partitions to increase maneuvering space;
14. Insulating lavatory pipes under sinks to prevent burns;
15. Installing a raised toilet seat;
16. Installing a full-length bathroom mirror;
17. Repositioning the paper towel dispenser in a bathroom;
18. Creating designated accessible parking spaces;
19. Installing an accessible paper cup dispenser at an existing inaccessible water fountain;
20. Removing high-pile, low-density carpeting; or
21. Installing vehicle hand controls.
Source: ADA Act of 1990.

Newly Constructed Facilities

Any newly constructed facility, or any facility of public accommodation occupied after January 16, 1993, must meet ADA guidelines. In order to ensure awareness and compliance with ADA standards, the U.S. Department of Justice makes available new stadium requirements in many documents via the Internet. In addition, sport facility managers may contact the Department of Justice (U.S Department of Justice, n.d.). While specific guidelines, such as installation of an elevator if a stadium has more than three stories and when each floor has more than 3,000 square feet, apply to other types of buildings, certain stipulations, such as a requirement that 1% of seating must be wheelchair seating locations, are specific to sport facilities (U.S. Department of Justice, n.d.).

In detailing what constitutes an accessible stadium, the Justice Department has highlighted key features, including such items as seating, concessions, access to playing fields and lockers, assistive listening systems, parking spaces, drop-off and pick-up areas, entrances, rest rooms, drinking fountains, signs, and visual alarms. Related to the ADA, an accessible stadium incorporates concepts such as dispersed seating (dispersed seating provides people with disabilities, their family, and friends with a choice of admission prices and views comparable to those of the general public) into the design and management of a sport stadium. In order to make a stadium truly accessible, sport facility managers must strive to optimize the game experience for fans with disabilities. In order to arrive at workable solutions that comply with local, state, and federal regulations, managers must foster dialogue between the government officials, stadium owners, and cross-disability groups.

Alterations

Justice Department regulations take into account that not all alterations must meet ADA requirements. For example, primary function areas, such as a sport exercise room, would have to meet ADA standards, while non-primary function areas, such as a mechanical room, would not (ADA Act of 1990). However, a "path of travel" to a primary function area should meet ADA requirements. In addition, the law stipulates accommodations need not exceed 20% of the total cost of renovation. With these cost-conscious realities in mind, the Department of Justice has put a priority on the following alterations:

1. An accessible entrance;
2. An accessible route to the altered area;
3. At least one accessible restroom for each sex or a single unisex restroom;
4. Accessible telephones;
5. Accessible drinking fountains.

The Justice Department has identified accessible entrances as a major priority.

(ADA Act of 1990)

Cost

It should be remembered the ADA calls for renovations or alterations or additions that are "readily achievable." Regulations are not intended to impose undue hardship on the sport business owner but rather to ensure inclusion and equal access. Therefore, an expense that would impose undue hardship—such as major structural renovations—may be avoided. However, all other efforts must be made to make reasonable accommodations. It should also be noted that ADA compliance and cost reduction can be achieved through tax deductions.

Two examples of available tax deductions include Internal Revenue Service (IRS) Code 190, which allows up to a $15,000 business deduction for qualified architectural and transportation barrier removal expenses, and IRS Code Section 44, which provides small businesses with fewer than 30 employees and less than $1 million in sales with a 50% credit for an accommodation's cost—as long as the total cost is between $250 and $10,250 in one year (Equal Employment Opportunity Commission, 1997).

Exemptions

Future sport facility managers should be aware of an additional point: while truly private—including religious—organizations are exempt from ADA requirements, if a private organization owns and operates a facility that is open to the public or advertises its facility usage or functions in a public medium, the organization may no longer hold private status (ADA Act of 1990). Taking this example one step further, if a private organization that conducts a public sport camp were to rent or lease a religious organization's facility in order to hold its camp, the private organization would still have to provide accommodation under ADA guidelines. As can be seen from these examples, sport facility managers need to be aware of relevant ADA-related case law.

ADA Case Law

The landmark case involving ADA legislation, specifically Title III accommodation for sport programs, was *Anderson v. Little League Baseball, Inc.* (1992). In this case Little League Baseball had enacted a policy to prohibit wheelchair-bound coaches from coaching from the coach's box, due to the potential of a collision between player and coach. As the court noted, individuals with disabilities must be provided equal access to recreation facilities, programs, and services, unless such participation poses a "direct threat" to the health and safety of others. Under scrutiny from the court, it was found that Little League's position was based upon stereotypes and misconceptions. In fact, Little League had not taken any steps in order to assess the merits of its own rule to determine if Anderson's being on the field actually represented a direct threat to the health and safety of others. As a result, the rule was abolished.

From a direct practical sense, this case serves to show that sport facility rules (like any other rules) cannot be made arbitrarily. Direct evidence of a direct threat to the health and safety of others must be shown as the basis for a disabled person's exclusion from an activity or a facility. If such evidence does not exist, and disabled patrons are prohibited from accessing a facility or event, the facility or event management and staff face the possibility of a lawsuit, and perhaps more damaging, a public relations nightmare.

Planning and Accommodations

Determining how best to ensure ADA compliance or implement reasonable accommodations begins with a thoughtful and careful facility evaluation. A consultant could be hired, or a staff member could be assigned to develop a facility evaluation checklist incorporating ADA guidelines (see Figure 6-1 for an example section) and to perform a facility evaluation.

Parking Areas Adjacent to Venue		
ITEMS TO CHECK	RATING (Y/N)	POTENTIAL PROBLEM
Americans with Disabilities Act (ADA) (See Note—below)		
(See ADA Guidelines for Stadiums)		
Accessible parking spaces for cars		
Accessible parking for vans		
Accessible parking spaces closest to accessible entrance(s) and on an accessible route to entrance(s)		
Ramps at appropriate rise and slope		
Guardrails and handrails where required		
Walkways wide enough to allow for wheelchair access		
Accessible passenger drop-off and pick-up areas		
Curb ramps		
Fire safety		
Fire lanes properly marked and kept clear		
Fire hydrant/sprinkler/standpipe/fire department connections accessible and clearly marked		
Protective caps are in place		

Note: Americans with Disabilities Act (ADA) Information

Parking Spaces

- When parking spaces are provided, accessible parking spaces for cars and accessible parking spaces for vans are required. Accessible parking spaces must be the closest parking spaces to the accessible entrances and must be on an accessible route to the entrances.

Accessible Drop-Off and Pick-Up Areas

- If passenger drop-off areas are provided, they must be accessible and an accessible route must connect each accessible drop-off area with the accessible entrance(s). Curb ramps must be provided if the drop-off area is next to a curb.

Figure 6-1. Example of Facility Evaluation Checklist

In any case, all applicable ADA requirements should be catalogued, and cross-disability organizations should be contacted for feedback and ongoing input. The developed checklist can be used to identify areas of concern, develop action plans to address the situation, and document scheduled completion dates. Performing an ADA-specific facility evaluation serves to (1) set a timeline for completion of the any identified alterations or renovations, and (2) provide documentation of the facility's due diligence in identifying and instituting reasonable accommodations.

When managing any type of sport facility, it is important to be cognizant of persons in wheelchairs, but to not limit one's thinking to only one type of disability. For example, it is also important to recognize the needs of those on crutches and those with visual, hearing, speech, mental, and/or physical-weakness impairments. For a sport facility manager, it may be a worthwhile exercise to tour the facility with cross-disability organization representatives. In addition to simply accompanying them, the manager could also develop an empathetic awareness by starting in the parking lot in a wheelchair and attempting to access all primary locations within the facility. Next, the manager could do the same while on crutches, then blindfolded, and so on. Such an activity could also be a useful staff exercise. In addition, staff training on issues of persons with disabilities is a very worthwhile experience. It may be necessary to hire a consultant to conduct such training, or to perhaps simply discuss the issues and how persons with disabilities should be treated. Finally, ongoing systematic facility evaluations should be performed to ensure that enacted accommodations are adequate. Implementing these steps will not only decrease the likelihood of litigation, but more important will maintain the facility as a place where all patrons enjoy equal access.

Area-specific Suggestions

Although there is no one all-inclusive list that can ensure ADA compliance, Table 6-3 highlights suggestions to assist future sport facility managers.

Table 6-3. ADA Compliance Suggestions

Parking Area
• Make sure there are adequate handicapped spaces and that all designated spaces allow for a wheelchair to be easily maneuvered between vehicles.
• Provide adequate signage that directs patrons to the nearest accessible entrance.
Entrance
• Minimum of 60 × 60 inches of level space to allow for adequate maneuvering.
• Doors should be relatively easy to open.
• Doormats should not impede entrance.
• Automatic door openers should be positioned so doors do not hit a disabled patron when opening.
• Floors should be covered with a non-slip surface or carpeting.

(continued on next page.)

Table 6-3.—Continued

Stairs
- Non-slip surfaces.
- Railings should extend 12 inches at the top and bottom of stairs.
- Handrail height should be between 34 and 38 inches and less than $1\frac{1}{2}$ inch diameter.

Elevators
- Visual and auditory travel-direction signals.
- Call buttons 42 inches from the floor and unobstructed.
- Door opening should be a minimum of 32 inches wide.
- Elevator should be no more than $\frac{1}{2}$ inch off level on any floor.
- Handrails should be 34 to 36 inches above the elevator's floor.
- Control panel should be no more than 48 inches above the floor.

Public Restrooms
- Mirrors and paper-towel dispensers should be 40 inches from floor.
- Area of 30×48 inches in front of commode for adequate maneuvering.
- Adequate directional signage throughout facility.

Water Fountains
- At least 27 inches high and 17 to 19 inches deep.
- Control buttons should be easy to manipulate.

Summary

The overarching goal of the Americans with Disabilities Act was to mainstream and incorporate individuals into society as much as possible to ensure equal opportunity. If reasonable accommodation can be made when possible, and if the idea of stereotyping can be eliminated to some degree, then the purpose of the ADA will have begun to take shape. It is up to the facility manager to be cognizant of areas where accommodations can be made, evaluate their reasonableness, and, if appropriate, take action. Doing so will not only prevent lawsuits, but can also make the facility a more open and welcoming venue for all who enter.

Developing reasonable solutions to achieve ADA accommodation begins by carefully examining the current state of affairs. When planning a facility to be handicapped accessible, it is important to be cognizant of persons in wheelchairs, but to not limit one's thinking to only one type of disability. Follow-up and ongoing facility and event evaluation can help ensure that facilities and accommodations are adequate, help prevent lawsuits, and, most important, maintain an environment where all patrons have equal access to facilities. Although specific guidance from the ADA can help establish guidelines for compliance in structure and various activities, ultimately it is up to sport facility managers to be knowledgeable of ADA guidelines, determine if accommodations can take place, evaluate their reasonableness, and, if appropriate, implement them.

Questions

After having read this chapter, the application exercise at the beginning of the chapter should now make more sense. In addition to thinking about that specific situation, the following questions should allow you to evaluate your knowledge and understanding of the Americans with Disabilities Act. The answers to these questions are not simply "Yes" or "No" propositions. As a future sport facility manager, you should be aware that little in our industry is cut and dried. However, by critically examining each situation, and using theoretical models and practical experience, you will be better able to ensure that your facility complies with the ADA and other federal, state, and local legal requirements.

1. How can you identify someone with a handicap as expressed by the Americans with Disabilities Act?
2. What would constitute measures that are not "readily achievable"?
3. How might you train your staff to be on ADA compliance and how to empathetically help disabled patrons have a great fan experience?
4. What are some options for deferring some of the cost of renovation?
5. According to material in this chapter, what is one of a facility manager's first priorities in making ADA alterations?

Relevant Web Sites or Web Links

- U.S. Department of Justice ADA Home Page
  www.usdoj.gov/crt/ada/adahom1.htm
- Americans with Disabilities Act Accessibility Guidelines (ADAAG) Checklist for Buildings and Facilities
  http://www.access-board.gov/adaag/checklist/a16.html
- ADA Document Center
  http://janweb.icdi.wvu.eud/kinder
- ADA Act of 1990
  www.usdoj.gov/crt/ada/pubs.ada.txt
- Notice Concerning The ADA Amendments Act of 2008
  www.eeoc.gov/ada/amendments_notice.html
- Executive Summary: Compliance Manual Section 902, Definition of the Term "Disability"
  www.eeoc.gov/policy/docs/902sum.html

7

Hiring Personnel

Application Exercise

Jim Drysdale, camp director of Summer Sport Camps for the past four years, has just received news that the camp's aquatics director of seven years, Stacy, has left to start her own camp. With only two weeks until the start of the summer season, Jim has to act quickly in order to hire another swimming director.

The first thing Jim must do is create a job announcement. However, since Stacy has been swimming director for seven years, Jim does not know exactly what her job entails. He has basically relied on Stacy knowing her job and allowed her a great deal of autonomy. However, knowing he needs to create a job announcement, he puts one together from memory and posts it on a local online job service. In the announcement, Jim includes the position title, the required qualifications, the details of the job, and the hourly pay rate, and lists himself as the contact person for further information.

Jim receives several interested applicants and sorts through their various credentials. He chooses to interview three individuals whose experience and credentials most closely match the position's duties and responsibilities. The first, Casey, has been a lifeguard for several seasons at Jim's camp. Jim knows Casey is a good worker, but is not sure if Casey is capable of assuming the swimming director's added responsibilities. A second candidate, Julie, is a former aquatic director who, after leaving the work force 10 years ago to raise her two children, wants to get back in the business. Jim wonders if Julie is ready for the demands of a 50-hour-a-week position. The final candidate, Martin, was the swimming director at a camp in another state the previous year. However, Jim is aware of reported improper conduct by staffers toward campers the previous year, though no legal action has yet been initiated at Martin's previous camp. Unfortunately, Jim has been unable to get in touch with the out-of-state camp's director to check on Martin's credentials or ask specific questions about the situation. The director is out of the country for the next week and has no access to emails or phone calls. Jim has to make a decision within the next two days, in order to hire a swimming director in time for his camp's opening.

If you were Jim, what would you do? In this situation, whom would you hire as your swimming director? What are the possible ramifications of making a hiring decision without performing due diligence in checking all the candidates' credentials? What are some possible implications of this hiring decision?

The various issues raised above will be discussed as we progress through this chapter. In addition, we will refer to this situation at the end of the chapter in our follow-up discussion.

Introduction

Utilizing sound hiring practices can significantly affect a sport organization's success, since the sport product by its very nature is people oriented. Fundamentally, any sport event, whether it is a college lacrosse match or the Super Bowl, is dependent—to some degree—on the sport organization's staff members' ability to interact with each other and the consuming public. In any business a hiring mistake can be costly, since employee turnover may adversely affect customers' perception of an organization's stability as well as impact the actual work environment.

Research into what was originally known as personnel management is most often said to have begun in the 1950s with the publication of Peter Drucker's *The Practice of Management* (1954), in which he coined the term "human resources." By the 1980s this notion that employees were valuable human resources was widely accepted. In 1989 Drucker described such management as human resource management (HRM), a combination of being a file clerk, housekeeper, social worker, and firefighter. Drucker contended HRM's overall goal must be to help an organization meet its short- and long-term objectives. During the same time period in which Drucker was articulating the fundamentals of HRM, two HRM models were being developed: Fombrun, Tichy, and Devanna's Michigan model (1984) and the Harvard model of Beer Spector, Lawrence, Quinn-Mills, and Walton (1984).

The Michigan model emphasized the link between human resource strategy and the business strategy of the firm. According to this framework, an organization's business strategy should define and determine the types of employees hired, how such employees are organized, and how their performance is evaluated. In other words, an organization's business strategy should lead its human resource (HR) strategy. In this model employees are just an organizational resource like any other. In addition, while employees should be used sparingly, they should also be fully developed and exploited (Sparrow & Hiltrop, 1994). In the Harvard model employees were not viewed as just another resource, but as equal participants whose understanding of and commitment to an organization's business strategy were critical. Within this view, a corporation's business strategy is part of, rather than leading, its HR strategy.

Therefore, to help ensure a sport organization's competitive advantage, sport managers must consistently apply strategic HRM best practices, while evaluating, motivating, promoting, and retaining employees (Billing, 2000). Arguably, the most important precursor to any of these HRM functions is practicing effective staff selection. In other words, hiring good people may be the most important HRM strategy.

Steps in the Hiring Process

Drafting a Job Analysis and Job Description

Before hiring the best possible employee, a manager must execute many preliminary steps. First and foremost is performing an adequate job analysis. A thorough job analysis includes a description of a particular job's tasks and roles. Specifying the duties and responsibilities of a position will ensure that prospective employees know what is specifically expected of them and are also aware of how the job fits into the organization's overall structure (Billing, 2000). To ensure creation of a balanced job analysis, current employees and other managers should be consulted and jointly involved in this analysis process. After a job analysis has been conducted, a formal job description can be developed, which provides a general position overview, details the position's major measurable responsibilities, and explains to whom the person reports and whom the person supervises (Billing, 2000). While job descriptions may vary depending on a particular situation, at a minimum a job description should contain the following elements:

- Job title
- Essential job duties and responsibilities
- Job qualifications
- Starting date
- Name and address of the contact person

Quite often an organization's job descriptions contain a collection of past duties, responsibilities, and tasks. Periodically, such job descriptions should be reviewed, evaluated, and updated to ensure recruitment efforts start with an accurate job analysis and job description. A well-written job description, based on a thorough job analysis, can

What would you include in a job description for security personnel at your venue?

help attract an appropriate applicant pool. It also allows interviewers and interviewees to prepare for specific questions, defines employee and employer expectations, makes a new employee aware of expected tasks, and provides information on promotion and evaluation criteria. In other words, a good job description provides a foundation for the new employee's success.

Recruiting and Retaining Employees

Before any discussion of how to recruit employees, a future sport manager needs to be aware that, by law, organizations, and any associated recruiters, must ensure their recruiting and selection processes are nondiscriminatory. Under Title VII (42 U.S.C. 2000e-2[a] [1]) and Executive Order 11246—as amended—employers cannot discriminate against applicants based upon their race, color, religion, sex, or national origin. In addition, it is illegal for employment agencies to fail or refuse to refer for employment based upon these bases.

Within these legal parameters, recruiting and retaining employees requires the use of both internal and external recruiting channels. Recruiting internally to fill a position by hiring a current employee has distinct advantages. Since most often such a hire is a promotion, such a hire may improve employee morale, because they see one of their own being rewarded. In addition, such a hire is often less risky, because management knows the employee's strengths and weaknesses and has had an opportunity to engage in a long-term evaluation. Such a hire also requires less time and financial expenditure. However, there may also be disadvantages, including creating chaos by promoting someone above her or his ability, creating tensions among co-workers, and failing to generate outside or disparate opinions.

An increasingly utilized internal recruitment channel—the internship—is a practical employment strategy that provides an opportunity for both the employer and intern to engage in an employment test drive for a limited period of time. Because an internship has agreed-upon beginning and end dates, neither the organization nor the intern has made a long-term commitment. However, at the end of the internship, if the organization wishes to offer the intern employment, it has gained a valuable employee, who has undergone on-the-job training throughout the internship. Although internships benefit both parties, it is important that both the organization and the intern are aware that interns are legally employees and that negligent conduct on the intern's part creates risks for the organization (Sharp, Moorman, & Claussen, 2007).

In today's highly competitive job market, external recruitment, or searching for an employee outside the organization, may make use of a variety of sources, including online employment web sites, traditional employment agencies, college placement centers, newspaper and web-based want ads, and professional associations. Recruiting externally most often involves publicly posting a job or position announcement.

Utilizing online or traditional employment services allows outsourcing of the recruiting process, including necessary Equal Employment Opportunity Commission (EEOC) record keeping. Such convenience may entail increased organizational expense and a loss of control over some recruiting elements, while not completely transferring an organization's legal responsibility for any discriminatory recruiting practices that the employment agency may undertake.

Because an organization can reach a large number of potential candidates, utilizing a college placement center for external recruitment has many advantages. It provides many of the benefits associated with a traditional employment agency, but at a reduced cost. The placement center can preliminarily sort resumes, providing the recruiter access to the best student applicants. In addition, since a recruiter can travel to one location to interview a number of candidates, instead of the organization having to pay a number of candidates' travel expenses, an organization can dramatically reduce its external recruitment expenses. As recruitment technology continues to develop, the number and type of recruiting channels will continue to expand. Regardless of where managers choose to recruit, by utilizing a variety of outlets, active recruitment of applicants from a variety of backgrounds and locations is possible.

Since the 1990s the Internet and other electronic data-processing technologies have become well established recruiting and job-seeking channels. According to a 2003 iLogos Research study, Internet job hunting ranked second in effectiveness to personal contacts and networks. In addition, the increasing use of the Internet as a recruiting channel had resulted in over 94% of the world's largest organizations having corporate "Careers" web sites (iLogos Research, 2003). These technologies allow job seekers and employers to easily explore the job market.

In addition to maintaining career web sites, an increasing number of companies are choosing to actively recruit online. Today, there are, literally, hundreds of job web sites, such as Monster.com, CareerBuilder.com, Yahoo!Hotjobs.com, as well as sport-specific sites, such as TeamWorkOnline.com and Bluefishjobs.com. In addition, since many companies post job openings on their corporate web sites, aggregator sites such as Beyond .com and Snagajob.com, which aggregate corporate sites, provide job seekers with a central site, eliminating their having to go from one site to another. In May 2009, Forbes.com reported, "In April, 2009 such sites attracted 57.2 million 'unique visitors,' up nearly 50% from the same period last year, according to Nielsen, an audience-tracking firm" (Marcus, 2009, para. 2). In light of changes and advancements in available recruitment channels, it seems reasonable, when possible, to solicit applications from both inside and outside an organization and make use of as many recruitment technologies as possible.

Gathering Information

Regardless of what recruitment channel is utilized, the application process should be as straightforward as possible. When used, application forms should be simple and straightforward, gathering as much necessary information as possible. In addition, a closing date for the particular position should be stated, as the EEOC requires reexamination of applicants' files for other jobs that may open in the future (Billing, 2000). If a resume and cover letter are required as part of the application process, the EEOC requires accepted resumes be kept on file for two years. Since there are many EEOC record-keeping requirements associated with applicant files, it is important for sport managers to be aware of what, according to the EEOC, makes someone an applicant and act accordingly. As outlined in the EEOC's *Q and A 15 of the 1979 Qs and As* (www.eeoc.gov), the precise definition of the term "applicant" depends upon the user's recruitment and selection procedures. An applicant is normally a person who has indicated an interest in being considered for hiring, promotion, or other employment opportunities. This interest might be expressed by completing an application form, or might be expressed orally, depending on the employer's practice.

Utilizing an Application and Conducting an Interview

In general, if an application form is utilized there are several categories a manager should ensure are included. In addition, when conducting an interview, there are some general guidelines for what questions should not be asked. In developing an application form and preparing for conducting an interview there are several steps that need to be completed. In addition to the EEOC web site (www.eeoc.gov), there are numerous web sites that offer lists of acceptable and unacceptable interview questions. We've provided a list of some such questions in Table 7-1.

Table 7-1. Acceptable and Unacceptable Questions

Subject	Acceptable	Unacceptable
NAME	• "Current legal name?" • "Have you ever worked under a different name?" • "Is any additional information, relative to a change of name, necessary to enable a check of your educational or work records?"	• "Maiden name?" • Questions about national origin, ancestry, or prior marital status.
AGE	• "Are you over the age of 18?"	• "Age?" • "Birth date?" • Questions that might identify the applicant's age, especially if the applicant is over age 40.
NATIONAL ORIGIN/ CITIZENSHIP	• "All offers of employment are contingent upon verification of identity and work authorization in the United States" • "Are you legally authorized to work in the United States?"	• Questions as to nationality lineage, ancestry, national origin, descent, parentage of applicant or applicant's spouse. • "What is your mother tongue?" or language commonly used by applicant. • How applicant acquired ability to read, write, or speak a foreign language. • "Are you a U.S. citizen?"

Table 7-1.—Continued

Subject	Acceptable	Unacceptable
RACE/COLOR	• None	• Questions that indicate applicant's race or color, complexion or color or skin, eyes or hair. • Direct or indirect reference to race, color, or racial groups.
RESIDENCE	• Place of residence	• "Do you own or rent your home?"
MARITAL STATUS/ FAMILY	• Whether applicant can meet work schedule or job requirements. • Should be asked of both sexes.	• Any inquiry about marital status, children, dependents, pregnancy, or childcare arrangements. • Name or address of relative, spouse or children of adult applicant. • "With whom do you reside?" or "Do you live alone?"
RELIGION	• Describe the work schedule and ask whether applicant can work that schedule.	• Questions about applicant's religion, religious days and hours to be worked. • "Does your religion prevent you from working weekends or holidays?"
MILITARY SERVICE	• Questions about knowledge, skills and abilities, acquired during applicant's military service, relevant to the position applied for.	• Specific questions about military service, such as dates, type of discharge, or service in foreign military services. • "What type of discharge did you receive?"
REFERENCES	• "By whom were you referred for this position?" • Names of persons willing to provide professional references for applicant.	• Questions of applicant's former employers or acquaintances that elicit information specifying applicant's color, race, religious creed, national origin, ancestry, any physical or mental disability, medical condition, marital status, age, or sex.

(continued on next page.)

Table 7-1. — Continued

Subject	Acceptable	Unacceptable
DISABILITY/ MEDICAL CONDITIONS	• May ask applicant's ability to perform job-related functions and with or without reasonable accommodation, only if the question is asked of all applicants. (NOTE: The interviewer must have already thoroughly described the job.)	• Whether applicant is handicapped or has a disability. • "Have you ever been hospitalized? If so, for what condition?" • "How many days were you absent from work because of illness last year?"
ARREST AND CONVICTION RECORDS	• "Have you ever been convicted of a crime?" • "If so, when, where and what was the disposition of the case?" • The answer, if yes, will not be used to discriminate against any applicant. • (May ask about record of convictions if all applicants are asked.)	• "Have you ever been arrested?"
Source: Table information based upon EEOC guidelines: www.eeoc.gov.		

Utilizing the guidelines in Table 7-1 or developing questions from other sources, the application and interview process can still help weed out the not-so-good applicants from the great ones. Keeping in mind that each interview involves an expenditure of time and money, and that having too many choices is really the same as having no choices, it is a good idea to select between three and five candidates to invite for formal interviews. In addition to contacting candidates invited for an interview, all applicants not selected for an interview should be sent a professional rejection letter in a timely fashion. Candidates selected for an interview should be called and arrangements should be made for conducting the interview; an itinerary should be provided to everyone involved in the interview process. Any necessary accommodations and meals should be above average, but not extravagant.

In preparation for the interview, the panel should develop a set of questions to guide the interview and keep the process on target. Examples of possible interview questions are listed in Table 7-2.

These questions are simply examples of possible interview questions. Rather than using these questions verbatim, it is important to develop questions that will allow the interview committee to get to know each candidate and determine the best fit for the advertised position. By utilizing these types of questions, taking careful notes, and perhaps (with the interviewee's permission) taping the interview, interviewers can obtain a great deal of relevant information from interviewees.

Table 7-2. Sample Interview Questions

- What were/are your last/present job duties?
- Could you describe a typical day at your past/present job?
- What attracted you to this type of work?
- What aspects of the job were challenging?
- What aspects of the job gave you the most trouble? Why?
- If you had it to do all over again, would you still go into the same kind of work? Why? Why not?
- How do you feel about the progress you made?
- Why did you decide to make a change?
- What do you think might be the toughest aspects of this job if you were to accept the position? What do you anticipate will be the most enjoyable aspects? The least enjoyable?
- What do you think your greatest contribution to the job and our organization will be? Where and how do you think you would be able to make your greatest contribution?
- What do you feel were your most significant accomplishments on your past/present job?
- Which of your accomplishments in your past/present position are you most proud of?
- What personal accomplishments and attributes make you the proudest?
- What are your goals in your present position for the next one, two, and three years?
- What would you have liked to have accomplished in your past/present position that you have not been able to? What prevented you from accomplishing these goals?

For Recent College Graduates

- How did you feel about the college you attended?
- What made you decide on your major?
- Were there any school-related accomplishments of which you feel particularly proud?

Testing Applicants

There are many different types of tests and selection procedures that employers utilize to screen applicants. These tests include cognitive tests, personality tests, medical examinations, credit checks, and criminal background checks. While many managers and companies have applicants take personality tests as part of the application process, there are—as one might expect—pros and cons with doing so. Choosing an appropriate test is the first challenge, since there are numerous tests that have been developed. In addition, whether to utilize a forced-choice or a normative test may be a decision for which a sport manager is not qualified. However, asking a candidate to submit to a drug test, if it can be shown to have a link to the safety of the employee and the people under his or her care, is perfectly legal For example, the position of gym supervisor or lifeguard could logically warrant a drug test. However, if drug testing is to be performed, no discrimination should be involved that would conspicuously subject or exclude any group from the drug test.

The use of tests and other selection procedures can be a very effective means of determining if applicants are qualified for a particular job. Sport facility managers may use specific tests designed to measure relevant knowledge, skills, or attitudes. It is likely that you will have to take some sort of test when applying for a sport facility position. However, use of these tools violates federal antidiscrimination laws if they are intentionally used to discriminate against candidates based on race, color, sex, national origin, religion, disability, or age (40 or older). In order to provide guidance for the use of testing in the employee selection process, the EEOC has developed a list of best practices. These practices are listed in Table 7-3.

Table 7-3. Employer Best Practices for Testing and Selection

• Employers should administer tests and other selection procedures without regard to race, color, national origin, sex, religion, age (40 or older), or disability.
• Employers should ensure that employment tests and other selection procedures are properly validated for the positions and purposes for which they are used. The test or selection procedure must be job-related and its results appropriate for the employer's purpose. While a test-vendor's documentation supporting the validity of a test may be helpful, the employer is still responsible for ensuring that utilized tests are valid under the Uniform Guidelines on Employee Selection Procedures (UGESP).
• If a selection procedure screens out a protected group, the employer should determine whether there is an equally effective alternative selection procedure that has less adverse impact and, if so, adopt the alternative procedure. For example, if the selection procedure is a test, the employer should determine whether another test would predict job performance but not disproportionately exclude the protected group.
• To ensure that a test or selection procedure remains predictive of success in a job, employers should keep abreast of changes in job requirements and should update the test specifications or selection procedures accordingly.
• Employers should ensure that tests and selection procedures are not adopted casually by managers who know little about these processes. A test or selection procedure can be an effective management tool, but no test or selection procedure should be implemented without an understanding of its effectiveness and limitations for the organization, its appropriateness for a specific job, and whether it can be appropriately administered and scored.

Source: From "Employment Tests and Selection Procedures" (http://www.eeoc.gov/policy/docs/factemployment_procedures.html).

Checking References

Reference checks are usually performed to confirm application details, check for prior discipline problems, discover new information about an applicant, and help predict whether the applicant will be a good fit for the job. Reference checks can be conducted either before or after an interview. While reference checks are useful, many times former employers are unwilling to give information, or are leery about giving unfavorable information that could be used by former employees as grounds for a defamation lawsuit based on a negligent referral (van der Smissen, 2007). Generally, defamation cases involving references have arisen when an employer gives negative, untrue, and inconsistent information about a current or former employee. For example, if an employee had a satisfactory performance evaluation on file, but the former employer, in responding to a reference check, said the employee was subpar, this would be a basis for a defamation lawsuit. As a result of such litigation, some organizations, as a matter of policy, will provide only minimal and clearly documented information, such as job title, dates of employment, or final salary level, when asked to provide a reference. In response to these concerns over the past several years, many states have passed laws to protect employers who provide "good faith" job references for current or former employees (van der Smissen, 2001a).

On the other end of the spectrum, if former employers refuse to give information, and the employee is subsequently hired and found to be incompetent, the present employer may decide to sue the former employer (referent) for failing to disclose important information about a poorly performing employee (van der Smissen, 2001a). Another important consideration related to checking references is the concept of negligent hiring, under which employers may be held liable for an employee's negligent acts committed within the scope of their employment. Since employers have a duty to protect their employees, customers, clients, and visitors from injury caused by employees that an employer knew or should have known posed a risk of harm to others, an appropriate background check or investigation—based upon the specific job—should be conducted. In determining how extensive a background check should be conducted, factors such as the degree of unsupervised contact with customers, clients, or other employees should be taken into consideration. It is legitimate to conduct a background check that investigates whether an applicant has a history of violent or dangerous tendencies.

In addition to being sometimes difficult to obtain, references often have limited usefulness. Since the reference giver's motivations cannot be known, a reference's accuracy should always be questioned. Since too often they are unreliable predictors of job success, the best use of reference checks is to screen out people when specific negative information is discovered (e.g., falsification or exaggeration of information reported on the job application and in the interview). A reference check's real value is supplementing the available information on a candidate, in order to minimize the likelihood of hiring a clearly unsatisfactory employee.

In addition to the general concepts discussed above, many state employment commissions or departments publish interview checklists. Table 7-4 is an example of an interview checklist.

Table 7-4. Interview Checklist

✔ Verify past employment (check references) on only those candidates under serious consideration after final interviews.
✔ Inform candidates you plan to check references and get their verbal permission. Check references by phone, not by email or postal service. Some organizations and people tend to be reluctant about putting less than positive remarks on paper.
✔ Call as many former employers as possible. Whenever possible try to talk to the applicant's direct supervisor.
✔ Begin the conversation in a friendly manner, but maintain a strong sense of professionalism. Identify yourself (name, title, organization), why you are calling (say you are calling to "verify past employment" rather than "requesting a reference"), and move right into your questions.
✔ Limit your inquiries to verifiable job-related information. It is inappropriate to inquire about areas not related to actual on-the-job performance, such as hobbies, social activities, religious or political beliefs, marital status, children, residence, medical status or disability, and any past legal actions, including worker's compensation claims, civil rights charges, and safety complaints.
✔ If you check the references of more than one finalist, make sure you ask the same general questions about each candidate.
✔ Ensure that reference information is weighted in the same way for all candidates. What disqualifies one candidate should be the basis for disqualifying any applicant.
✔ If negative information is uncovered, consider its source and check its accuracy with other sources before using it to make a decision about the applicant.
✔ Assure the person you're speaking with that any information will be shared only with officials involved in the hiring process and not otherwise disclosed.
✔ Document the information gathered from your reference check(s), noting even those reference requests for which you obtained no information.

Making the Hire

After a final candidate has been selected, negotiating salary and benefits and finalizing an employment contract take place. During this process, both employer and employee need to be up-front and honest. However, an employer needs to also be truthful about the job's working conditions, promotions, and other personnel issues. If not, the employer may be guilty of fraud

After the offer has been made and accepted, an employee or occupational manual should be provided. A policies and procedures and employee training manual should be typeset so that it is easy to read, with some graphics, have a color-coded table of contents, and perhaps a question and answer section It is also a good idea to have an employee verify, via signature, she or he has, in fact, read the manual.

The manual or handbook's contents should include company history, philosophy, and mission, organizational chart, EEO/Affirmative Action statement, working hours/days, pay, raises, benefits, and sexual harassment policy. Since this type of document contains time-sensitive material, an employee handbook should be regularly updated. The final step in the hiring, or "on-boarding," process is the preparation and signing of an employment contract and an employee beginning work. For an expanded look at contracts, see Chapter 8.

Summary

Sound hiring practices can significantly affect the effective and efficient management of a sport facility. Since sport organizations are so people oriented, hiring appropriate personnel throughout the various levels within the business is crucial (Billing, 2000). Developing and conducting a thoughtful and thorough hiring process provide the best chance for hiring great employees. Throughout this chapter we have focused on many facets of the hiring process, including such elements as:

- Drafting a job analysis and job description
- Recruiting and retaining employees
- Gathering information
- Utilizing an application and conducting an interview
- Testing applicants
- Checking references
- Making the hire

None of the identified strategies will guarantee mistake-free hiring. However, by implementing a hiring program that includes elements discussed in this chapter, the likelihood of finding great employees can be increased.

Questions

After reading and thinking about the material presented in this chapter, address the following questions.

Application Exercise Questions

At the beginning of this chapter, the application exercise involved a summer camp director who was looking for a swimming director.

1. What specific qualifications would you look for in an applicant?
2. Are there any mistakes that Jim may be possibly making in regard to the three finalists?
3. Is there any way to solve some of the problems that Jim faces with respect to Martin?
4. What steps in the hiring process has Jim forgotten?
5. Whom would you hire for the job?

Chapter Questions

1. Briefly explain the differences between the Michigan and Harvard human resource management models.
2. Explain and discuss the basic steps in the hiring process.
3. What are some permissible questions that can be asked during an interview?
4. What are some impermissible questions?

Relevant Web Sites

www.businesstown.com/hiring/hiring-top-asp

www.toolkit.cch.com/textPO5_0001.asp

www.hrzone.com/topics/hiring.html

www.smallbiz.biz.findlaw.com/hr/hiring/

www.onlinesports.com

www.teamworkonline.com

8

Contracts

Application Exercise

Premium seating has become a mainstay in sport facilities. Premium seating may be either luxury box or club seating with excellent game sight lines services and amenities such as special parking, wait staff, and/or private up-scale restaurants. Premium seating is a prime source of revenue for sport facilities and oftentimes requires seat-holders to agree to multi-year contracts. As is the case with any extended contract, sometimes premium seat patrons may want to end a premium seat contract prematurely. Since premium seating revenue is important for facility maintenance, operation, and renovation, sport facility/organizations attempt to ensure such agreements are upheld.

A case that encapsulates many premium seating issues was New Boston Garden Corporation v. Baker (1999 WL 98099 [Mass. Super. 1999]). In this case, Mr. Gary Baker signed a 3-year, 18-page contract, which entitled him to sit in a club seat, to watch the National Basketball Association's (NBA) Boston Celtics and the National Hockey League's (NHL) Boston Bruins. For this privilege, Mr. Baker agreed to pay $18,000 per year. However, due to personal problems (including marital difficulties and his son being diagnosed with cancer), and the fact the teams were not performing up to his expected standards, Mr. Baker reneged on the agreed-upon contract. At the time, Mr. Baker was not the only fan dismayed by the teams' performances. An average of 2,000 seats per game went unsold.

Needless to say, the management group for the home of the Celtics and Bruins, the New Boston Garden Corporation (NBGC), was in dire need of contracts such as the one Mr. Baker signed being fulfilled. As a result, NBGC sued Baker for breach of contract.

If you were the judge in this case, how would you rule? Are there mitigating circumstances that make this a difficult case? As we explore contracts related to sport facilities, keep this case in mind. In times of economic downturn, situations such as this are becoming more common. Understanding contract essentials is always important for sport facility managers, but in economic hard times, contractual issues become increasingly part of a sport manager's professional life.

Contract Law Basics

In today's sport industry, contracts are a ubiquitous fact of life. Generally contacts are used to formalize relationships involving exchanges of personal services or goods. In the sport industry, contracts may involve television and sponsorship coverage, contest scheduling, equipment purchases, players' and coaches' contracts, facility leases, licensing agreements, and athletic grant-in-aids. Reading this chapter does not substitute for the need to obtain legal representation for contractual matters. However, this chapter's contract fundamentals provide an overview and information that can help avoid troubling situations. By understanding contract principles, a sport facility manager can also more easily explain his or her need for legal counsel and help in establishing a well-written contract.

At its most basic, a contract is an agreement between two or more parties that creates enforceable obligations recognizable at law (Garner, 2004). However, while an agreement or promise—either clearly expressed or reasonably implied—is a necessary element, a contract also includes other elements, such as physical acts, recitals of fact, and transfer of property rights (Garner, 2004). Businesspeople negotiate and agree to informal and formal contracts each and every day. Not every agreement made in the course of a business day needs to take the form of a formal written contract. To do so would be time and labor intensive and also prohibitively expensive. However, it is important for a sport facility manager to recognize that in certain situations an unspoken, poorly drafted, or assumed agreement can expose the organization, and the manager, to legal and financial liability. The purpose of this chapter is to assist in the process of determining when it is necessary to obtain or consult legal counsel and draft a formal written contract. This section is designed to educate the sport facility manager so he or she may, when necessary, secure and retain competent legal counsel and communicate effectively with an attorney during the process of practicing risk management as it relates to contracts. In addition, once a contract is drafted and agreed to, it is important for managers to be aware of their obligation to faithfully implement the contract and also be aware of the ramifications of not fulfilling the contract.

Offer

An offer is a promise to do, or refrain from doing, something in the future. Usually, the promise made by the offeror is conditioned on an act, or return promise, being made by the offeree in exchange for the offeror's initial promise or performance (Garner, 2004). An offer has material terms, described by Sharp, Moorman, and Claussen (2007) as (1) the parties involved, (2) the subject matter, (3) the time and place for the subject matter to be performed, and (4) the consideration (price to be paid). In many negotiated business transactions involving a contract there is often an initial offer and then a counteroffer, which outlines different terms. As the back-and-forth negotiation process continues, the parties exchange roles as offeror and offeree.

Acceptance

Acceptance occurs when the offeree accepts the offeror's proposal. Acceptance of an offeror's terms may take the form of expressed act(s) (such as signing a contract or paying cash) or may be implied by conduct authorized or requested by the offeror (Garner, 2004). Only the person to whom the offer is made can accept it. An offeree cannot reject an offer and then attempt to accept it. It is important to remember that once an offer has been rejected, the offer no longer exists. In addition, in certain situations the acceptance of an offer does not have to be expressed in words or by actions. This is called acceptance by silence (Garner, 2004).

Consideration

Even though parties have agreed on a contract, consideration makes the contract binding. Consideration involves the exchange of value; one party gives up something of value in exchange for the other party doing the same. An example of consideration is when a soft drink company, in consideration for its name being associated with the contest and the advertising exposure resulting from the football game broadcast (as well as, perhaps, an agreed-upon number of in-game advertisements), agrees to sponsor a half-time field goal kicking contest. In exchange, the company might agree to pay $1 million to a contestant who makes a 50-yard field goal and also provide in-store displays that advertise the upcoming football game and invite fans to buy tickets to attend the game. (Note: As part of its risk management plan, the soft drink company should contract with a promotional insurance company for a policy that would pay the $1 million prize if the contestant actually makes the field goal.)

Capacity

Capacity refers to the ability or power of a person to enter into an agreement or contract. Specifically, capacity involves the satisfaction of legal qualifications (i.e., of legal age, possessing soundness of mind) that qualify someone to enter into a binding contract. Capacity is an important concept in contractual situations involving minors.

Intent and Specificity

There must be serious intent on the sides of both parties for a contract to be enforceable (Sharp, Moorman, & Claussen, 2007). If the other requirements of a contract have been met, but the parties never intended to create a legally binding document, then there is no contract. In addition, the terms of a contract must be precise enough to be followed. If not, the contract will be considered void.

Legality

Very simply, a contract must be legal for it to be binding. Making sure a promotion is legal is sometimes overlooked. For example, a charity raffle, unless it is conducted in accordance with state and local laws, is an illegal lottery. As a result, any sponsorship or promotion contract associated with such an illegal lottery would be called into question.

Breach

Breach of contract occurs when an obligation specified in a contract is not met. Such a breach may take the form of failing to perform as promised, repudiating a promise, or interfering with another party's performance.

Damages

In order to remedy a situation if a contract were broken, the courts may award compensatory packages or liquidated damages (money) in order to fulfill the obligation (Sharp, Moorman, & Claussen, 2007). The amount of compensation to be paid in a breach situation is determined based on the situation at the time of the contract, not at the time of the breach. In addition, if a contract is broken, the courts may order the party in breach (except in cases of a contract involving personal services) to fulfill the contract, when appropriate. This is called specific performance (Garner, 2004).

Types of Contracts

Bilateral Contract. In this type of a contract, each party promises to perform an act on the condition that the other party will also perform an act. Within this type of agreement, a conditional exchange of promises has been met. For example, one person would pay $1,000 to a facility if the other person would grant gym space for a specified day and time.

Unilateral Contract. In this particular case, there is not an exchange of promises. The situation in this example is that only one party promises to perform an act, while the other party is not bound to accept the offer. However, if they do accept, then the first party is obligated to hold up their end of the deal. For example, in between games during a volleyball match, spectators may be invited to participate in a game of skill to see who can serve into a specified area for a prize. This is a unilateral contract due to the fact the spectators are not required to participate, but if they do, and if they win the game of skill, then they are legally entitled to the prize.

Errors in Contracts

Misrepresentation

A contract can be voided if the facts were intentionally or unintentionally misconstrued (Cotten, 2007). However, this process must take place in a reasonable amount of time.

Undue Influence/Duress

If a person has been unfairly persuaded to enter into a contract, the person who was in the less powerful position can generally void a contract. Under similar circumstances, if a person were forced into forming a contract, by fear of loss of life or limb or through economic hardship, that contract is considered voidable.

Mistake

In the case of a mistake, the parties may be allowed to rewrite the contract. Courts do not normally act to protect contracting parties from mistakes in judgment. However, unless the mistake was mutual, or if a unilateral mistake is unconscionable (i.e., the mistake is profoundly discriminatory to one of the parties, results in an arbitrary or needless burden, or contains intentionally obscure language), such a mistake is not cause to void a contract (Cotten, 2007). The courts will investigate the varying explanations for the mistakes and make a ruling on the merits of each individual case. The simple lesson here is to be very careful when forming a contract, as mistakes could come back to haunt you.

Integration and Parole Evidence

Many times a contract will contain an integration clause that states the signed contract will be upheld "as is," and no other previous agreements that would add to or detract from the contract will be allowed (Garner, 2004). If this clause is in place, the parole evidence rule states that no other information, even if it were discussed beforehand, will be considered binding if that information is missing from the signed document (Garner, 2004). In sum, the contract will be upheld as written.

Delegation of Duties

If one party is unable to fulfill the contract as promised, they may delegate their duty to another party (Garner, 2004). However, if the second party is unable to meet the contract specifications, the first party may still be held liable (Garner, 2004). For example, it would be reasonable for a facility manager to contract with a sporting goods supplier for an order of premium leather basketballs. If the supplier could not fill the order, it would be legal to delegate the duty to another supplier. However, if the second supplier could not or did not fill the order, the original supplier would be liable for a breach of contract.

Breach of Contract

Defenses

A contractual breach occurs if one party to the contract no longer wishes to fulfill their contractual obligation. There are three legitimate defenses for contractual breach: (1) impossibility of performance, in which the contract cannot be performed, has become illegal, or if one of the contracted parties has died; (2) frustration of purpose, which occurs when the contracted matter—due to unforeseen circumstances—no longer has any value; and (3) contractual impracticability in which the cost of fulfilling the contract has, through no fault of the breaching party (e.g., act of God, war, embargo), become unreasonable and, therefore, impractical.

Remedies

Most often, a contractual breach will be remedied by awarding monetary damages or equitable relief. Specific to sport facilities, seeking monetary damages may be an expedient and favorable contractual breach remedy. Such damages are calculated utilizing the classifications of expectation, reliance, or restitution interests (Garner, 2004). Expectation and reliance interests focus on the non-breaching party, while restitution concentrates on the breaching party. In computing monetary damages utilizing expectation interests, the idea is to reasonably predict what the injured party's future position would be, had the contract been performed. Such a judgment involves computing lost profits, adding incidental/consequential damages, and subtracting any avoided expenses

(Restatement § 347). While reliance interest also focuses on the injured party, it strives to restore the party to a predicted past position had the contract not been made in the first place (Restatement § 349). It is designed to force the party in breach to return any benefits obtained from partial fulfillment of the contract (Restatement § 373).

Relevant Facility Operations and User Agreements

A sport facility manager needs to be aware of several relevant user agreements. Each type of agreement will contain specific elements or general clauses. Examples of such agreement and appropriate elements are listed in Table 8-1.

Table 8-1. Key User Agreement Elements

Type of User Agreement	Elements
Lease Agreement	• Right to use and occupy • Rental fees • Fee for additional services • Revenue sharing • Nonassignment clause • Choice of law clause • Hold harmless clause • Indemnification clause • Insurance clause • Force majeure clause • Damage clause
Game Contracts	• Location, time, and place of event • Financial arrangements • Eligibility and game rules • Termination provision • Force majeure clause • Broadcast rights provision • Insurance and indemnification provisions • Complimentary tickets • Promotional rights
Contracts for Services	• Independent contractor provisions • Insurance provisions • Indemnification provision

Source: Developed from user agreement concepts covered in Sharp, Moorman, & Claussen, 2007.

Before putting fans in the stands, facility managers must ensure that all contractual obligations have been met.

Examples of Sport Facility–related User Agreements

Independent Contractor Agreement

Quite often sport facilities will hire or outsource an organization to perform a certain service or undertake a specific project. The independent contractor performs the assigned or contracted work and is free to choose the method for accomplishing or completing the service or task. As a general rule, an employer is not liable for the negligence of an independent contractor (Restatement [Second] of Torts § 409 [1965]). However, there are a number of exceptions to this general rule, and the exceptions have in many cases invalidated this rule. Comment b to section 409 of Restatement (Second) of Torts states that exceptions to section 409 "are so numerous, and they have so far eroded the 'general rule,' that it can now be said to be 'general' only in the sense that it is applied where no good reason is found for departing from it."

Even if an organization contracts with an independent contractor for a service or task, the organization still retains certain obligations. Initially, the organization must ascertain that the independent contractor is competent to provide the service or complete the project. In addition, the employer retains responsibility for safely maintaining any business premises open to the public (Restatement [Second] of Torts § 425 [1965]). As a sport facility manager, it is crucial for you to be aware that an employer—and in many cases the contracting organization—may retain liability associated with promotions, such as pyrotechnics or fireworks, deemed to include "inherently dangerous activities." (Note: Such a determination is subject to the court's discretion.)

There are several factors courts will use to determine whether a true independent contractor relationship exists. First, the degree of control asserted by the employer over the contractor's activities will be scrutinized. Second, to what degree did the employer retain the right to terminate the agreement? Third, how was the contractor paid and how were taxes withheld from the contractor's compensation? Fourth, did the service or project involve specialized skills? Fifth, did the contractor supply his or her personally owned tools, material, or equipment? Since courts use these questions in determining whether a true independent contractor relationship exists, a sports promotion manager should determine the answer to these questions in assessing the viability of any such agreement.

Facility Contract

A facility contract allows the contracted person(s) to use the facility for a set period of time, for a set fee, and for a designated purpose. An important facet of this type of a contract is an indemnification agreement. This type of agreement holds the facility owner harmless for the events contracted and expresses a provision that the contracted person(s) possess insurance for the event is usually required (Sharp, Moorman, & Claussen, 2007). Contracts of this nature must be very specific as to the responsibilities of all parties involved. For example, considerations should be given to such items as rent amount, method of payment, services provided by rental, promotion, set-up, personnel, time of event, warm-up policies, potential conflicts among multiple lessees, radio and TV arrangements, and insurance (Sharp, Moorman, & Claussen, 2007).

Game Contract

A game contract is generally between two schools that identifies one game, or a series of games, to be played (McMillen, 2007). Included in this contract would be such items as location, date, time, provisions as to officials, guarantees (remuneration), broadcast rights, complimentary tickets, and termination clauses with compensation in the event of nonperformance in mind (Sharp, Moorman, & Claussen, 2007).

Event Contract

Even though it is referred to as an "event" contact, such an agreement often encompasses more than a single event. It is frequently associated with the numerous ancillary events associated with, or surrounding, a major event (McMillen, 2007). For example, an event contract for a particular college basketball tournament may, on the surface, appear to be a single-event proposition. However, upon further examination, the event contract may include not only multiple-game contracts, but may also agreements involving personnel (e.g., security, officials; emergency care professionals, and food service vendors); facility lease agreements; licensed merchandise sales; pre-, post-, and in-game activities; and other sponsorship opportunities associated with the larger event.

Sponsorship Agreement/Contract

Like any business relationship, a sponsorship agreement or contract should serve to protect the best interests of all parties involved. In addition to the basic contractual principles discussed below, there are several elements specific to sponsorship agreements of which a sport facility manager should be aware. As in any agreement, a sponsorship agreement should specify the rights and duties retained by all parties. The contract

Several types of user agreements are necessary when a facility hosts an NCAA championship event.

should clearly identify and define terms unique to such an agreement. For example, a definition for the term "presenting sponsor" will not be found in Black's Law Dictionary; it must be defined in the agreement. Descriptions of all relevant ancillary elements, including such items as signage requirements and specific declarations and parameters of sponsor categories for which exclusivity may be granted, should be included. Clarification of attendant liability of all parties to the contract is an important element as well. As part of most sponsorship agreements, sponsors will require that a sports property/entity lists them as a co-insured on all insurance policies. In addition to such transference via insurance, sponsors may ask to be released from liability through the signing of a waiver agreement

A sponsorship agreement should also detail any agreed-upon event and/or associated promotions ownership. By drafting a noncompetition covenant or promise "not to engage in the same type of business for a stated time in the same market," such an event or promotion owner can be better protected (Garner, 2004). In order to withstand judicial scrutiny, such covenants should be reasonable in scope, time, and territory. Another important element that should be included in a sound sponsorship agreement is protection of the future rights of all contractual parties. Since many events/promotions occur more than once, it is in the best interests of both sponsors and the sports entity that owns the event, as well as the facility in which the event/promotion will be held, that a long-term relationship be created and nurtured. Through inclusion of a right of first refusal or preemption clause, in which the existing sponsor has the right to meet the terms of any other prospective sponsor's proposal (as part of a multi-year sponsorship agreement), all parties' interests can be more easily met. Such a clause does not preclude the sport entity/facility from receiving full-market value for associated sponsorship packages, but does provide an existing sponsor—if its objectives are being met by a continued association with the event—with the opportunity to extend an existing agreement (Garner, 2004).

As is the case with any agreement, simply using a boiler-plate template as the basis for a sponsorship agreement is not recommended. While using a template can be a good first step, even though it costs more to have an attorney involved in any contractual process, it is likely to be—in the long run—more cost-effective to utilize a licensed attorney to finalize such agreements.

Licensing Agreement

Similar to sponsor agreements, a licensing agreement is a contractual agreement that gives someone permission to engage in a specifically defined activity or to use a certain property owned by someone else. A license is a means to protect ownership or proprietary rights to property. Licensing agreements involve property right situations, including copyrights, patents, and trademarks. A licensing agreement should be part of a comprehensive licensing program. Almost all sport franchises, organizations, or events have well-established licensing programs.

For example, according to information found on its web site, the National Collegiate Athletic Association (NCAA) retains the exclusive right to sell souvenir products at all events held in conjunction with its 88 NCAA championships (National Collegiate Athletic Association, 2009). However, the NCAA does not manufacture and actually sell these souvenir products. Instead, it has assigned its souvenir merchandising rights to Event 1, Inc., a subsidiary of GEAR for Sports, Inc. As part of the agreement between GEAR for Sports, Inc. and the NCAA, Event 1, Inc., has the "limited" right to sell NCAA licensed merchandise at on-site venues, at team hotels, and at events associated with NCAA championships (National Collegiate Athletic Association, 2009).

In order to more clearly understand licensing agreements, it is helpful to outline the various licensing agreement elements. Any licensing agreement should first clearly define the scope of the license. As the paragraph above demonstrates, the NCAA by licensing its products has assigned to Event 1 only a limited right to use that property; the NCAA retains the ultimate ownership rights. However, it is important to remember that the NCAA has not assigned to Event 1 the right to sell other merchandise, such as posters, women's apparel, headwear, T-shirts, video games, or many other licensed merchandise on the premises of its events. Those rights have been assigned to other companies. Most often, license agreements are nonexclusive. Such nonexclusivity allows the NCAA to assign rights for T-shirts, fleece garments, and youth and toddler clothing to several competing companies (i.e., Nike, Lee Sport, Jan Sport, Champion, etc.). This nonexclusivity results in more effective market penetration of NCAA licensed merchandise. As a sport facility manager, it is critical that you are aware of such licensing agreements. This will help ensure that unlicensed vendors (also known as "bootleggers"; see Chapter 14) do not infiltrate an event.

It is also important that a licensing agreement includes provisions specifying and controlling the revenue streams generated by the sale of licensed products. It is critical that merchandise management, control, and accountability guidelines be specified in an agreement. The amount of any one-time licensing fee, royalties, or maintenance charges should be listed. Table 8-2 details topics that should be covered in a licensing agreement.

Table 8-2. Licensing Agreement Topics

• Length of the agreement	• Liability insurance
• Definitions	• Payments
• Prohibitions	• Statements
• Warranties	• Inspection audit
• Limitations	• Events of default and/or termination
• Guarantees	• Representations
• Assignments of rights, including rights to transfer or sublicense	• Indemnifications
	• Remedies
• Use of registered trademarks	• Jurisdiction and venue
• Copyright of ancillary materials	• Confidentiality
• Protection of copyrights	• Relationship of parties to agreement

Summary

Contracts are a crucial part of today's sport industry. Contracts may be used for contest scheduling, equipment purchases, player and coaching contracts, facility leases, licensing agreements, and teams or officials failing to show for a game. By understanding basic contract principles, facility managers can assist legal counsel in drafting well-written and well-served contracts.

Contract law is primarily based in common law court decisions and various codifications. A contract is an agreement between parties enforceable under law. The two main types of contracts are called bilateral and unilateral. The elements of a contract include meeting of the minds, offer, acceptance, consideration legality, capacity, and intention to create legal relations. The contract itself involves an opening, representations and warranties, operational language, other clauses, termination, entire agreement and amendments, and a closing. Some common errors within contracts include misrepresentation, undue influence/duress, and mistakes. To uphold a contract as written, an integration clause is included and the parole evidence rule invoked. A breach of contract is most times remedied by a damages amount. Facility, game, event, and sponsorship contracts are examples of types of sport facility usage agreements and are crucial to ensuring sport events are handled with diligence, care, and understanding.

Application Exercise Revisited

As you remember, the case of New Boston Garden Corporation v. Baker involved a multi-year contract dispute centering upon preferred or premium seating. Due to personal problems and team performance, Gary Baker attempted to dissolve his 3-year, $18,000 contract. The facility was against this, as revenue from premium seating is the most important source of funding for facility operation and construction. A breach of contract claim and lawsuit followed.

The decision in this case is compounded in difficulty due to the confounding and colliding factors of personal life and private interest. Certainly, Mr. Baker's personal problems were not to be dismissed. However, personal issues are not enough to warrant a breach of contract. For NBGC, suing Mr. Baker may have been a publicly unpopular course of action, but allowing Mr. Baker to breach the contract would have had far-reaching legal consequences.

Baker's arguments would most certainly have been based upon personal turmoil. In addition, Baker argued that he offered to amend the agreement to buy fewer tickets, or have the contract terms shortened. In addition, Baker was upset that NBGC did not adequately advertise the premium seating, or reduce its prices despite a poor season. Mr. Baker contended that if NBGC had done these things and allowed him to resell his seats he would not have breached the contract. The arguments from NBGC stemmed from a breach of contract claim alleging that a valid agreement had been entered into, and the requirements of a contract had been met. In addition, consideration had been exchanged, NGBC had the seating available, Baker did not fulfill his part of the bargain, and NGBC suffered damages as a result. On appeal, NGBC won, and Baker was ordered to pay restitution. From a practical perspective, fans must understand there are no warranties or representations in such a contract that guarantees a winning team. On the facility manager's side, by the same token, if a contract is poorly worded, the courts will award judgment against the creator of the contract. In this particular contract, the wording was clear and the contract upheld. Therefore, proper language and suitable counsel are always important. In the end, frequent and appropriate communication between the patron and the facility manager, including addendums or adjustments to contracts, will hopefully keep these and other types of cases out of court.

Questions

1. What are the basic elements of a contract? For each element, can you offer a definition and a brief description?
2. What are two basic types of contracts?
3. List some common contractual errors.
4. What is contractual breach? What are some remedies to contractual breach?
5. Three common user agreements were outlined in this chapter. For each, list at least three elements.
6. List at least six topics that should be included in a licensing agreement.

Relevant Web Sites

www.sportsbusinessnews.com

www.sportsbusinessjournal.com

www.sportslawnews.com

www.sportbusiness.com

www.nflpa.org

www.nhlpa.com

www.ncaa.org

9

Risk Management

Application Exercise

You have been hired as the risk manager for Pikes Peak Field (PPF), a 12,000-seat, multipurpose stadium in Colorado Springs, Colorado. The stadium hosts a variety of small concerts as well as being the home to the Colorado 14'ers, a Women's Professional Soccer (WPS) team. The facility operations manager at PPF hired you specifically because during the interview you spoke of your ability to present a viable risk management plan.

Your objective is to create a specific event risk management information plan for the 14'ers. This information may be gleaned from interviewing a member of a facility management team from any stadium to which you have access. Further information may be obtained from newspaper articles, the Internet, any of your class notes, this textbook, your professors' reserve materials, and so on. You will need to research the WPS and familiarize yourself with professional soccer. How the plan will be implemented is up to you, but remember that you are the risk manager, so if the plan does not work, it is your reputation (and job security) that will be affected.

You need to include all of the following:

1. *Date and type of event.* When will the event take place? Who will the 14'ers opponent be? Will it be a preseason, regular season, or postseason game? Is the opponent a major rival?
2. *Risk management.* Who is in charge of managing the plan? How will the plan be communicated to the PPF employees? What are the five most common risks that will occur at the 14'ers matches? What are their classifications? What is the most significant treatment used to reduce the risks? How do you plan on dealing with inherent risks to your event? Are all staff members aware of the risk management plan? Do they have any input?
3. *Insurance.* What types of insurance have you as the risk manager purchased?
4. *Staffing needs.* Does a policy manual exist? What type of personnel and staffing needs exist for the match? Do you need to utilize volunteers? Where will they be recruited? Will you use independent contractors? In what areas will the volunteers be utilized?

5. *Facility considerations.* How many spectators do you anticipate for the event? When will the gates open? Who makes the decision to open the gates? How many locker rooms will be used? Where are they located in relationship to the field? What happens in case of a power outage? Are there any hidden dangers of which the patrons need to be made aware? Do adequate numbers of restrooms exist?

6. *Maintenance.* Who provides the maintenance? What types of maintenance are available?

7. *Business operations.* Who will handle the cash? How will the money be transported from the box office, food and beverage stands, and merchandise store to the bank? Is there a cash pick-up from any of those locations during the event? Who will count the money?

8. *Evaluation of the event.* When will the evaluation take place? Who will be present? Is a standard form used? How long are the evaluations kept? Does an event file exist? What constitutes the file?

Introduction

Slip-and-fall accidents account for 15% of all accidental deaths in the United States; only automobile accidents result in more deaths. In addition, 66% of all incidents at U.S. stadiums and 66% of all claims dollars paid out each year are a result of slip-and-falls (Powers, 2006). A large number of these accidents could have been avoided with the implementation of a proper risk management plan. The focus of the facility industry has shifted in the past decade and risk management has become a vital component. Ten to 15 years ago, when there were fewer national venues, most facilities dealt with an

Risks at a football stadium are completely different than those found at a swimming pool.

average number of events whose influence was mostly regional. The current number of facilities has increased exponentially, and the sport and entertainment events scheduled in them have produced global interest. Some of these events include the Fédération Internationale de Football Association's (FIFA) World Cup, the Australian Open, the National Collegiate Athletic Association's (NCAA) Final Four tournaments, Professional Golf Association (PGA) championships, major concert tours, and conventions. These various events have become extremely popular, resulting in increased event attendance and accompanying media coverage. Each event has its own unique risks that result in the need of a comprehensive risk management plan. Although event managers must be proficient in many areas in order to successfully stage an event, no area is more important than understanding and implementing an effective risk management plan.

Definition of Risk Management

Risk management has a variety of definitions. A brief overview finds that risk management has been defined as the control of financial and personal injury loss from sudden, unforeseen, unusual accidents and intentional torts (Ammon, 1993). Later Wong and Masteralexis (1999) termed it "a management strategy to maintain greater control over the legal uncertainty that may wreak havoc on a sport business" (p. 90). Finally, a recent (2009) definition stated that risk management is the process of analyzing exposure to risk and determining how to best handle such exposure (Investor Words, 2009).

The losses or risks mentioned in these definitions can be either physical or financial in nature. Not only must sport facility managers attempt to minimize bodily injuries; they also need to minimize the risks that create the potential for lawsuits. Financial

Risks come in many shapes and sizes. (Photos courtesy Todd Seidler.)

losses resulting from incidents such as vandalism, poorly written contracts, stolen equipment, and sexual harassment claims must also be identified and managed. Therefore the primary goal of a risk manager must be to reduce those risks that contribute to bodily injuries and/or monetary losses while effectively managing a sport facility. This goal may sound easy, but it becomes a very complicated and difficult task.

The DIM Process

The DIM process has been utilized by multiple practitioners to establish effective risk management programs (Ammon & Brown, 2007). This simple process involves three basic steps: (1) *d*eveloping the risk management plan, (2) *i*mplementing the risk management plan, and (3) *m*anaging the risk management plan. The steps used in creating a risk management plan are similar no matter the size of facility or events it contains. Thus, facility managers at ice rinks, convention centers, municipal golf courses, minor league baseball parks, and international stadiums would use the same fundamental concepts. The DIM process, when used as an anticipatory technique rather than as a reactionary procedure, will assist any organization in diminishing the chances for litigation (Ammon & Brown, 2007).

Developing the Risk Management Plan

Developing a risk management plan consists of three separate steps: (1) identifying the risks, (2) classifying the risks, and (3) selecting treatments for the risks.

1. Identifying the Risks

   During the identification stage, a facility or risk manager must determine the various risks or losses that may occur during any given event. This information may be captured by surveying the attendees, inspecting the facility, talking to the current employees, or discussing potential risks with other facility managers who have similarly sized venues.

   An effective risk management plan is similar to a group of numbers in an equation. The numbers by themselves won't provide an answer, but adding some of the numbers together and subtracting others will result in the correct answer. Similarly each facility contains a variety of factors that impact the probability of various types of losses. The first variable in our risk management equation is the facility's *standard operating procedures* (SOPs). The SOPs are guidelines or methods utilized to manage the facility on a day-to-day basis. In addition, the utilization of these SOPs will assist a facility or risk manager to identify various risks.

   A second variable in our risk management equation pertains to the venues staff. A well-trained staff, knowledgeable about proper risk management procedures, can assist the risk manager in identifying potential risks. Unfortunately, the facility staff may also be risks themselves. For example, a nonobservant personal trainer may provide an inadequate spot during a lifting sequence by a member of the fitness center. A poorly trained lifeguard may not prohibit boisterous children from chasing each other on a wet pool deck. An athletic department may hire an inexperienced athletic trainer who misdiagnoses an athlete's injury. A football coach, with no background check, may previously have been sued for sexual assault. In each of these situations, the staff members themselves have become the risk. Risk identification for the facility's staff begins when interviewing prospective employees. The sport facility manager needs to demonstrate special vigilance that each employee meets the qualifications of the position before being hired (see Chapter 7).

Once the obvious factors have been identified, the sport facility manager must be watchful for additional risks. Additional variables in our risk management equation are applicable to most sport facilities and include the following: weather, event or activity type, patron demographics, and facility location. Risks may occur in a variety of locations, including indoor or indoor sport venues, professional or intercollegiate entertainment facilities, and privately or publicly owned buildings. It is important to remember that each facility, school, clinic, event, and program is different and has its own unique risks or areas of potential loss. Therefore, monitoring these risks needs to be constant and ongoing. It is equally important to remember that when identifying risks, special considerations should be taken, since the risk could involve either a financial loss or personal injury. Many of these risk factors affect and interact with each other. This can be demonstrated through the following example:

Once each of these factors has been considered, an athletic department administrator or sport facility manager has now identified potential risks or losses that may arise due to a high school football game. However, as mentioned earlier, developing a risk management plan is a three-step process. The second step is to *classify* these

Risk identification may include design flaws. (Photos courtesy Todd Seidler.)

A high school football game has been scheduled for the coming weekend. Several factors must be identified. In what part of the country is the high school located? What time of year is it? Obviously, a game played in a southern state early in the season may have to contend with hot, humid weather. If so then liquids need to be available for both spectators and players. A game in a northern state, later in the season, may have cold, snowy conditions. If a snowstorm approaches the stadium, the parking lot and sidewalks must be salted so patrons do not fall and injure themselves. Time of day the game will be played is an additional factor to be considered. Previous research has demonstrated that sporting events held at night have more crowd problems than those played during the day (Ammon & Unruh, 2007). Is the game between two fierce rivals, or is it a non-conference affair between teams who have never played each other before? This situation becomes even more significant if problems have occurred at previous sporting events between the two schools. If so, proactive measures need to be implemented before the game commences. All of these illustrations are real-life risks that have occurred at football stadiums throughout the country. If the activity were an intercollegiate women's basketball game or an age group swimming meet, a completely new set of risks or potential losses would need to be identified.

identified risks. The purpose of the classification stage is to determine the severity of loss arising from the risk and the frequency of occurrence of the risk.

2. Classifying Risks

After the risks or losses have been identified, they must be classified. The risk manager takes each of the previously identified risks and quantifies it in terms of frequency and severity. The frequency of the risk is dependent on the number of times the risk or loss may occur. The risk manager will select each identified risk and assign a frequency designated as "often," "average," or "seldom." The severity of the risk is determined by the intensity of the loss and should be classified as "catastrophic," "critical," "moderate," or "low." The level of severity and amount of frequency are determined by the risk manager, based on his or her previous experience. It is important to remember that both financial and personal injury losses need to be classified in terms of their frequency and severity.

Every activity is classified in a distinct manner, and each is dependent on the risks considered *inherent* to the activity. Inherent risks normally are risks or potential losses that are associated with the specific activity or sport. If the inherent risks were deleted, the resulting activity would be different from the original. For example, an inherent risk in rock climbing is falling. An inherent risk of swimming would be drowning, and an inherent risk of attending a baseball game would be being hit by a foul ball.

Non-inherent risks must be decreased as much as possible by the venue manager since the courts will not accept an "assumption of risk" defense if the spectator did not know, understand, and appreciate the *inherent* risk (see Chapter 10). For example, in YMCA adult basketball, a sprained ankle would be classified as "often" in frequency and "low" in severity because a sprained ankle is common to the game of basketball. However, for those individuals participating in an age group swimming

What risks can be identified at a basketball game? How would do you classify these risks? (BigStock Photo)

program, a sprained ankle would be classified as "seldom" in frequency. The difference is because a sprained ankle would *not* be an inherent risk for those engaged in a swimming program.

A matrix can be created that allows a consistent approach to the classification process. Once a risk has been identified, the matrix below (Table 9-1) gives the facility manager nine different categories in which to classify the risk. Twelve categories are a sufficient number; too many categories create unnecessary complexity; too few can cause some risks to be mislabeled. By placing the identified risks in the matrix, the risk manager would have successfully completed the classification stage. It should be noted that risk assessment is an ongoing process always subject to change. For example, as previously mentioned, one week a high school football game may be played during the afternoon, and the next week the game may be held at night. On the other hand, one week's game may be against a weak opponent with no play-off implications whereas the next week's game may be for the conference championship. The risk manager must be aware of such changes and assess each risk accordingly. Table 9-1 provides a matrix with some risks from our high school football game example placed in their proper categories.

Table 9-1. Risk Category Matrix

		SEVERITY			
		Catastrophic Loss	Critical Loss	Moderate Loss	Low Loss
FREQUENCY	High	None	None	• Inebriated fan injured while involved in a fight • Player sprains an ankle in pile-up	• Employee theft at concession stand • Spectator evades admission fees by sneaking into stadium
	Medium	None	• Heat exhaustion or frostbite	• Slip-and-falls in/around stadium • Player tears ligament in knee from loose sod on field	• Vandalism of stadium • Accidents in parking lot due to lack of signage
	Seldom	• Spectator suffers fatal sudden cardiac arrest	• Player breaks neck while performing improper tackle • Player's valuables stolen from locker room	• Discarded coals from tailgate barbeque start fire	• Pipes in bathroom spring leak due to cold weather • Food poisoning from poorly stored mayonnaise

3. Treating the Risks

The third stage in developing the risk management plan is to determine a *treatment* for each identified and classified risk. The type of treatment chosen for the various identified and classified risks normally depends on the nature of the risk and the likelihood of the risk occurring. Although it is often difficult to determine the severity and frequency of losses involved, a risk matrix can also assist in this identification process.

Avoidance

As depicted in Table 9-2 risks should be avoided when they could cause a catastrophic or critical loss with medium or high frequency. Ideally, a facility manager should be able to identify these types of risks before an accident occurs and avoid them completely. For a sport venue, avoidance means that a specific activity should not be started or the activity should be discontinued if it is presently being offered. Obviously, using a piece of equipment that has previously caused personal injury and/or property damage would not be prudent. For example, some pieces of equipment (such as trampolines) have a reputation for causing moderate to severe injuries. Once this is danger is recognized, a gym or fitness center would choose not to purchase a trampoline or if it currently owned one, it would do away with it. Decreasing or eliminating the number of athletic or recreational activities is not an attractive option. Therefore, avoidance should only be implemented as a last resort when danger is substantial and frequency of injury is significant. For example, in our football scenario, cancellation or postponement of the game would occur in the event of severe weather (impending lightning storm), bomb threat, or a power outage that makes further play impossible.

Transfer

Table 9-2 illustrates that the second type of risk treatment, *transfer*, occurs in almost every instance with the exception of catastrophic/critical loss with medium/high frequency (would use *avoidance*) or low loss and medium/low frequency (would use *retention*).

Table 9-2. Risk Treatment Matrix

		SEVERITY		
		High Loss	Moderate Loss	Low Loss
FREQUENCY	Often	Avoid	Transfer & Reduction	Transfer or Retain & Reduction
	Average	Avoid or Transfer & Reduction	Transfer & Reduction	Retain & Reduction
	Seldom	Transfer & Reduction	Transfer or Retain & Reduction	Retain & Reduction

While every risk carries some degree of danger, they should not always be considered immediate concerns and therefore do not always have to be avoided. For our purposes transfer is simply the shifting of the financial responsibility for an injury or loss from the facility manager/owner to a third party. Transfer occurs when the risk is not severe enough to avoid the risk but it is greater than what the venue can assume on its own.

Why transfer some risks and avoid others? First of all, the combination of severity and frequency may not be large enough to warrant avoiding the risk. Nevertheless, the risk may be large enough to cause substantial monetary damage to the sport facility. One option is to transfer the risk to an insurance company. After being paid a *premium*, the company will cover of any type of financial loss that may occur up to the limits of the *policy*. It is important to recognize that the insurance company transfers financial liabilities from the *policy-holder* to the *insurer*. Therefore, the definition of insurance is the transfer of financial risk from one individual to an outside organization. Insurance is the most well known and popular type of transfer. In order to comprehend the concept of insurance an understanding of basic terminology is paramount:

Adjuster: a representative of the insurance company who determines the amount of financial responsibility an insurance company owes to the policy-holder.

Agent: a representative of the insurance company who sells and services the policy to an interested party.

Claim: after suffering a financial loss, a policy-holder notifies the insurance company to cover the financial liability according to the stipulations of the policy.

Deductible: the amount of money (liability) the policy-holder owes before the insurance company becomes liable. The deductible is inversely related to the premium.

Insured: the individual who purchases the insurance policy from an insurance agent. This individual files a claim with the insurer after a financial loss occurs that is covered by the policy.

Insurer: the insurance company who provides the policy and agrees to cover the financial liability of the policy-holder.

Personal liability insurance. Two main types of insurance will be relevant for sport facility managers: personal liability and property insurance. If a spectator, participant, or employee is injured by something the facility manager did or did not do, then the individual was injured personally and can sue to recover appropriate damages. The following are examples of what could be covered under this type of insurance policy:

- Crowd management staff injures an innocent third party while trying to eject a violent intoxicated spectator.
- At Y Camp, instead of closely supervising a group of middle school basketball players, the YMCA supervisor is texting his girlfriend. A fight breaks out during the game and a player sustains a broken nose during the fight.
- The screen behind home plate at a minor league baseball park has a hole in it. A foul ball flies through the hole and hits a spectator in the eye, causing a visual impairment.

All of these incidents would be covered under the personal injury clause of the insurance policy. Although there is no safe amount of coverage, most facilities have a minimum of $1 million worth of insurance.

Policy: a contract between the person (insured) purchasing the insurance and the organization (insurer) offering to provide the coverage.

Premium: a payment (monthly, quarterly, or yearly) to the insurance company offering the coverage. The size of the premium is inversely related to the size of the deductible. To put this issue into perspective, an insurance company is a "for profit" business. The company gambles that the revenue acquired through *premiums* is greater than the expenses paid out for *claims*. If it pays out more than it accrues, you can rest assured that the company's premiums will be increasing fairly soon! Because insurance companies are in business to show a profit, it is important to realize that insurance companies often find that it is less expensive to settle lawsuits than litigate the claims. During a lawsuit, settlement occurs when an insurance company (when it is the defendant) determines it to be financially advantageous to offer the plaintiff a financial settlement to drop the case. After calculating the cost of a trial, the insurance company comes to the realization that paying the plaintiff is a cheaper solution than litigating the case, even if the company believes it would win the case. If the plaintiff agrees to the settlement, the money changes hands and the case is over. In this instance there is no awarding of guilt by the court. If plaintiffs believe that even with a weak case the insurance company will settle with them for a substantial sum, this strategy may actually backfire by increasing the number of lawsuits. As insurance companies gain the reputation of paying off claims, the number of suits will continue to grow. An additional problem that occurs because of settling lawsuits involves individual employees defended by the organization. If the sport or recreation organization pays off the claim, the employee has no opportunity to prove his or her innocence. This stigma can be quite traumatic and remain with the employee for a long time.

Property Insurance. The building, its amenities (locker rooms, ticket booths, check-in counters, snack bars, swimming pools, exercise facilities, etc.), equipment, and furniture all have a specific value. Weather and acts of God can wreak havoc with a sport facility. In addition, some individuals who visit sport venues are immoral or corrupt individuals who show no respect for other people's property. Alcohol may also play a part in clouding some spectators' judgment. The damage could be a result of vandalism, theft, or destruction. Property insurance will help defray the costs to repair the loss. Two types of property insurance are relevant. *Named perils* insurance will cover only the specific risks spelled out in the policy. As indicated, this coverage will be only for certain events that are specifically mentioned in the insurance policy. Examples include wind, hail, fire, and lightning. Most *named perils* are natural occurrences and are virtually uncontrollable. *All-risk* policies are broader than *named perils* policies and will insure most any loss unless the insurance company says it isn't covered. Some risks caused by terrorism, earthquakes, and floods require specific policies that must be purchased separately and are not usually covered by a general policy.

Property insurance should be purchased to protect events as well as facilities.

Waivers: A waiver is a document by which the signer voluntary gives up the right, by contract, to sue a service provider for negligence. The waiver implies that a person agreeing to accept the risk of harm (the signer) caused by another's actions (the provider) must understand and comprehend the nature of the risk. Because the document is a contract, the intent of the waiver must be unambiguous and definite. Well-written waivers can protect against ordinary negligence in 46 states in the United States (Cotten, 2007). However, a waiver generally does not protect a private business or state entity from liability against gross negligence or reckless misconduct. In most states waivers are unenforceable for minors.

Indemnification clauses: Indemnification clauses are included in most contracts that sport and recreation managers sign with organizations that lease the facility or when they rent equipment. These clauses, sometimes called "hold harmless agreements," allow the organization management to be compensated by the individuals renting the facility, if any damage occurs during the event. Thus the risk during the event is *transferred* to the outside organization.

Retention

Retention is the third treatment a sport facility manager can select.

A venue that chooses retention becomes financially responsible for any injuries or financial risks that may occur to their stakeholders or to the venue itself. This expense must be planned for in advance and the budget must provide funds to pay for expenses that may be incurred by the organization. Normally this treatment is used for minor injury pay-outs, first aid treatment, ambulance service, and other low severity types of risks. It is important to realize that another form of retention involves the use of insurance deductibles because the deductible is the amount of risk retained by the organization. Deductibles can be a financial boon to sport facility managers since insurance premiums decrease measurably as the size of the deductible increases.

Some risks are easily mitigated and therefore are retained.

Reduction

Reduction is the fourth and final treatment a facility manager will try in order to reduce the risks.

This treatment involves trying to restrict the risks, therefore diminishing the number of lawsuits. Requiring employees to undertake more training, using preventive maintenance instead of waiting for an accident to occur, and compiling extensive records through the collection of accident forms, participation forms, and instructions are examples of reduction treatments. In addition, proper signage is an absolute necessity for preventing property damage and bodily injury. Signs build a support network between fans and event staff. All of these reduction treatments need to become part of the standard operating procedures (SOPs).

Any time an activity is offered, reduction must be utilized in addition to the transfer, retention, and avoidance methods previously discussed. Table 9.2 illustrates that when a risk manager decides to retain or transfer the risks, he or she must be ready to also include a reduction treatment that will ensure that each situation is handled in a manner that will reduce the chance of liability. No one reduction treatment will work all the time, and each different activity may require a different action.

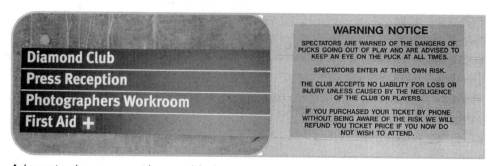

Adequate signage must be provided.

CLARIFYING STEPS IN THE DIM PROCESS

A hypothetical situation can help to clarify each of the steps in the DIM process.

Allison Connors, a recent sport management graduate, has been hired as the adult program coordinator at her hometown YMCA. The program has been beset by several negligence suits in the past three years, and one of her responsibilities is to implement a risk management plan for the adult program at the YMCA. Allison's first priority is to develop the plan. After several weeks of reading reports and records, observing various activities, analyzing operational policies and procedures, talking to participants, and questioning other YMCA directors, Allison begins to make a list of the risks she has observed and identified. The adult program at the YMCA includes a men's soccer league, which Allison decides poses some potential physical hazards that need to be addressed. There has been a rash of reported injuries, mostly involving twisted ankles, jammed fingers, skin abrasions, and occasionally small lacerations. After identifying these risks Allison classified them as low-medium frequency and low severity. When selecting a treatment for the risks, Allison must decide among four options. First, she could eliminate the soccer league to ensure that the risks didn't occur, but this would not be sensible. The decision would be unpopular with the participants and could potentially cause some participants to drop their

membership. Second, Allison could amend the Y's insurance policy to cover these types of injuries. That would transfer the risk to an outside agency, but would increase the cost of the YMCA's insurance policy considerably. She could also transfer the risk by having each participant sign a waiver. Since this is an adult league, such documents could provide considerable protection. Third, she could retain the risk and pay for any of the identified minor injuries from the adult program's operating budget. If the potential injuries were classified correctly retention would be a possible choice. Finally, Allison could attempt to avert the risks through reduction measures. Educating the participants about proper stretching techniques, training the league referees to keep better control of the games, and instituting certain safety rules might significantly reduce the injuries. However, Allison's best options might be to select two of the approaches—transfer (by requiring that participants sign a waiver and assumption of risk statement) and risk reduction (by instituting the measures to reduce risk). In Allison's situation transfer and risk reduction offer realistic, yet achievable, solutions for her identified risks. Allison would proceed to develop her plan by identifying, classifying, and selecting treatments for her other risks.

Implementing the Risk Management Plan

The next step in the DIM process consists of implementing the risk management plan. As previously stated, communication of the risk management plan is critical for implementation, and the employees of the facility or organization are the primary group who need to be made aware of the plan. The best way to implement the plan is for all employees to be included in the development of the plan. This sense of ownership will emphasize the importance of the plan. That way each employee has a shared responsibility to communicate the plan in order to ensure the success of the plan. Encouraging the employees to make suggestions will increase the sense of ownership and thus the rigor of the risk management plan.

The easiest way to communicate the plan occurs when an employee is initially hired. Placing the risk management plan in the orientation handbook provides the new employee with a firsthand look. A note of caution: do not place the entire plan in the notebook. It will be too comprehensive. Place only the sections that are pertinent to the individual employee. This will take a certain amount of organization on the part of the facility or risk manager, but will be an investment for the future.

After several months of employment, employees should receive inservice training on the risk management plan. These instructional periods help identify specific employee training needs that have arisen since the initial employee orientation meetings. The job tasks of various personnel may have become very specialized since employment, such as those involving aquatic areas, the use of chemicals, and technical equipment operation. Additional insurance coverage, redesigned operational techniques, and new safety measures are often discussed and practiced during these in-services. Motivational techniques and team building strategies may also be implemented during these sessions.

In our scenario, Allison implements her plan by providing a condensed risk management manual to each employee, including contracted personnel such as referees. The books explain appropriate policies, rules, and regulations, and emphasize emergency care procedures. In addition, she conducts training sessions for the league referees to make certain they understand and enforce the local safety rules instituted by the program. Allison also implements an emergency medical plan for which her supervisory personnel are well trained.

Managing the DIM Plan

The final step of the DIM process is to manage the plan. A risk manager or safety committee must be selected and provided with the authority to motivate and lead. Some facilities will hire one individual to take on the responsibility of a risk manager. Other facilities, due to budget constraints, will divide the responsibilities among a group of current employees. The person or persons selected to take responsibility for the risk management plan should be chosen very carefully. First, they must recognize the need for such a plan. Second, they must understand that by managing risks properly, they are improving the spectators' overall experiences and ultimately the reputation of the facility, which translates into repeat customers. Without comprehending the connection between these two elements, the success of the risk management plan is questionable.

Facility management and ownership must also buy into the idea of risk management. They must be willing to assist the risk manager or safety committee with verbal and financial support. Without upper management's support, a risk management plan will not succeed. The risk manager or safety committee must be given the freedom to act independently, but within the philosophy of the facility. As previously mentioned, risks are constantly changing and shifting due to the activities and programs employed by various organizations. Therefore, risk management plans must also evolve and fluctuate; they are never static.

Risk management is a necessity for facility managers today. Even though many risks can be identified, classified, and treated, some hazards will still exist and accidents will occur. It is unreasonable to expect a facility manager to eliminate all injuries and finan-

After risks have been identified a risk manager must have the authority to mitigate them. (Photos courtesy Todd Seidler.)

cial losses. However, by developing an extensive risk management plan, implementing the plan, and bestowing the authority to manage the plan upon a concerned risk manager, sport managers can diminish a number of dangerous risks.

In our scenario Allison was hired with the understanding that her duties as adult program coordinator would include the duties of a risk manager. She is fortunate that the YMCA's policy statements provide her with the essential authority to carry out these various responsibilities and to manage the plan effectively. She established an employee risk management committee to assist her in the management of the risk management plan. Once the risk management plan was developed, Allison sought needed help, advice, information, and support from the employee risk management committee. From this input, Allison manages the plan and makes regular modification in her plan.

Summary

1. Many experts recognize event management as a growth industry, and risk management is acknowledged as an important component of a successful event.
2. Risk management is defined as the ability to control both financial and personal injury losses from sudden, unforeseen, unusual accidents and intentional torts.
3. The DIM process is a tool used to establish a proper risk management program and involves three basic steps: (1) *d*eveloping the risk management plan, (2) *i*mplementing the risk management plan, and (3) *m*anaging the risk management plan.
4. In developing the plan, each risk is identified and classified by frequency and severity. Then it is assigned to a specific treatment. These treatments include avoiding the risk, transferring the risk, retaining the risk, and reducing the possibility of loss with standard operating procedures (SOPs).
5. Insurance is the most common method used to transfer the risk to another party. Other types of transfer include waivers, independent contractors, and indemnification clauses.

6. When a facility retains a risk, it becomes financially responsible for any injuries or financial losses that may occur.

7. Requiring employees to use preventive maintenance, compiling extensive record keeping, and using signage are reduction techniques that become part of a facility's standard operating procedures (SOPs).

8. Implementing the risk management plan pertains to the ability to communicate the plan to others, namely, the facility employees.

9. Facility management and ownership must be willing to assist with verbal and financial support in order for the risk manager or safety committee to manage the plan.

Questions

1. Why is risk management so vital to facility managers in the 21st century?
2. Identify and define the various stages involved in the DIM process.
3. How can a risk manager identify the risks in his or her facility?
4. Identify and provide an example for each treatment of a risk management plan.
5. What is an inherent risk? Is it important to know if the risk is inherent? Why or why not?

10

Premises Liability and Negligence

Application Exercise

On October 18, 2005, Charlie Brown and three fraternity brothers ostensibly entered Jefferson Davis Stadium to watch a college football game. However, their primary motivation was to participate in an annual fraternity frolic known as "Drunk as a Skunk," in which costumed fraternity members attempt to enter the running track surrounding the football field during half-time and run a quarter-mile race. The group members, including the plaintiff (Charlie Brown), were prevented by security personnel on three separate occasions from gaining access to the field and the running track.

Prior to as well as during the course of the game, Brown consumed a quantity of "trash can punch," a mixture of Kool-Aid fruit punch and 180-proof grain alcohol. In compliance with university policy, the group brought their "recipe" into the stadium in four, 1-gallon containers. The university's policy prohibited the consumption of alcoholic beverages during football games, but allowed containers into the stadium as long as they were 1-gallon size or less. This directive was enforced by crowd management staff that performed visual searches of all packages and containers as patrons entered the stadium gates. Anyone deemed visibly intoxicated was escorted out of the stadium. Security personnel made no attempt to ascertain the nature of the fraternity members' beverage. Prior to passing out, the plaintiff had an encounter with security officers and stumbled into one, prompting a direction being given to the other members of the group to "get him up in the stands and back to his seat." One of the security staff observed the plaintiff was drunk and recommended he be taken home. During the course of the game, as he continued to consume the punch, Brown became progressively intoxicated and eventually fell asleep in the stands.

Upon waking, Brown and his three "brothers" climbed over a wall and continued onto a grassy bluff area. There, the plaintiff tumbled, rolled, and even attempted to lay down a second time and go to sleep. The group then proceeded to the opposite side of the stadium and made another unsuccessful attempt to gain entrance to the track.

Brown then rushed back to the walkway at the top of the stands and, with the others in pursuit, darted along the walkway and vaulted over the 4-foot wall at the far end of the walkway, apparently without realizing there was a 30-foot drop to the concrete steps below. Brown sustained severe and permanent injuries to his ankles and knees as a result of his fall.

Plaintiff Brown brought a negligence action against the university. The local district court entered judgment on jury verdict in favor of the university and Brown appealed.

Appplication Questions

1. Does Charlie Brown have a case?
2. Is the crowd management group potentially responsible for Brown's injuries?
3. Was the university negligent?
4. What "duty" did the university owe to Charlie?

Premises Liability

Sport and entertainment events provide enjoyment for millions of fans each year. In addition, these experiences provide multiple challenges for sport and entertainment facility managers. Our litigious society mandates managers have a firm grasp of negligence concepts and understand that litigation may well follow an incident. *Premises liability* is a term that describes these legal parameters. The definition of premises liability that we will use in this text is *the legal responsibility a facility or event manager owes to the individuals utilizing the venue.* It is important to remember that facilities come in a variety of shapes and sizes. Therefore, stadiums (like Jefferson Davis Stadium), arenas, theaters, convention centers, amphitheaters, golf courses, ski areas, skate board parks, and fitness facilities fall under our definition of a facility. In order to fully understand premises liability a comprehension of negligence must first be acquired.

Many sporting activities, including soccer, involve the risk of injuries from collisions.
(Photo courtesy of *The Times Georgian* and Kendra Waycuilis.)

Definition of Negligence

Negligence falls under the general body of law called torts. Negligence deals with avoidable accidents that should have been anticipated and prevented by taking reasonable precautions. When negligence is used as a cause of action, the injured party (plaintiff) claims he or she was injured as a result of action or inaction on the part of the service provider (defendant). While the defendant may not have intended to harm the plaintiff, negligence is something a defendant did or did not do that resulted in the plaintiff being injured.

Elements of Negligence

Most jurisdictions recognize that four distinct elements must be proven by the plaintiff to establish a negligence claim. These elements consist of *duty*, *breach of duty*, *proximate cause*, and *damages*. All four elements must exist in order for a person to be found negligent.

Duty

Venue managers possess a general *duty* to do what a reasonably prudent person in a similar situation would do. In order for a duty to exist three criteria must be established. First, there must be a "relationship" between the service provider and the injured party that requires the service provider to protect the plaintiff from unreasonable risk of harm (van der Smissen, 2007a).

In any particular situation in which a level of professional expertise is involved, there may be many such relationships (club owner/member, coach/player, facility manager/ vendor, event coordinator/concert attendee are all examples of the many types of relationships relevant to sport facilities).

Second, these relationships involve "types of specific duties." These duties require a professional to abide by specific standards of care established or adopted as the standards of professional behavior in the particular industry. The existence of a relationship and the degree of care required are determined by examining similar conduct of other professionals in the field and providing a safe environment for patrons (Wong, 2002). Examples of these various types of duties include inspecting the facility and playing surfaces; ensuring that all equipment is maintained properly; providing proper medical assistance to employees, fans, and athletes/entertainers; supervising participants; warning participants;

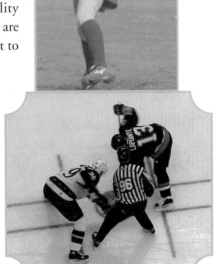

Softball and hockey are two examples of activities that may involve a duty on the part of the facility manager.

and spectators of inherent risks of the activity; and, ensuring that the design of the facility is appropriate for the activity being conducted.

The third criterion that must be established to determine if a duty exists pertains to the "status" of the plaintiff. The four general types of patrons are *invitee, licensee, trespasser,* and *recreational user.* An invitee is someone who has paid a fee or can be expected to pay a fee in the future for the use of the facility. A spectator purchasing a ticket for a game or an individual purchasing a lift ticket at a ski resort would both be examples of business invitees. Furthermore, a guest at a health club or a person browsing in the pro shop would be considered a business invitee since this individual would be providing an economic benefit to the facility. A facility manager owes the highest duty of care to an invitee to inspect the premises, provide a safe environment, and reasonably foresee dangers that could arise.

In contrast, a *licensee* is someone who has been allowed, without expectation of monetary exchange, to use the premises. The facility manager does not have to afford a licensee the same degree of care as an invitee. Therefore, the premises operator only has the duty to warn of dangers that may not be readily apparent to the user. For example, a landowner who allows community members to hike and bike on his property needs only to warn about dangers that would not be readily apparent (Sharp, Moorman, & Claussen, 2007). In this situation, the facility owner need not inspect, foresee, or give warnings of obvious dangers. Patrons would be considered licensees at a community softball field, at a public park, or while watching a celebration parade from a city sidewalk.

A *trespasser,* or someone who enters the premises without permission, is owed only the duty not to intentionally harm.

A *recreational user* is an individual who uses another person's property with her or his permission. The recreational user does not pay a fee for this opportunity. A landowner does not owe any type of duty to a recreational user to keep the premises safe or to post warnings about hazardous situations (Sharp, 2007).

The situation often determines the duty owed. As a result, a facility manager must be cognizant of particular situations that could potentially arise in a given activity, how they might be viewed from a legal perspective, and whether that particular activity warrants a special relationship to the patron.

These standards of care outline what a *reasonably prudent professional* (RPP) would do. With this in mind, it is critical that sport managers are knowledgeable about the standards of care in the facility management industry. Since the standard of care may change, it is the manager's responsibility to read the relevant literature and attend professional conferences to understand the duty of care that is owed. Coaches, referees, and facility

Business invitees occupy seats during a Phoenix Suns game.

The duty owed to participants is situational. For example, football coaches owe a duty of care to football players to provide water during practices.

managers cannot eliminate all risks associated with the sport. Some risks, such as the risk of collision, are *inherent*. Professionals in the sport industry can be expected to owe a duty to participants consistent with an accepted standard. For example, soccer fields should be maintained to a certain acceptable standard. This will require inspections before a game is played to ensure a safe playing surface.

While every particular situation is unique, standards of care are used to measure a particular professional's conduct in a given situation. Therefore, in a sport or recreation setting a venue manager should possess and use the degree of knowledge, ability, and skill possessed by competent professionals in the facility management industry.

Breach of Duty

The next element a plaintiff must prove in a negligence case is *breach of duty*. Once a duty has been established, then a breach of that duty must be proven for a negligence case to continue. Quite simply, breach of duty is when something the defendant (service provider) either did (*commission*) or did not do (*omission*) to meet the obligation of the standard of care of a reasonably prudent professional (RPP). For example, in order to provide a safe workout environment for its patrons, a fitness center has a front desk employee whose job it is to verify that anyone entering the facility is a member. One day the front desk employee, instead of performing her task, is busy talking on her cell phone. An adult male nonmember enters the fitness center while the employee is chatting on the phone and she neglects to verify the individual's membership card (omission). Subsequently, this nonmember proceeds to assault a member in the facility's locker room. The employee's act of omission breached the duty of care owed to the injured facility member as a result of the fiduciary relationship that existed. In addition to the duty owed as a result of official, legal, or fiduciary relationship, a court may determine

There are often standards associated with teaching sports skills.

negligence, resulting from breach of duty, based on expert testimony that the professional's conduct did not meet the RPP standard.

Proximate Cause

Proximate cause is the connection or bridge between the breach of duty and the harm that occurred (Wong, 2002). In other words, there must be a connection between the negligent act and the injury. For instance, if a facility manager at a baseball field used an unsafe material for the warning track, a breach of duty would occur. If a player were injured on a properly manicured infield, it would not be an act of negligence because there was no proximate cause between the breach (warning track on the outfield) and the injury that occurred on the infield. The act need not be the sole cause of the injury, but should be a "substantial factor" (van der Smissen, 2007a, p. 41). To put it another way, for causation to occur the service provider/professional must have done, or not done, something that could be reasonably expected to result in an unreasonable risk of harm. While there may not be an absolute linkage of cause and effect between a service provider's actions and the injury, the court's judgment will be the benchmark. Furthermore, if the act was not an essential element of the harm, and the injury would have taken place regardless, a negligence claim would be negated.

Sport and recreation participants often rely on the knowledge and judgment of service providers.

Damage

Damage is the last part of the negligence equation, and has a double meaning. First, damage refers to the physical or emotional loss suffered by the injured party. These losses fall into four basic categories: (1) economic loss (medical expenses, lost wages), (2) physical pain and suffering, (3) emotional distress (fright, anxiety, humiliation), and (4) physical impairment (temporary or permanent) (van der Smissen, 2007a). Second, "damage*s*" refer to the compensation the plaintiff receives in order to return to the way they were before the injury. This is termed "to be made whole again." Even though some injuries cannot physically be "made whole," the court system will assign some type of monetary compensation for the negligence.

Defenses against Liability

In order to decrease liability exposure, a facility manager should plan ahead by anticipating, identifying, and resolving potential risks (Cotten, 2007a). However, no facility manager can account for every imaginable risk. Therefore, it is important to identify various recourses available to a facility manager in the event of a negligence lawsuit. In this section, several possible defenses against liability are listed and briefly discussed. In addition, waivers and releases, and their use as a defense against liability, are covered in greater detail at the end of the chapter.

Possible defenses against negligence include the following:

Negligence elements not met

In order for a negligence suit to have merit, all four elements (duty, breach, cause, and damage) must be present. If any one of these items is missing, there is no negligence (Cotten, 2007a).

Primary assumption of risk

Under the doctrine of assumption of risk, the patron voluntarily put himself or herself in harm's way; the risk associated with the injury is inherent to the sport; and the participant knows, understands, and appreciates the potential risks associated with the activity (Cotten, 2007a). For example, in *Alwin v St Paul Saints* (2003) a plaintiff (Ronald Alwin) was returning from a restroom while attending a minor league baseball game when he was struck by a foul ball. The Minnesota Court of Appeals stated that since Alwin assumed the risk by attending an inherently dangerous sport (baseball), he could not recover damages for his injuries when he was struck by the foul fly ball. It is expected that foul balls will often fly into the stands at a baseball game, so patrons must remain alert—even when leaving the restroom.

Contributory negligence

Only a handful of states allow contributory negligence. In its pure form contributory negligence can be used if the participant in some way contributed to his or her own injuries. Any fault on the part of the plaintiff will completely bar them from receiving any type of compensatory award.

Facility lease agreements

Lease agreements are basically rental contracts (see Chapter 8) between the facility and the agency or organization interested in using the facility. Most of these agreements will contain an *indemnification agreement*. This clause will stipulate that the organization leasing the facility will reimburse or hold the facility manager harmless for any damages or consequential litigation resulting from the event. The facility manager will still be responsible for any damage related to the facility itself.

Independent contractors

In most jurisdictions independent contractors or agencies that have been outsourced are responsible for the hiring, employment, and training of their staff, while the facility manager exercises little control over them. The independent contractor will be responsible for any litigation resulting from their employees' actions if individuals were behaving as they had been trained; this is known as acting within the scope of their employment.

Comparative fault

In this negligence defense, the amount of award is reduced by the amount of fault by the plaintiff. In most cases plaintiffs can recover up to the point at which they are 50% at fault; beyond that they are barred from recovery (similar to contributory negligence) (Cotten, 2007a).

Immunity

Immunity in the legal sense occurs when individuals or organizations are exempted from being found negligent for their actions or those actions taking place on their property. Four types of immunity pertain to premises liability.

Recreational user statutes. This protects landowners who let others use their property without any type of fee. If patrons are charged a fee, their status reverts to that of an invitee and the landowner loses any immunity. The rationale behind the law was to encourage landowners to open their land to the general public. For facility managers, this would not protect against injuries on the playing field, but it has been used successfully as a defense in the event that spectators were injured (Cotten, 2007b).

Volunteer immunity statutes. A volunteer is classified as someone who donates her or his time and services. Prior to passage of the Volunteer Protection Act of 1977, volunteers were treated like any other employees. However, after passage of this Act, in most jurisdictions, volunteers are protected from liability as long as they were acting within the scope of their employment. In addition, in order for this Act to apply, volunteers must be licensed (when appropriate); the harm caused must not be due to the operation of a motor vehicle; and, when appropriate, volunteers must undergo safety training (Cotten, 2007b).

Good Samaritan statutes. Good Samaritan statutes have been enacted "to provide immunity from liability for certain parties who voluntarily and gratuitously come to the aid of injured persons" (Cotten, 2007b, p. 78). However, if a person is an employee of a facility, this defense would not apply, since as an employee, the person has a responsibility to provide help.

Statute of limitations. The time allotted for a negligence claim to remain viable varies by state. However, a minor's time clock does not start until she or he reaches the age of majority, despite when the action was committed. Youth sports camps provide an example of a minor having an extended statute of limitations. A 16-year-old minor injured at a football camp due to a facility's negligence would have his statute of limitations "clock" begin after he turned 18 years old.

Waivers and Releases

If sport management students were to ask several lawyers or sport law scholars, "What are *waivers* and *releases*, and why should I use them?" they might receive several slightly different answers. Both waivers and releases involve a plaintiff rescinding her or his right to sue a service provider for negligence that resulted in the plaintiff's injury. Cotten (2007c) described a waiver as "a contract in which a participant or user of a service agrees to relinquish the right to pursue legal action against the service provider in the event that the ordinary negligence of the provider results in an injury to the participant" (p. 85). In all of these definitions, individuals signing the waivers or releases are basically giving up their right to sue someone else for negligence.

Since the focus of this section of the chapter involves the use of a waiver as a defense to negligence, the term "waiver" will refer to any document that seeks to transfer liability from a service provider to a participant or spectator. While various terms ("waiver" and/or "release") may be used, the concept of transfer of liability is constant.

A waiver is a *contract* where one agrees not to pursue legal action for an injury occurring as a result of negligence (Cotten, 2007c). In contrast, an *agreement to participate* is not in the form of a contract. Typically, agreements to participate spell out inherent risks and provide instructions to participants, but they do not include an *exculpatory clause* barring the signee from suing. Since agreements to participate are not contracts, they may be signed by a minor (Cotten, 2007a). Any transfer of liability document (waiver) normally seeks to primarily protect the service provider/professional from liability for ordinary negligence as defined above. A signed waiver indicates a participant acknowledges that, if injured, he promises not to sue the service provider. If he does sue the service provider, the defendant will produce the waiver to the court as his defense. The waiver is a contract, so it is important that it is treated as such by both parties. In addition, waivers can indemnify the facility, if they are properly drafted and signed by the appropriate people as justified by that particular state's laws (Cotten, 2007c).

Each state has a different set of standards for how rigorous a waiver must be, but "in at least forty-six states and Washington, DC, a well-written, properly administered waiver, voluntarily signed by an adult, can be used to protect the recreation or sport business from liability for ordinary negligence by the business or its employees" (Cotten, 2007c, p. 85). Because of its potential importance, a waiver should not be considered a formality. An attorney should be involved in the preparation of the waiver because if properly written, presented, and signed it can be a valuable tool in achieving the transfer of liability.

Waivers, however, have certain limitations. For instance, a waiver cannot be contrary to public policy. If a waiver is not in the best interest of the general public, a court will not uphold it. In addition, if both parties to the waiver do not have equal bargaining power, the waiver will be void. With the exception of four states, waivers cannot attempt to waive liability for extreme negligence, gross negligence, reckless misconduct, or willful and wanton conduct (Cotten, 2007c).

Since minors cannot be bound by a contract they sign, minors cannot waive their right to sue. However, courts in 10 states (Alaska, California, Colorado, Connecticut, Florida, Georgia, Ohio, Massachusetts, North Dakota, Wisconsin) have recently upheld waivers signed by a parent on behalf of a minor child (Cotten, 2007c).

The specific format of a waiver may vary from state to state or from jurisdiction to jurisdiction. This present discussion is not intended to demonstrate how to write a waiver, but to make the reader aware of the importance of waivers. It is important for sport managers to remember that a licensed attorney who has experience or specializes in the appropriate area of law should review any waiver or release document. Some areas that are considered minimum criteria that generally have to be met for a waiver to be enforceable are listed in Table 10-1.

Table 10-1. Necessary Elements for a Waiver to Be Enforceable

✔ It should be clearly labeled as a waiver.
✔ It must be clearly written and understandable. Also, the font point size should be large enough to be easily read.
✔ It must be filled out correctly, accurately, and completely. Signers must understand they are giving up their right to sue in the event of injury.
✔ It can only involve relinquishing the right to sue for ordinary negligence (not gross negligence except in Florida, Illinois, Kentucky, and Pennsylvania) (Cotten, 2007c).
✔ There must be consideration or exchange of value involved in the contract.
✔ The parties involved should be clearly specified (who is relinquishing rights and whom the waiver is protecting).
✔ The person signing the contract must have the capacity to contract (waivers signed by minors are unenforceable) (Cotten, 2007c).
✔ Both parties must have equal bargaining positions.
✔ Inherent risks should be mentioned. In most cases individuals must have an awareness and understanding of an inherent risk before relinquishing their right to sue.
✔ Mentioning the word "negligence" in the body of the waiver makes the waiver stronger in many states.

Responsibility for Liability

After a plaintiff proves the elements necessary for negligence and the defendant produces a defense, it is important to determine who would be held responsible, or liable, if the negligence occurred. In the past, suits primarily targeted those with *deep pockets*. This term refers to those individuals involved in the lawsuit with the largest number of financial resources (normally insurance). However, due to the litigiousness of our society individuals have begun to sue not only the individual with the deepest pockets, but anyone else remotely associated with the particular incident. For a facility or event, those potentially responsible in a negligence suit are the employees, the administrative or supervisory personnel, and the corporate entity (Cotten, 2007d).

Employee

In many situations, the employee is the person who commits a negligent act. The employees are the associates who are in direct contact with the patrons in the form of coaches, ushers, referees, fitness specialists, lifeguards, and concessionaires. If the plaintiff can demonstrate that the employee had a duty, breached that duty, and that breach was a proximate cause of the injury, then the employee will be considered negligent and therefore legally responsible.

Administrative or Supervisory Personnel

The administrative or supervisory role is one that is more complicated and convoluted than that of an employee. (See Table 10-2). Ordinarily, the supervisor is not considered negligent for the actions of her or his employees. However, if a supervisor had knowledge, or should have had knowledge, of a particular employee's actions and failed to resolve the situation, if the administrator failed to enforce safety regulations, or if the administrator practiced inappropriate employment and hiring practices, the administrator may be liable.

A weight room supervisor is responsible for establishing rules and regulations for the safety of patrons.

Table 10-2. Five Categories of Responsibilities for Administrators

1. Hiring and training competent personnel and discharging unfit employees
2. Providing proper supervision and having a supervision plan
3. Directing certain services in the manner they should be completed
4. Establishing rules and regulations for safety and complying with policy and statutory requirements
5. Remedying dangerous conditions and defective equipment or giving notice of this when there is knowledge of the conditions
Source: van der Smissen, 1990.

The Corporate Entity

The corporate entity determination of liability falls under the context of *respondeat superior* or vicarious liability. In each situation, the general rule is if an employee is found to be negligent in the course and scope of his or her duties, then the employer might also be negligent. If, however, the employee were negligent in a situation outside of her or his normal duties, the employer would not be held liable. Traditionally, interns, volunteers, or trainees will be viewed by the courts as actual employees, if at the time of the negligent act, the individuals were acting under the control of the corporation. However, athletes in a university setting, even though they may be receiving a scholarship, are not considered employees of the institution. Therefore, the university would not be vicariously liable for their actions (Cotten, 2007d).

Facility Liability

Other methods of limiting corporate liability specifically with regard to facilities exist. If a facility is leased by an outside group, the determination of liability lies within the parameter of whether the injury was premise related or activity related (van der Smissen, 1990). If the cause of the injury were directly related to the facility premises, the facility owner would most often be liable. If, however, the injury was activity related, and the owner of the facility had no control over the activity, then the facility owner would most likely not be liable (van der Smissen, 1990). This shifting of liability from the facility manager to the outside organization is accomplished by way of an *indemnification clause*. These types of clauses are included in the language of the rental contract to protect the facility manager/owner from risks associated with the activity. In the same manner, if the service is outsourced to an independent contractor (someone outside of the organization who is paid for a particular service), this generally shifts liability away from the corporation and onto the independent contractor. Properly written contracts can shift liability to the events, and properly written waivers can be helpful in attempting to shift liability away from the facility to the participants.

Premise-related Issues

As mentioned previously, if the cause of negligence were related to a facility premise issue, the facility manager would more than likely be held liable.

Inspection of Premises

Premises liability is a major concern for sport/entertainment facility managers. A variety of items influence the duty of care owed to the patrons at such facilities. The frequency of events, the demographics of the attendees, and the quality of the facility's maintenance program affect liability issues for facility managers. An additional concern for these managers is the age of the facility. As a facility ages, the treatments utilized to reduce the possibility of premises liability must also change. It comes as no surprise that the risks in venues are constantly changing and shifting due to the activities and programs scheduled at the facility. Therefore, the venue's inspection plan must also evolve and fluctuate; it should never be static.

Industry standards dictate that a facility must have a properly implemented inspection schedule, performed by trained employees and documented through the use of detailed forms. Once an inspection plan is implemented, it should be assessed annually, but potentially more often depending on the types of risks. The lack of an itemized maintenance schedule, the absence of specific inspection forms, the inability to investigate the status of a playing surface, and the failure to ascertain what specific repairs have been accomplished are all examples of the lack of an effective inspection plan. Specific details regarding required actions to undertake when maintenance issues are identified should be included within the inspection plan. Often, maintenance issues occur after-hours or when key personnel may not necessarily be in the facility. Written instructions to remedy—or at the least mitigate potential risks—should be included in the maintenance inspection plan.

Regular inspections will point out a variety of potential accidents, but in addition to formal maintenance inspections, facility personnel should always maintain their awareness when in the facility. Slip-and-fall accidents account for more than 66% of all sport facility incidents. These accidents result in more than two-thirds of all claims dollars paid in any given year. According to National Floor Safety Institute (NFSI), slip-and-fall accidents result in more than $20 billion in insurance claims each year. An average claim costs $3,900 to settle and $100,000 to litigate (Powers, 2006). Often, slip-and-fall accidents can be avoided if personnel maintain an eye for potential dangers.

Previous court decisions found that a facility manager is liable if he or she had *actual* notice or *constructive* notice of a condition unreasonably hazardous to spectators. Constructive notice occurs when a defect exists that is so inherently dangerous that facility management should have known about it. Constructive notice places a higher duty on facility managers and dictates that action is taken when the facility manager *should have been aware* of the problem. This is also termed "foreseeability." Actual notice, on the other hand, is when a defect is plainly visible or could be discovered during an inspec-

A facility manager is responsible for the upkeep of premises so that they are reasonably safe for all users. (Photo courtesy of Todd Seidler.)

tion. Actual notice dictates that a facility manager has specific information about a maintenance problem before action needs to be taken by the manager (Sharp et al., 2007).

As previously discussed, the number and type of events scheduled in the facility, the maintenance and care provided to the facility, and other extraneous items such as the weather will all impact the life span of a facility. A ballpark figure for the life expectancy of most facilities is around 30 to 40 years, depending on when a given facility was built. However, the equipment *inside* these facilities, such as chairs, risers, dasher boards, and HVAC systems, are not as impervious to daily wear and tear as the exterior of the facility. Therefore, conducting inspections of equipment, playing surfaces, and facility components becomes a huge responsibility for venue managers. These inspections not only mitigate potential risks, but regular maintenance inspections also increase the likelihood that the facility and its equipment will increase their life span.

Provision of Medical Assistance

Almost every facility will have various activities with which it is associated. In order to protect patrons from harm, and the facility from legal action, it is important to note the proper conditions under which an activity should take place. A primary responsibility of a facility manager includes providing adequate and appropriate medical attention. This includes the presence of an adequate number of trained medical personnel. At the very least every employee and volunteer should be competent in basic first aid and cardiopulmonary resuscitation (CPR). Depending on the event, distance to outside medical facilities, and other factors, highly qualified medical personnel such as certified trainers, emergency medical technicians (EMTs), and medical doctors may be needed on-site throughout the event. Many jurisdictions mandate that a certain number of highly qualified medical personnel be present at specific events.

Emergency Care

Developing a plan to handle medical emergencies may be a prime determinant in assessing liability in a negligence situation. Therefore, the facility manager must understand the duty to provide emergency care and what that potentially entails. While planning an event the questions of who, what, when, and how regarding medical care should be addressed. In addition, assessment of risk, training of personnel, regular review of the emergency plan, and consent to give emergency care should take place prior to activity participation. Finally, an understanding and rehearsal of the plan need to be implemented (see Chapter 12).

Recently, in many jurisdictions access to *automatic external defibrillators* (AEDs) has also become a requirement. There are no statistics available for the exact number of sudden cardiac arrests (SCAs) that occur each year. However, it is known SCA is the leading cause of death and disability in the United States (Lucas, Davila, Waninger, & Heller, 2005). There is a direct link between the lapse of time from the onset of the attack to the beginning of defibrillation and the likelihood that the victim will survive. Many patients will survive a sudden cardiac arrest if defibrillation is achieved in less than three minutes. In fact when an AED is employed within 3 to 5 minutes, the survival rates for SCA can be as high as 48 to 74% (American Heart Association, 2004).

Supervision

Inadequate supervision is listed as the cause of action in 80% of the negligence cases pertaining to sports events (van der Smissen, 1990). Facility supervision not only includes supervising spectators and participants at a sporting event, but also warning these individuals about the inherent risks in the facility.

Inherent Risks

All sports and physical activities have certain *inherent risks*. An inherent risk is integral to a particular sport or activity. Without the inherent risk the sport or activity would be different. For example, breaking your leg during a fall is an inherent risk of skiing. Participants assume certain inherent risks, but sport event and facility clients expect certain duties from sport managers. They expect event and facility managers to be experts and protect them, whenever possible, from certain risks associated with a particular sport event or activity. These risks may range from an errant puck leaving the rink and striking a spectator to a NASCAR stock car crashing over a barrier at a racetrack. While it may not be possible to eliminate all risks from sport and recreational activities, all sport managers must be aware of the need to identify these risks, and remove or reduce them whenever possible (see Chapter 9). As a sport manager, it is important that you are aware of participant, spectator, and sponsor expectations and are familiar with methods for removing or transferring potential liability exposures associated with sport and recreational activities from yourself and your organization (see Chapter 2).

Supervision normally falls into one of three categories:

1. General Supervision—this consists of the general overseeing of a group of individuals. The person providing the supervision usually will stand in a location that permits observation of the entire group but may actually roam among the group depending on the activity. Supervising a weight room, playground, or athletic practice are examples of general supervision.

2. Specific Supervision—this type of supervision is "constant and continuous," and is generally used with small groups or at those times when specific instruction is necessary. Specific supervision is also utilized in a high-risk activity, such as when a gymnastic routine is being taught. The person providing the supervision is normally fairly close to the individual being supervised.

3. Transitional Supervision—this occurs when the supervision transitions from general to specific and back. This will be dependent on the type of equipment being utilized, the age of the participants, and their skill level (Gaskin & Batista, 2007).

Though certainly important, the number of supervisors is not necessarily the primary factor in assessing liability for supervision; rather, the *quality of supervision* is the key. Mismatching participants and having the supervisor become an active participant would be examples of poor quality supervision. To avoid poor quality supervision, a supervisory plan outlining supervisory ratios, locations, qualifications, and functions should be developed (Gaskin & Batista, 2007).

Human Resources Law

Negligence applies not only to incidents that occur on the field or court. There are many aspects of human resources law. Negligence in the office or work setting can occur in many situations. A facility manager could be liable if an employee perceives a *hostile work environment*. A hostile work environment is present when interference with work performance occurs or an intimidating environment is created. In this scenario, five elements are necessary: (1) the employee is part of a protected class—based on sex, race, age, religion, disability, or ethnicity; (2) the harassment was unwelcome; (3) the harassment was based on a protected class; (4) the harassment affected the employment situation; (5) the employer knew, or should have known, of the harassment and failed to take corrective action (van der Smissen, 2007b). While a court will decide if a hostile work environment existed as a matter of law, it is important to understand that the perception of the plaintiff is the deciding factor, *not* the intention of the defendant(s) (van der Smissen, 2007b).

An additional example of harassment is that which occurs specifically due to gender. This is known as *sexual harassment*. Several examples of sexual harassment in sport have received extensive media attention. In January 2007 Anucha Browne Sanders, a marketing executive, filed suit against Madison Square Gardens (MSG) for sexual harassment. She alleged that the president of Basketball Operations (and head coach) Isaiah Thomas sexually harassed her and other female employees. She worked for MSG from 2000 to 2006, when she was fired for what MSG termed poor job performance. A jury awarded Browne Sanders $11.6 million, finding that Thomas and MSG had sexually harassed the plaintiff. However, the jury decided that only MSG and Chairman James Dolan should pay. Dolan owes $3 million; MSG owes $2.6 million for retaliation and $6 million for condoning a hostile work environment (espn.com, 2007).

A former University of North Carolina student-athlete won a $385,000 settlement against legendary women's soccer coach Anson Dorrance. The January 2008 settlement resolved a decade-old sexual harassment claim (Steinbach, 2008).

In February 2008 the former women's basketball coach at Fresno State University accepted a $6.6 million jury award emanating from a sexual harassment lawsuit. She had claimed she was groped by athletic department superiors and retaliated against for threatening to expose the school's unequal treatment of female athletes and coaches (Steinbach, 2008).

A former NASCAR official, Mauricia Grant, filed a $225 million lawsuit in June 2008 against NASCAR, alleging both racial and sexual discrimination. Grant claimed during 2005–2007 she endured 23 incidents of sexual harassment and 34 incidents involving racial and gender discrimination. While NASCAR maintains Grant was fired for poor job performance, the plaintiff alleges she was fired in retaliation for her harassment claims (Allen, 2008).

Finally, facilities may be held liable for negligent hiring, negligent supervision of employees, negligent referral, and negligent retention of employees. For these reasons, it is important to conduct background checks on potential, and in some cases, current employees, and if necessary, take corrective action (van der Smissen, 2007b). For a more in-depth discussion of this topic, see Chapter 7.

Summary

1. The importance of a facility manager understanding negligence cannot be overstated. In fact, more lawsuits in this field are based in negligence liability than any other category (van der Smissen, 2007a).

2. Negligence, which falls under tort law, is an "unintentional act that injures" (van der Smissen, 2007b, p. 36).

3. To determine liability, the person accused of negligence will be compared to others of similar occupational status (reasonably prudent professional—RPP) to determine prudence of action (Wong, 2002).

4. To be found negligent the plaintiff must prove "duty," "breach of duty," "proximate cause," and "damage." If any of these elements is missing then there is no negligence.

5. A general defense to liability exists when any one of the elements of negligence has not been satisfied (Cotten, 2007a). Barring that situation, a variety of other defenses exist that can help the facility manager in the event of a negligence suit.

6. One common defense for negligence is the use of waivers or releases. A waiver or release of liability is a contract. The participant agrees to relinquish the right to pursue legal action against the service provider in the event that the participant is injured as a result of provider negligence.

7. Although the enforceability of waivers may vary from state to state, there are certain minimum criteria that can be used to evaluate the enforceability of a waiver. A licensed attorney should review any waiver or release document before it is used.

8. Responsibility for facility negligence will generally rest with employees, administrative or supervisory personnel, and the corporate entity (Cotten, 2007d).

9. Responsibility for negligence may also be predicated upon whether the situation was "premise-related or activity-related" (van der Smissen, 1990). Premise-related

situations are generally those that involve facility upkeep and patrons (Sharp, 2007).

10. Developing an emergency management plan requires all levels of the organization to be aware of the plan. In addition, all personnel must be aware of their responsibilities and trained to properly execute the necessary actions when faced with specific situations.

11. Proper supervision should be emphasized, since inadequate supervision is alleged in 80% of the cases (van der Smissen, 1990).

12. Facility managers need to know what happens in an office setting just as much as what happens on the field. Developing harassment policies and effective hiring procedures will help create a respectful and efficient workplace environment and will prevent negligence lawsuits alleging harassment (van der Smissen, 2007b).

Practical Application

Evaluating a Liability Release and Express Assumption of Risk Document

Using the principles discussed in this chapter, examine the Liability Release and Express Assumption of Risk document (Figure 10.1) and answer the following questions:

1. Is the document clearly labeled as a waiver/release?

2. Is it clearly written and understandable?

3. Is the font point size large enough to be read?

4. What steps should be taken to fill it out correctly, accurately, and completely?

5. Do you think the person signing the release will understand that it is a release from liability in the event of injury?

6. Does the release involve only relinquishing the right to sue for ordinary negligence, not gross negligence or intentional torts?

7. Is there consideration or exchange of value involved in the contract?

8. Are the parties involved clearly specified? (In other words, is it clear who is relinquishing rights and whom the waiver is protecting?)

LIABILITY RELEASE AND ASSUMPTION OF RISK AGREEMENT

Please read carefully and fill in all blanks before signing.

I, _____ , hereby affirm that I am aware that skin and scuba diving have
Participant Name
inherent risks which may result in serious injury or death.

I understand that diving with compressed air involves certain inherent risks; decompression sickness, embolism or other hyperbaric injury can occur that require treatment in a recompression chamber. I further understand that the open water diving trips which are necessary for training and for certification, may be conducted at a site that is remote, either by time or distance or both, from such a recompression chamber. I still choose to proceed with such instructional dives in spite of the possible absence of a recompression chamber in proximity to the dive site.

I understand and agree that neither my instructor(s), _____ the facility through which I receive my instruction, _____ , nor International PADI, Inc., nor its affiliate and subsidiary corporations, nor any of their respective employees, officers, agents, contractors or assigns, (hereinafter referred to as "Released Parties") may be held liable or responsible in any way for any injury, death, or other damages to me, my family, estate, heirs or assigns that may occur as a result of my participation in this diving class or as a result of the negligence of any party, including the Released Parties, whether passive or active.

In consideration of being allowed to participate in this course, I hereby personally assume all risks of this course, whether foreseen or unforeseen, that may befall me while I am a participant in this course, including but not limited to the academics, confined water and/or open water activities.

I further release, exempt and hold harmless said course and Released Parties from any claim or lawsuit by me, my family, estate, heirs, or assigns, arising out of my enrollment and participation in this course including both claims arising during the course or after I receive my certification.

I also understand that skin diving and scuba diving are physically strenuous activities and that I will be exerting myself during this diving course, and that if I am injured as a result of a heart attack, panic, hyperventilation, drowning or any other cause, that I expressly assume the risk of said injuries and that I will not hold the Released Parties responsible for the same.

I further state that I am of lawful age and legally competent to sign this liability release, or that I have acquired the written consent of my parent or guardian.

I understand the terms herein are contractual and not a mere recital, and that I have signed this document of my own free act and with the knowledge that I hereby agree to waive my legal rights. I further agree if any provision of this Agreement is found to be unenforceable or invalid, that provision shall be severed from this Agreement. The remainder of this Agreement will then be construed as though the unenforceable provision had never been contained herein.

I, _____ BY THIS INSTRUMENT AGREE TO EXEMPT AND RELEASE MY
Participant Name
INSTRUCTORS, _____ , THE FACILITY THROUGH WHICH I RECEIVE

MY INSTRUCTION, _____ , AND INTERNATIONAL PADI, INC., AND ALL RELATED ENTITIES AS DEFINED ABOVE, FROM ALL LIABILITY OR RESPONSIBILITY WHATSOEVER FOR PERSONAL INJURY, PROPERTY DAMAGE OR WRONGFUL DEATH HOWEVER CAUSED, INCLUDING, BUT NOT LIMITED TO, THE NEGLIGENCE OF THE RELEASED PARTIES, WHETHER PASSIVE OR ACTIVE.

I HAVE FULLY INFORMED MYSELF OF THE CONTENTS OF THIS LIABILITY RELEASE AND ASSUMPTION OF RISK AGREEMENT BY READING IT BEFORE I SIGNED IT ON BEHALF OF MYSELF AND MY HEIRS.

_____   _____
Participant's Signature   Date (Day/Month/Year)

_____   _____
Signature of Parent or Guardian (where applicable)   Date (Day/Month/Year)

G PRODUCT NO. 10072 (Rev. 11/01) Version 2.0   © International PADI, Inc. 2002

FIGURE 10-1. Example of Liability and Express Assumption of Risk Document. © International PADI, Inc. (Reprinted with permission of International PADI, Inc.).

11

Crowd Management

Application Exercise

Connor and Allison Sanders attended a Nebraska State University (NSU) football game at Ethanol Stadium in Omaha on October 6, 2002. For approximately three years, the Sanders were season ticket-holders whose seats were located in the south end zone behind the goalpost. During the last quarter of the October 6 game, the NSU kicker attempted a field goal. The ball flew directly toward Mrs. Sanders, and when she attempted to move away from the approaching ball she was pushed from behind by several fans who were trying to catch the football. Mrs. Sanders fell down and severely injured her right shoulder.

Previously, Mr. and Mrs. Sanders and other patrons seated in the stadium's end zone section had lodged complaints with Ethanol Stadium's Guest Relations Office and security personnel about the lack of security and crowd management in their seating area during field goal and extra-point attempts. They complained the football regularly cleared the stadium net and landed in the stands, which caused fans to scramble for the ball, resulting in a danger to the welfare of other patrons seated in their section.

It was undisputed that the defendants—Nebraska State University and Event Staff Services (ESS)—were responsible for providing security services at Ethanol Stadium during home games. Mr. and Mrs. Sanders filed a complaint asserting negligence against ESS as well as Nebraska State University alleging the defendants breached a duty of care owed to Mrs. Sanders by failing to supervise security guards at Ethanol Stadium and failing to regulate crowd management in the end-zone seating area.

Summary judgment was granted by on October 11, 2005. Thereafter, the plaintiffs filed an appeal challenging the trial court's grant of summary judgment in favor of the defendants (see Chapter 10).

During the appeals process the Nebraska Supreme Court held that facility managers are responsible for risks that are common, frequent, and expected, and in no way affect the duty of sports facilities to protect patrons from foreseeably dangerous conditions not inherent in the game. Facility operators can't guarantee a spectator's safety, but the court held they are liable for spectator injuries when the manager fails to use reasonable care in the construction, maintenance, and management of the facility. Thus, it becomes clear that the main question for the court was to decide whether the injury resulted from an inherent risk to the football game.

In this case Mrs. Sanders, seated in her appropriate seat, was pushed from behind by aggressive fans, causing her to fall and sustain serious injury. The lower court concluded the risk of being trampled by a group of fans pursuing a souvenir was common to the game of football and was reasonably foreseeable based on Mrs. Sanders's experience. Although this type of unruly, improper fan conduct may have previously occurred in Mrs. Sanders's section of the stadium, the Nebraska State Supreme Court found that being trampled by fans scrambling for a ball was *not* an inherent risk for spectators at a football game. The Supreme Court held the lower court's reliance on Mrs. Sanders' prior knowledge of fans scrambling for a football and her report of this behavior was an attempt by the defense to demonstrate that these types of actions were common to a university football game. By creating the notion that "if it happened before, it must be customary," the trial court concluded that if a spectator was injured at a football game and had prior knowledge of the risk of injury, the risk was automatically an inherent part of the spectator sport and recovery was prohibited. This inappropriately forced Mrs. Sanders to ensure her own safety and protect herself from the behavior of aggressive fans despite the presence of the defendant, whose primary obligation was to provide appropriate crowd management.

In this case the risk of being trampled or shoved is not the same as a fan's risk of being struck by an errant puck at a hockey game, falling down or being bumped by other skaters at a roller skating rink, or being hit by a batted ball while watching a baseball game. These types of incidents involve risks that are inherent to the activity itself and are specific to the activity at any type of appropriate venue. They are, therefore as a matter of law, risks assumed by spectators and participants who attend the sport events. The Nebraska Supreme Court held that an assault of displaced fans is *not* a common, frequent, or expected occurrence to someone sitting watching a football game. Therefore, it cannot be said that the injuries suffered by Mrs. Sanders resulted from a risk that any spectator would be held to anticipate and against which a sport facility did not have a duty to protect. Certainly this matter would compel a different result had Mrs. Sanders been injured by the football itself rather than by other fans scrambling to grab a souvenir.

Application Questions

1. Who won this case?
2. Do you agree with the court's decision? Why or why not?
3. What could have Nebraska State University have done to prevent this case from going to court?
4. What does "summary judgment" mean?
5. Should the crowd management company (Event Staff Services) been granted summary judgment? Why or why not?

Adapted from *Telega v. Security Bureau, Inc.*, 719 A.2d 372; 1998 Pa. Super. and Hayden v Notre Dame 716 N.E.2d 603: 1999 Ind.App.

Introduction

In the past few years you may have read some of these headlines online or in your hometown newspaper: "Bombs Found in Crackdown of 'Ozzfest,'" "Two Moscow Concert Bombers Kill 14," "At Least 12 Dead in Mexico Club Stampede," "Rolling Stones' Concert Interrupted by Bomb Threat," "Olympics Security Costs at $107 Million So Far," "Judge Dismisses Bears Pat-Down Search Lawsuit." These examples demonstrate that tragedies take place throughout the world at sport and entertainment events. The summer and winter Olympics, the Fédération Internationale de Football Association's (FIFA) World Cup, the Monte Carlo Grand Prix, the Australian Open, the Ryder Cup, the Six Nations Championship Rugby match, the Super Bowl, the Stanley Cup, and the ICC World Twenty20, as well as world championships

> Crowd management is a critical factor in the safety and security of an event conducted at a sports and entertainment facility. Appropriate crowd management not only contributes to the event day experience of the ticket-holder, but it ensures that good order is maintained. September 11th has changed how crowd management is conducted at sports and entertainment facilities, but the ticket-holder may only notice the changes at the entry points into a facility, where the ticket-holder may be "patted down" and his belongings closely scrutinized. The other significant changes are refined policies, new and improved technology, and an increase in staffing and the training of the event staff.
>
> —William D. Squires
> Past-President
> Stadium Managers Association

in basketball, baseball, and softball are examples of mega-sporting events from around the world. Increased awareness of these events has not only augmented public knowledge of the various host facilities, but has also illuminated the importance of proper crowd management strategies to prevent, reduce, or mitigate potential disasters.

You may have witnessed fans rushing onto the athletic field or court at the end of an exciting home college football or basketball game. Since such incidents have become commonplace they are "foreseeable" to a reasonably prudent professional (RPP) facility manager. Injuries resulting from these *crushes* emphasize the need for proper crowd management plans in order to prevent or mitigate their occurrence. In addition to the fact that we live in a litigious society, spectator safety is one of a professional sport facility manager's responsibilities. As a result, proper crowd management training is crucial for future sport facility managers. A specific event's crowd management procedures are tailored to that event. Take, for example, the previously mentioned example of college students rushing a field or court. While we know none of you have ever done this, the important thing is to point out that no matter what strategies are employed to keep spectators off a field, injuries may occur. For example, in 2000 a number of attendees rushed onto the field after a University of Texas at El Paso (UTEP) football victory. During the ensuing celebration an attendee (Mr. Moreno) hung from the goal post, while other individuals tore it down. As a result, Mr. Moreno was injured. Moreno (plaintiff) sued UTEP as well as the University of Texas System (defendants) alleging the goal post was defective. In addition, he alleged the defendants failed to erect barriers to control the crowd (*University of Texas at El Paso v Moreno*, 2005).

In order to prevent actions that could lead to this type of litigation, universities may proactively address the issue. One university that anticipates its home crowd rushing the field after a major victory may decide to simply purchase collapsible goalposts. Instead of—or in addition to—the collapsible goalpost option, another university might implement extensive crowd management plans in an attempt to prevent fans from rushing the field. This option could include armed personnel, dogs or horses, and peer-group security positioned at the access points to the field. Other universities may take a third type of approach. For example, The Ohio State University's chief of police stated in 2002, "It's a futile attempt to keep a crowd of 20,000 students off the field. If [an on-field celebration] happens, we let them go out and celebrate" (Deckard, 2005, p. 194). Other universities experience problems with fans running onto the court after a basketball game. The Southeastern Conference (SEC) experienced a number of such instances with fans charging onto the court after big victories. In response, in 2004 the SEC implemented a policy for football and men's and women's basketball games that if fans swarm onto the court after a game the home university is fined $5,000 for a first offense, $25,000 for a second, and $50,000 for a third (Associated Press, 2005).

What Is Crowd Management?

Simply put, crowd management is an organizational strategy designed to assist facility or event administrators in providing a safe and enjoyable environment for their guests by implementing the facility or event's policies and procedures. A crowd manager's duties include managing the movement and activities of crowds/guests, assisting in emergencies, and assisting guests with specific concerns related to their enjoyment and/or involvement with the event by communicating with guests in a polite and professional manner. A facility manager must recognize the importance of developing and implementing an effective crowd management plan in order to protect the event's image and reputation. Such a plan, however, will assist facility management only in *supervising* or *managing* a crowd, not *controlling* it. Trying to control a crowd is a difficult and potentially dangerous endeavor, whereas supervising or managing a crowd is not only often achievable, but also safer.

Having attended athletic or entertainment events, most of you can guess that a number of items influence the actions/movement of a crowd: venue-seating arrangement, facility size, crowd size, time of day, climate variables (heat, humidity, etc), fan-intoxication levels, patrons' ages and gender, and the specific athletic or entertainment event all have an effect on a crowd's actions and movement. For example, a seating configuration known as *festival seating* actually is somewhat of a misnomer, since the area in front of the stage is devoid of seats. If you attend a festival-seating concert you are able to move up next to the barricade in front of the stage (or as close as you can get). As some of you may have experienced, this type of proximity to the stage can be very enjoyable. Unfortunately, as past incidents have shown, it can also be deadly. Due to tightly packed conditions, you can become trapped in the crowd and find it nearly impossible to move. You won't be able to move forward or backward, or extricate yourself from this "sea of humanity." Oftentimes, a dangerous phenomenon known as a *compression wave* is set in motion as the crowd begins to slowly sway back and forth. The wave is forceful enough to actually knock individuals off their feet. Asphyxia or other injuries can rapidly occur as other patrons, in order to remain upright, are forced to step on top of those unfortunates on the floor.

While, as you can see, festival seating can sometimes lead to fatalities, some concert promoters and venue managers value festival seating, since more patrons can be accommodated on the floor than in seats. It is hard to imagine, but some individuals actually place a higher priority on their financial bottom line than on the ticket-buying public's safety. Fortunately, the facility management industry is—albeit slowly—confronting this issue.

Large crowds accompany mega-events; they can also be dangerous.

Other dangerous crowd movements can also take place during a concert or athletic event. A *stampede* occurs when patrons hurriedly move *away* from something of perceived danger, such as a fight, a brandished weapon, or a fire. Conversely, a *crush* occurs when patrons move *toward* something of perceived value, such as a goalpost, popular athlete, or band member. A crush or stampede can prove equally as tragic as movements associated with festival seating. Once a crowd begins to move en masse, it may be nearly impossible to extricate oneself, and injury or death may occur.

Why Is Crowd Management Necessary?

Significant liability issues exist at every event, and the inability of facility managers to provide a safe and secure environment due to poor crowd management strategies is an invitation for disaster. Unfortunately, many facility managers do not realize that crowd management strategies should affect many facility decisions from the facility design through the completion of the event. Van der Smissen (1990) emphasized the importance of crowd management when she described it as part of the *duty of care* facility managers owe their patrons to protect them from unreasonable risk of harm from other individuals. However, even though facility management has a *duty* to provide a safe environment to spectators, this duty of care to protect does not extend to "unforeseeable" acts committed by third parties. Thus, some crowd activities do fall outside a facility manager's responsibility.

Our society's litigious nature has resulted in a variety of groups (plaintiffs) filing lawsuits against venue managers. These plaintiffs may include athletes, spectators, or independent contractors, such as game officials, concessionaires, uniformed law enforcement officials, and members of peer-group security companies. The litigation usually revolves around claims of some type of negligent behavior, including negligent hiring of security personnel, negligent design of the facility, negligent supervision, or negligent training (Ammon & Fried, 1998). For example, in 1996 while taking photos at a heavyweight boxing match at Madison Square Garden (MSG) a photographer for *Sports Illustrated* was injured during a post-match riot. He sued MSG alleging negligence in failing to provide adequate staff to prevent the riot and control the riot once it commenced (*Iacono v MSG Holdings*, 2005).

If a case goes to court, the jury will ask to see the crowd management plan. They will also ask about the appropriate special training the crowd management staff received. All documentation specific to the crowd management plan will be scrutinized. Therefore, it becomes vital that evidence of background checks, orientations, training, or any type of employee certification be documented by the individuals responsible for providing the crowd management staff.

Foreseeable Duties

The concept of *foreseeability* is also a key element in determining if a venue manager or crowd management provider was negligent (Ammon, 1993; Ammon & Fried, 1998; Sharp, 1990; van der Smissen, 1990). Foreseeability is defined as "reasonable anticipation that harm or injury is a likely result from certain acts or omissions" (Garner, 2004, p. 649). If the facility manager fails to foresee a crowd-related incident that would have been foreseen by a reasonable, prudent facility manager, such injuries resulting from the incident leave facility owners, the venue manager, and the crowd management provider vulnerable to a lawsuit. Therefore, a prudent facility manager should anticipate rather than react. A facility manager's philosophy must be proactive, or *anticipatory*, in an attempt to recognize potential crowd management problems well before they actually occur. If, under similar circumstances an injury situation has previously occurred at an event, then operating under the doctrine of foreseeability, it is likely that if no actions are taken to manage the circumstances (due care), injuries may occur again. Van der Smissen (1990) stated that "the reasonable and prudent professional must be able to foresee from the circumstances a danger to the participant, a danger which presents an 'unreasonable risk of harm' against which the participant must be protected" (p. 45).

However, the November 2004 fight, between players and fans, during an Indiana Pacer and Detroit Pistons National Basketball Association (NBA) game demonstrated foreseeability is a complex concept. The president of Staff Pro, Cory Meredith, insinuated the complexity when he stated, "Security's job has never been to watch the players. It's been to protect the players and keep the fans from getting too close; security is really just to act as a deterrent" (Gotsch, 2004, p. 3).

As mentioned in Chapter 9, Risk Management, the duty of care owed to a group of spectators depends on their *status*. Most fans and athletes are classified as *invitees*. An invitee usually provides the owner of the property with some monetary benefit (i.e., purchasing a ticket and buying food and beverages). These individuals are owed the greatest degree of care from any known defects or problems. An invitee enters onto the

Table 11-1. Specific Duties of a Crowd Manager

• Coordinate the event and facilities
• Understand and comprehend facility risk management plans
• Assess crowd for potential problems
• Manage changing crowd behavior and demeanor
• Use good guest service techniques
• Respond to guest concerns
• Implement facility/event policies and procedures
• Assess potential problem guests
• Emphasize appropriate reaction to problem guests
• Resolve credential/ticketing/seating problems
Source: Ammon, 1993.

property of another with the owner's encouragement unlike a *trespasser*, who is owed the least degree of care.

A seminal court decision that has far-reaching implications for facility managers regarding the issue of foreseeability and spectator status is *Bearman v. University of Notre Dame* (1983). In October 1979, Mr. and Mrs. Bearman were walking across a University of Notre Dame parking lot after attending a Notre Dame football game. An intoxicated spectator fell on Mrs. Bearman from behind, breaking her leg. No security or facility personnel were present at the time of the accident. The Bermans sued Notre Dame, stating Mrs. Bearman was an invitee and the university had a duty to protect her from the negligent acts of a third party. The university maintained the incident was an unforeseeable accident. The Indiana Court of Appeals, however, disagreed and stated that Notre Dame allowed alcohol to be consumed during tailgate parties in the parking lots. With the presence of alcohol, it was foreseeable that some individuals could become intoxicated and pose a general danger to others. Therefore, the court found that the university had a duty to protect its invitees from negligent third-party acts.

Development of Crowd Management

Crowd management is not a new concept. The techniques of monitoring crowd flow and fan safety while maintaining facility security have existed for thousands of years. For example, centuries ago if you attempted to "invade a Roman pitch" you might have been killed by a gladiator or fed to the lions. In subsequent years, crowd management, while not necessarily less dangerous than during Roman times, has evolved into a more humane enterprise.

Bill Graham on the West Coast and Barry Fey in the Midwest were two early rock-'n'roll band promoters and are most often credited with understanding the need for implementing appropriate crowd management tactics. Initially, in the early to late 1960s, uniformed law enforcement officers were utilized to provide crowd management for rock bands. Unfortunately, most of these police officers were trained to solve crimes, protect citizens from criminals, and ticket traffic violators. They were not trained in effective crowd management techniques. In addition, as a result of differing cultural norms, many police personnel did not relate to the bands or the bands' fans. This antipathy often became problematic, to say the least. Fey and Graham introduced the concept of using *peer-group security* personnel. Peer-group personnel (i.e., people of the same general age, physical appearance, or cultural background as concert goers) received specific training relevant to rock events and were more able to relate to the ticket-buying fans. The strategy of utilizing these part-time employees to provide basic crowd management services did not alleviate every problem, but the advent of peer-group security did introduce the concept of professional crowd managers (Ammon & Unruh, 2007).

As time progressed crowd management continued to evolve. Instead of the promoters providing peer-group security, crowd management companies came into existence. Promoters, facility managers, and event managers began to *outsource* their crowd management needs. This meant they contracted with an outside agency to provide the necessary staff. This allowed facility managers to concentrate on other priorities. Currently, 62% of the National Collegiate Athletic Association's (NCAA) largest universities outsource their game-day operation staff (Phillips, 2006). The outsourced company is responsible for the proper, training, planning, and deployment of the crowd management employees. Some events still use uniformed or off-duty law enforcement officers, but due to high salaries, improper training, and promoter concerns, using uniformed security for crowd management duties is no longer the industry standard. However, at most events uniformed security is still used to provide security services and to arrest intoxicated or unruly individuals. In addition, because of heightened concerns since September 11, 2001, the pendulum has swung back to facilities employing more armed law enforcement officers.

In 1967, Contemporary Services Corporation (CSC) became the pioneer in peer-group security. Since its inception, CSC has expanded to 36 branch offices and 175 cities and has provided service to various political, sport, and entertainment venues and events, including the 2004 Summer Olympics and Paralympics in Athens, Greece. At every major sporting event a familiar yellow shirt or jacket emblazoned with "Event Staff" helps spectators know that some measure of security is being provided. Landmark Event Staffing Services

> Crowd management has constantly evolved over the last 40 years with the introduction of peer-group security to address the needs of the ever-changing entertainment world. A huge emphasis was placed on hospitality and guest relations and attention to the different responsibilities relative to the diversity of entertainment and its requirements. Since 9/11, the concentration has been on additional instruction relative to terrorist threats. During this period the new architecture, with multiple levels, suites, added size and functions, the facilities have become labor intensive. These factors have created a greater demand for continuing education and training; however, the end result is a more mature and professional crowd management industry.
> —Damon Zumwalt
> President/CEO
> Contemporary Services Corporation

CSC staff conduct a search at the Super Bowl.

is one of the newer crowd management companies whose management brings over 50 years of experience to the industry. Located in six states across the U.S., Landmark employees are trained in the latest techniques pertaining to crowd and risk management as well as guest services. The reputation of Landmark has already made its mark by securing clients in the entertainment industry, intercollegiate football and basketball venues, NFL stadiums, and MLB baseball parks across the country. Another company that provides security, primarily on the West Coast, is StaffPro. It services over 3,000 concerts, sporting events, conventions, and special events every year (Contemporary Services, n.d.; Landmark, n.d.; Staff Pro, n.d.).

Global Crowd Management Concerns

Sport and entertainment has become a global enterprise. Unfortunately, so have the associated problems. As a result, crowd management plans need to be in place at various events around the world. The information discussed in this chapter is similar to course material from other classes in many ways. However, unlike most other course information, failure to implement crowd management techniques discussed in this chapter can lead to disaster and tragedy. It would be safe to assume sport event tragedies have occurred as long as there have been sport events. One of the first documented sport event disasters took place on April 5, 1902, in Glasgow, Scotland at Ibrox Park. During a soccer match between England and Scotland, one set of stands (seating area) collapsed, resulting in 25 deaths and 517 injuries ("Crowd Disasters," 2008).

Most sport management students recognize that football (called soccer in the United States) is the most popular sport in the world. The Fédération Internationale de Football Association (FIFA) estimates that there are 400 to 500 million soccer players worldwide. If FIFA's estimates are correct that means that more than 10% of the world's population is in one way or another involved in soccer (Peiser & Minten, 2003). There has been a corresponding level of violence at soccer matches worldwide. One tragic incident in South Africa resulted in 43 deaths and more than 100 injuries. Ten years later, in a second incident 42 people died at a game between the *same* two teams. The continent of Africa has witnessed more than its fair share of soccer disasters. During a match in the Republic of Congo, local law enforcement personnel fired tear gas into the crowd, which caused the crowd to stampede from the threatening gas, resulting in eight deaths. In addition, at a soccer stadium in Ghana, supporters of one team began to throw objects on the field with five minutes left in a soccer match. Police again fired tear gas, which sent the panicked crowd stampeding to the main stadium gates, which were locked. It was estimated that more than 70,000 spectators were crammed into a stadium designed to hold 45,000. The ensuing riot resulted in the deaths of 126 fans (Selzer, 2001).

Soccer is not the only area in sport/entertainment that has witnessed crowd disasters. During a February 2008 Indonesian rock concert, 10 teenagers were trampled to death as hundreds of music fans tried to force their way out of the facility. People inside the packed venue tried to escape the crush as hundreds of others were pushing their way inside. It was estimated that more than 1,500 individuals were inside, which was about 500 more than the building's capacity ("Crowd Disasters," 2008).

As you may have learned in an earlier class, for many years violence at British soccer matches was almost a foregone conclusion. These incidents prompted government officials to examine every possibility to curb this problem. This type of violent crowd behavior has become known as *hooliganism*. Historically *hooligans* have attended soccer games to prey on opposing fans and fight their counterparts from the opposing team. In response, British authorities have implemented a variety of techniques over the past 15 to 20 years, such as issuing fan identity cards and maintaining databases of identified hooligans. For example, during Euro 2004 British police, with the assistance of Portuguese immigration officials, identified nearly 2,700 well-known hooligans. These individuals were subjected to banning orders prohibiting them from entering Portugal during the soccer tournament (Euro, 2004).

British police often escort potential trouble-makers into the stadium.

An additional concern for European facility managers is stadium overcrowding. For many years stadium designs throughout Great Britain and Europe were significantly different from those in the United States. You may be familiar with the U.S. model in which fans purchase a ticket for an individual reserved seat, in a specific section and row. In addition, the U.S. model often has home team fans on one side of the stadium and the opposing team's fans on the opposite side of the venue. However, the European model is quite different. For many years European fans purchased a ticket for a certain area of the stadium where there were no seats but simply *terraces*. These terraces were actually rows of terraced concrete risers (think of a U.S. stadium without the seats) where the fans stood throughout the entire match. Since designated home and visitor fan sections were not always on opposite sides of the stadium, 10- to 12-foot-high fences kept fans separate from each other. These cordoned-off areas were called *pens* and in most cases facility managers did not employ appropriate crowd management techniques to control the number of individuals entering these fenced-in areas. This type of stadium design not only led to large-scale taunting between the various pens, but overcrowding provided a recipe for disaster as a result of a crowd surge.

An example of a pen at San Siro Stadium in Milan, Italy.

Europe sustained a number of crowd disasters as a result of overcrowded stadiums, but the final catalyst for change was the 1989 Hillsborough disaster, which claimed 96 lives. As a result of this tragedy, Great Britain has one of the most stringent pieces of legislation pertaining to crowd management in the world. The *Taylor Report* was a comprehensive investigation of British football that resulted in eliminating the terraces in Barclays Premier League (the top level of soccer in Great Britain) stadiums. Any stadium hosting Premier League games now must be an *all-seater*. In addition, while standing areas are still permitted in lower-division stadiums, the trend is toward the U.S. model at all levels. Another theme that emerged from the report was a connection between crowd safety and customer comfort; in other words, the report found that fans will respond to the environment in which they find themselves (Nuttall, 2001).

Terrace in a German stadium.

North American Crowd Management Problems

North America has been believed by many to be immune from event violence. Our sport facilities have not been forced to deal with the extreme bouts of violence witnessed in other parts of the world. However, we have had our share of difficulties. One of the first tragedies occurred in 1979, when 11 concertgoers were killed as a result of a crowd crush before a Who concert at Cincinnati's Riverfront Stadium. In 1991, three teenagers died at an AC/DC concert in Salt Lake City after being crushed by the crowd as a result of a compression wave. Later the same year a crowd stampede at a rap concert on the campus of New York's Harlem City College resulted in the deaths of nine attendees. Finally, pyrotechnics during a 2002 Great White concert in Rhode Island ignited flammable foam lining the walls of the venue. The consequent blaze and crowd stampede resulted in 100 deaths (Tucker, 2006).

In the United States, some of the most violent actions have involved spectators at professional games. For example, an opposing team's equipment manager was knocked unconscious after being hit in the head with an ice-ball thrown by a fan at a New York Giants game. Similarly in 2001, a Denver Broncos player was hit in the eye with a snowball (containing a battery) while walking off the field after a game. In addition, the 2001 National Football League (NFL) season witnessed two games being temporarily halted after irate fans protested referee calls by littering fields with plastic beer bottles in Cleveland and New Orleans. Crowd problems became so prevalent during Philadelphia Eagles' games that officials put a courtroom in Veterans Stadium in 1997 to immediately prosecute violators. During the summer of 2002, Major League Baseball (MLB) fans witnessed two spectators jumping onto the field at Comiskey Park to attack a Kansas City Royals coach and again in 2003 when a fan jumped on the field at Comiskey Park and assaulted the home plate umpire.

Fans who trespass on the field of play demonstrate a willful disregard for the safety of themselves, the athletes/entertainment group, and innocent parties. Politicians in numerous communities have proposed legislation designed to reduce these field/court intrusions. New York State imposes fines up to $25,000 for fans who "strike, slap, or kick participants in an athletic contest" ("Legislative Effort," 2004, p. 7). Maryland passed legislation that defines the "playing field" as any "field, court, rink, track, bench area, sideline, foul territory, bullpen, dugout, coach's box, penalty box, or other area where an athlete or athletic team or league personnel may be present and where access to the general public is generally prohibited" ("Legislative Effort," p. 7). Those who trespass during a game in Ohio face only a misdemeanor violation with a $100 fine and no jail time. New legislation will increase the fine to $1,000 and impose a mandatory 6-month jail sentence (Sherborne, 2005).

Sometimes players have gone after overzealous spectators as they did during the summer of 2001 at Wrigley Field, when a dozen Dodgers chased a fan who had pilfered a cap from one of the players. Many remember hearing about one of the more recent player-spectator incidents that took place in 2004 during an NBA basketball game between the Indiana Pacers and Detroit Pistons. After a foul was committed during the game, a Pistons fan threw a cup of beer on Ron Artest of the Pacers. Artest charged into the stands and a melee broke out between players and spectators. Nine players received suspensions of various lengths and five fans were charged. This incident motivated the NBA to increase the level of crowd management provided between players and spectators (Gotsch, 2004).

Crowd Management Operational Procedures

Facility operations are the policies and procedures utilized by facility staff to maintain the normal day-to-day functions of the facility. Due to the possibility of terrorist attacks at facilities where large numbers of spectators congregate, security-related operational costs have increased exponentially. Insurance claims from the attacks on September 11, 2001, have been estimated to be around $40 billion (Baugus, 2003). The enormity of such insurance industry losses not only limits the availability of terrorist insurance, but also ensures increased premiums for an indefinite period. Therefore, any measures that can reduce facility risks may help reduce insurance premiums. Along with insurance companies, facility mangers recognize the importance of periodically reviewing facility operations. Such evaluations involve examining a variety of policies and procedures, including the type of search policy, parking concerns, vendor credentialing, alcohol policies, team transportation, and individual event-staffing requirements. In addition to terrorist threats a variety of other vulnerabilities exist for which crowd management operational procedures must be developed. Threats to effective sport/entertainment facility operations run the gamut—from emotional and violent fans, mentally ill criminals, and disgruntled employees, to frustrated local community members who object to the traffic congestion and noise generated from sport/entertainment events (Abernethy, 2004). As a result, measures must be implemented to reduce or control as many of the aforementioned risks as possible. Some of these procedures will now be briefly discussed.

Vulnerability Self-Assessment Tool (ViSAT)

If you are interested in a career as a facility manager, one professional organization you should consider joining is the International Association of Assembly Managers (IAAM). It is a professional organization comprised of members from auditoriums, arenas, convention centers, exhibit halls, stadiums, performing arts theaters, and amphitheaters. Their mission is to "educate, advocate for, and inspire public assembly venue professionals, worldwide. IAAM is the preeminent source for all public assembly related research, information, services, and life-safety issues worldwide" (IAAM, n.d., para. 1–2).

After September 11, IAAM members were concerned with providing the best protection for their venues. As a result, IAAM developed position statements entitled "Best Practices for Safety and Security." These protocols were the basis for development of training materials and resources for IAAM members. The IAAM also contacted the Department of Homeland Security (DHS) and asked for its assistance in developing a self-assessment tool for venue managers (Durham, 2006). The partnership resulted in the development of the Vulnerability Self-Assessment Tool (ViSAT). ViSAT is an online program designed to be integrated with a facility's standard operating procedures. This tool allows venue security managers the opportunity to assess the vulnerabilities of their public assembly facilities. ViSAT is modeled after programs successfully used by the Transportation Security Administration (TSA) to identify vulnerability at airports and other transportation facilities. ViSAT has been "adapted to incorporate industry safety and security best practices for critical infrastructure to assist in establishing a security baseline for each facility" (Launch, 2005, p. 1).

Searches

Due to previously mentioned problems, and in response to the threat of terrorism, many changes have taken place in facility operations at venues across the United States. If you have attended a sporting event in the past two to three years you have undoubtedly noticed that the number of security personnel has increased, more searches are being conducted, and different search techniques are being utilized. Traditionally most facilities have performed a search for cans and bottles as patrons enter a venue. Most typically a crowd management staff member would request that all bags be opened and

visually inspected. Crowd management staff rarely touched anything. As a result of 9/11, many facilities began prohibiting patrons from bringing anything into the venue except a woman's purse or a diaper bag, as long as a baby was present.

While no terrorist incidents at sporting events have occurred in the United States, other incidents around the world have prompted an in-

Many sport venues allow for a visual search.

creased attentiveness regarding searches. In July 2003, 2 female suicide bombers killed 17 during a concert outside Moscow. They had been stopped for a search at the gates of the venue. In March 2004 the bombings of the Madrid commuter train system killed 191, and in July 2005 extremists (many of whom were British citizens) set off a series of explosions in the London public transport system that killed 52 commuters. As a result of these incidents, facilities that have never previously employed a search now are using a visual search in an attempt to prevent prohibited items from entering the facility. Searches at facilities in the United States may continue to become more intrusive, and some groups such as the American Civil Liberty Union (ACLU) will undoubtedly react. However, some venues have actually relaxed their restrictions due to the lack of any actual terrorist attack. No matter the philosophy, a visual search demonstrates the conscientiousness of facility managers and provides their guests with a feeling of security.

From a legal perspective two cases highlight the importance of pat-down searches and their impact on facility managers. In 2005, the Supreme Court of North Dakota held that a mass pat-down search of spectators at college ice hockey games was unconstitutional (*State of North Dakota v. Seglen*, 2005). The court found the existence of signs in an arena did not establish the plaintiff's consent to the search and that physical pat-down searches by campus police were more intrusive than a limited visual search. Previously various courts have ruled that a search of a person's belongings without her or his consent was viewed as illegal. Even though the facility was privately owned the officer conducting the search was found to be acting in an official capacity as a University of North Dakota police officer, so the Fourth Amendment applied.

Many of the claims of illegal searches allege a violation of privacy rights and rely on the Fourth Amendment's guarantee of freedom from unreasonable searches. In determining if a search is reasonable and therefore legal, the courts look at three factors: (1) if the conduct was considered to be state action; (2) if the conduct could be considered a search; and (3) if the search was reasonable (Miller, Stoldt, & Ayres, 2002).

The second case evolved from the NFL implementing a "limited" pat-down search policy in every NFL stadium before the 2005 season due to potential threats by terrorists. Raymond James Stadium (home of the Tampa Bay Buccaneers) halted their searches after Gordon Johnston, a season ticket-holder, sued the Tampa Bay Sports Authority (TSA), the government agency that runs Raymond James Stadium. Similar to the Seglen case, Johnston claimed that the pat-downs were a violation of his Fourth Amendment rights. Tampa is the only NFL city where the pat-downs have been successfully challenged in court, though lawsuits were also filed in Chicago, Seattle, and San Francisco (Estrella, 2005). Johnston successfully challenged the NFL policy in two state courts and one federal court. However, in June 2007 a three-judge panel of the 11th U.S. Circuit Court ruled that Johnston gave up his right to challenge the searches when he consented to them. The court concluded that Johnston, as well as other fans, knew they were going to be subject to searches before they entered the stadium. Knowing this information, in the judge's opinion, was considered voluntarily

> Crowd management in America today is a unique dichotomy of the "Disney" experience and Army boot camp. On the one hand, guests of sports and entertainment events expect to be dazzled by the food, drink, and architecture of the space beyond whatever is happening on the field or stage. On the other hand, bag searches, pat downs, and rules, regulations, and limits on everything from what to bring, how to behave, and what you can consume are commonplace. TEAM Coalition strives to help facilities, leagues, teams, and concessionaires provide an experience where responsible behavior is the standard for all guests and all employees. Irresponsible behavior is not tolerated.
>
> —Jill Pepper
> Executive Director
> TEAM Coalition

submitting to the search. The court stated, "considering Johnston's ticket was only a revocable license to attend games, there is in the court's opinion at least a question concerning whether Johnston had a constitutional right to pass voluntarily through the stadium gates without being subjected to a pat-down search, even if he had not consented

Table 11-2. Components of an Effective Search

- Outsource the search to an established crowd management company that provides qualified and knowledgeable staff.
- Locate detailed and easy-to-read signage outside every facility entrance, including any employee entrance. The signage must specifically identify what will be searched and the alternative if a patron chooses not to be searched. This information should also be on the back of each ticket.
- Depending on the event and local statutes, conduct a visual, magnetometer, or pat-down search of every individual entering the venue (including employees)
- Staff conducting the search should ask permission to search each individual (including employees).
- Ensure a same-gender search (females searching females and males searching males)
- Provide refunds to any patron choosing not to consent to the search.
- Respond to patron concerns regarding the search procedure.

Source: Ammon, Miller, & Seidler, 2008.

to one" (*Johnston v Tampa Sports Authority*, 2007). It is also important to realize that a ticket is a license that can be revoked at any time for any reason by facility management. Depending on the specifics of the revocation, a refund is sometimes provided.

Obviously these changes are making attendance at sporting events more rigid and may affect whether you want to go or not. We live in an open society that enjoys a number of freedoms; however, these benefits may impact the safety of the individuals at a facility or event. As one crowd management expert recently stated, "Freedom becomes a little more restricted if you want to ensure a safe environment" (Tierney, 2001, p. 4).

Components of a Crowd Management Plan

A crowd management plan will ensure a safe and enjoyable environment for all spectators. As stated earlier, providing a safe and secure environment free from non-inherent risks for all patrons should be the philosophy of sport event facilities, and the crowd management policy should parallel this concept. When a facility undertakes the responsibility to provide crowd management services itself it is termed *in-house*. Other facilities will *outsource*, or subcontract, the crowd management services to an independent company. As previously mentioned, two of the most recognized crowd management companies are Contemporary Services Corporation (CSC), based in Los Angeles, California, and Landmark Event Staff Services (Landmark) based in Fort Collins, Colorado.

A proper crowd management plan may be accomplished through the implementation of six fundamental concepts.

Training Qualified and Knowledgeable Staff

The first component of an effective crowd management plan is the training of qualified and knowledgeable personnel. *Searchers* who inspect all ticket-holders are the first group of crowd management staff that will be noticed as a patron approaches a sport facility. These individuals attempt to identify and turn away prohibited items. These objects traditionally have included bottles, cans, coolers, cameras, weapons, fireworks, umbrellas, and alcoholic beverages. Depending on the facility, this search may be more of a visual screen, may be an actual pat-down search, or may use a *magnetometer* (known as a

metal detector or wand). As previously mentioned, because of the number of terrorist attacks over the past several years most venue managers have become more diligent with their searches procedures. In addition, in order for the venue's spectators to be motivated to return, they need to feel safe while at the facility.

Ticket takers who collect tickets from those entering the facility provide the second wave of staff a patron will encounter. The main role of the ticket

A thorough search is paramount for a safe environment inside the sport venue.

taker is to ensure that everyone entering the event has a valid ticket for that day's event. The ticket-taking function may also be accomplished in-house or outsourced.

Ushers traditionally are the third wave of crowd management personnel a patron will notice upon entering a facility. Ushers may also be in-house or outsourced, often by the same company providing the general crowd management staff. However, they should not be utilized as crowd managers. An usher has three duties. The first is to be knowledgeable about the layout of the facility, in order to assist the guests in finding their seats. An usher's second responsibility is be familiar with the location of important facility services, such as the lost and found, first aid, restrooms, concession stands, authorized smoking areas, and exits. Finally, ushers should be trained to identify patrons who require medical assistance, potential crowd altercations, and food or beverage spills. This can be accomplished by learning the 20/20 rule: an usher's section should be scanned once every 20 seconds and they should be located so they can react and respond to any portion of their section within 20 seconds (Powers, 2007).

The previously mentioned peer-group staff provides the final wave of crowd managers and must be clearly identifiable to a patron entering the facility. These individuals are trained to handle crowd disturbances caused by unruly behavior and intoxicated or obnoxious fans. Peer-group security is always placed at important locations of access to the floor or field of the facility. They are placed there to verify individuals' credentials as they attempt to access the field or floor of the event. These individuals are also stationed at positions of importance, such as VIP rooms, dressing or locker rooms, and the press box.

Any student knows the importance of technology. Therefore it shouldn't be surprising that facility managers have begun to assist crowd managers with the implementation of new equipment. *Radio frequency identification* (RFID) is a wireless form of technology that automatically tracks any item possessing a RFID tag. Each tag has an accompanying chip that sends radio waves to a transponder. This technology may assist in reducing ticket fraud, restrict VIP access, and speed up the time a ticket-holder stands in line. Some drawbacks include the cost of the equipment and the fact that in some facilities transponders have trouble recognizing RFID signals (Boardman, 2007). In addition, a wristband with a barcode that is read by a hand-held reader could accomplish similar results at a fraction of the cost.

Implementing an Emergency or Evacuation Plan

All members of the crowd management staff, from searchers to peer group, must be thoroughly trained to ensure they possess a clear understanding of their duties and authority (including the legal ramifications of their actions). In addition, due to recent court decisions a background check of each staff member is paramount. Failure to do so may be considered negligent hiring and cause unnecessary litigation for a crowd management provider. The second component of an effective crowd management plan must address the specific procedures used to implement an emergency plan. An effective emergency plan can "ensure that minor incidents don't become major incidents and that major incidents don't become fatal" (American College of Sports Medicine

[ACSM], 1992, p. 29). To be viable, an emergency plan should have an *anticipatory* as well as a *reactionary* component. The anticipatory component should pertain to inspections, preventative maintenance, and potential crowd congestion as contained in the previously discussed SOPs (see Chapters 9 and 12). For example, a good ingress through turnstiles should net around 660 people per hour, but that is for spectators who already have tickets. If fans are purchasing a ticket as they come through the turnstiles, a facility manager would need to anticipate a much slower ingress (Nuttall, 2001).

The reactionary component of an emergency plan pertains to the procedures implemented after an emergency occurs. As discussed in Chapter 12, emergencies take many forms, such as medical problems (from minor injuries to life-threatening accidents), impending weather (lightning, tornadoes), natural disasters (earthquakes, floods), fires, bomb threats, power outages, and terrorist activities. A common priority of a crowd management plan must be an emphasis on guest safety and staff preparation to assist guests with special needs. In the past, it was assumed that all customers were mobile, that they had normal vision and hearing, and that they had no physical disabilities. In recent years, however, facility and event managers have not only acknowledged patrons' differences, but have endorsed making facilities accessible and accommodating for everyone who wishes to enjoy them. Venue managers must ensure that a emergency evacuation plan will effectively evacuate people with disabilities during an emergency situation.

Ejecting Disruptive, Unruly, or Intoxicated Patrons

The third component of an effective crowd management plan pertains to procedures involved with the necessary ejecting of fans. Examples of behaviors that could result in an ejection include disruptive or unruly behavior, intoxication, possession of forbidden items, evasion of admission fees, or entering prohibited areas of the facility (locker rooms, the field/floor, or VIP areas). However, it is important to remember that ejection duties should remain the responsibility of *trained* crowd management staff (peer-group security) and, in some jurisdictions, uniformed law enforcement. It is important to reiterate that facility ushers should *not* be used in this undertaking; their responsibilities should be to enhance communication and customer satisfaction. The individuals responsible for the actual ejection (ejectors) must understand the concepts of *reasonable person theory* and *excessive force* and how—as ejectors—they may be sued for negligence by the person being ejected, if the ejection is done incorrectly and viewed by the court as unreasonable. As most of you realize, our society has become quite litigious and the concept of "reasonable force" and proper procedures to be followed when ejecting unruly patrons have been increasingly scrutinized. In order to provide additional guidance recent legislation in Ohio included language that specifically states a facility manager can use "reasonable force to restrain and remove a trespasser from a restricted portion of the place of public amusement" (Sherborne, 2005, p. 5).

Removing disruptive or intoxicated fans will provide a safer spectator environment and help to protect a facility manager from potential litigation. Most spectators want to enjoy the event and will assist crowd management staff in dealing with disruptive or intoxicated individuals. In fact, it is not uncommon for patrons to point out to staff members other individuals who have exhibited inappropriate behavior. It has been the authors' experience that many times upon the removal of an overly disruptive individual, the spectators in the immediate vicinity will actually applaud the ejection.

Every ejection must be properly documented. This is a crucial step in the ejection process, and can assist in providing a valuable defense for the crowd management employee and venue management if subsequent litigation ensues. A digital photograph should be taken of the person being ejected as an additional step in the ejection process. This measure more accurately portrays the ejected fan's condition and further protects the employees from unnecessary harassment. With today's technology numerous facilities, such as Safeco Field and M&T Bank Stadium, also use digital video to capture the arrest or ejection process.

Establishing an Effective Communication Network

The fourth component included in effective crowd management plan is the implementation of a competent communication network. Effective communication has been found to be a critical aspect in providing spectator safety, enjoyment, and security. Establishing a centralized *command post* will provide directors from various groups, involved in an event's management, a location to discuss ongoing event concerns in an efficient and timely fashion. Generally these administrators are the main representatives from groups such as facility management, law enforcement, concessions, maintenance, medical, and crowd management. Providing access to such a location will facilitate as well as expedite communication and result in improved decision making. For example, these individuals will often utilize binoculars to identify disruptive or intoxicated individuals. In addition, many medical emergencies and areas of traffic congestion may be observed from the command post. Therefore, the site of the command post must be in a location that allows individuals the opportunity to view the overall event. Many stadiums position the command post in (or on top of) their press box or sometimes, depending on the size, the main scoreboard.

Command posts allow security and facility management representatives an opportunity to view what is happening during the event.

Multi-channel radios are an integral element of an effective communication system. Usually supervisors from various functional areas in the venue will be equipped with multi-channel radios, with each channel designated for specific groups (e.g., channel 1—facility management; channel 2—law enforcement; channel 3—medical services; channel 4—housekeeping; channel 5—crowd management; channel 6—open channel).

Unfortunately, radios have some limitations. If an event lasts many hours, a radio's battery may run down, necessitating a replacement. Therefore, battery chargers holding multiple batteries need to be on site. In addition, if batteries are improperly charged, their memory life can be reduced. Another problem relates to radio signals being muted by some facilities' construction materials. This results in dead-zones where radio communication is problematic. In addition, without the use of noise-dampening headphones, hearing a radio communication can be virtually impossible during noisy events such as concerts or athletic events with loud crowds. Finally, the training of staff using radios becomes extremely important. For example, with multiple radios being used simultaneously some individuals "step" on each other. This is when one individual is talking and another individual keys (presses) his or her microphone, causing the first individual's message to be drowned out, usually by static. This is somewhat alleviated with each group being assigned a specific channel (or frequency), though it still may occur if everyone isn't diligent in practicing proper radio etiquette.

Crowd management employees are normally the first individuals who become aware of an assortment of incidents during an event. Often employees will notify their supervisor, who in turn informs a command post member. Upon reaching a decision, the command post staff will radio the appropriate section supervisor with instructions on how to appropriately manage the problem.

Technological advances in communication devices utilized by crowd managers have taken place over the past few years. Several NFL teams use an apparatus similar to a pager. The mechanism is actually a transmitter with four buttons; (a) medical assistance, (b) ejection team, (c) maintenance; and (d) supervisor. Because of their simplicity, they don't have the drawbacks associated with radios. Similar types of pagers are being utilized in some venues as alternatives to radios.

Utilizing Appropriate Signage

The utilization of appropriate signage is the fifth component required for effective crowd management standard operating procedures (SOPs). Signage includes both *informational* and *directional signs* and provides a support network between facility patrons and crowd management staff. Spectators appreciate being treated fairly and—if previously informed—will normally follow facility directives pertaining to no-smoking sections, alcohol policies, and prohibited items.

Directional signs have a number of important uses. To begin with, as spectators approach the facility, road signs are used to indicate the correct exits from major roadways. The second layer of directional signs assists in providing parking information. Additional signs serve to indicate the correct gate or portal entrances, as well as direct ticket-buying

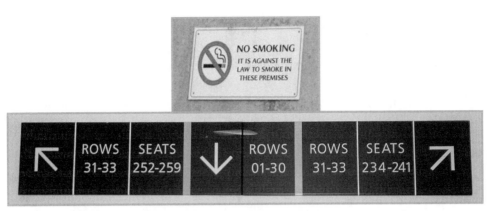

Signage should provide both directions and information.

patrons to the box office. Once inside, the venue directional signs indicate the location of concession stands, first aid rooms, telephones, restrooms, and seating sections.

The first level of informational signs identifies items that are prohibited in the facility. These signs will assist patrons in making informed decisions about what to bring into the search line and eventually the facility. Cans, bottles, backpacks, weapons, food, recording devices, and sometimes cameras are not allowed in many facilities. These items are prohibited for a variety of reasons, but traditionally because of safety or financial concerns. Spectators appreciate being treated fairly and will normally abide by facility directives if previously informed.

In response to the events on September 11, 2001, many facility managers prohibited all items from being allowed inside the venue. Since then most facilities have relaxed their policies to those in existence prior to 9/11.

Implementing and Evaluating the Plan

The sixth and final component in an effective crowd management plan is implementation and ongoing plan evaluation. Any plan is only as good as its implementation, evaluation, and reimplementation. Implementation should begin with training those involved in the event about the unique crowd management challenges before the event takes place. Each event has its own unique nuances and each of these specific activities contains potential problems. Event particulars such as VIPs attending the event, special promotions during an event (pyrotechnics are one of the latest quandaries), special half-time presentations, sideline guests, or band members coming down off stage and going into the crowd should all be discussed. Each staff member should understand how the activity might affect his or her event responsibilities. As was discussed in Chapter 2, after the event, all crowd management staff should come together for a debriefing. The director or supervisors should mention any major incidents and discuss what was done and/or what should have been done. Input from the event staff should be solicited on how to improve the plan. As stated earlier, a crowd management plan should be flexible and allow for change as needed. Without implementation and evaluation, a well-organized crowd management plan becomes ineffective.

New Developments in Crowd Management

Various criminal acts from petty pick-pocketing and ticket scalping to tragedies, such as the 1996 bombing at the Summer Olympic Games in Atlanta, have occurred at major sport events. Large-scale events are attractive targets for any terrorist or group wishing to draw attention to their cause. Potentially high risks associated with large crowds have motivated security and crowd management operations to develop more sophisticated and high-tech security systems.

Closed circuit television (CCTV) cameras with high-resolution zoom lenses have been mounted throughout most newly constructed sport facilities. These cameras feed back to a central viewing room within the stadium, where facility officials monitor parking lots, ticket gates, concourses, and seating areas for any indication of disruptive or criminal activity. Similar technology has proven successful in diminishing crowd violence at most British facilities, including Chelsea and Emirates Stadiums.

Several Super Bowls have been classified as *National Special Security Events* (NSSE). This classification has allowed the federal government to take over the control of Super Bowl security. During an NSSE, the Secret Service is put in charge and, along with the Federal Emergency Management Agency (FEMA) and the FBI, devises a comprehensive security plan. Very few sporting events have received a NSSE designation, but the existence of such a classification will allow the federal government the opportunity to implement specialized plans and utilize some of the best-trained security forces in the world.

Developments being tested at sport facilities have come from a variety of industries, including the correctional facility and defense, as well as law enforcement sectors. New technology has been developed since 9/11 that provides high-powered capabilities to facility managers for spectator protection. One of these is a type of x-ray machine (Bodysearch) that examines a person's clothing layer by layer to detect weapons. Bodysearch scans both sides of an individual in less than 30 seconds, and only dense items such as weapons or explosives appear on the image. The amount of radiation received during the scan is less than what is experienced during a long plane flight (Nuttall, 2001). These scans are also being implemented in the airline industry.

Summary

1. Mega sport events such as the Olympics, major tennis and golf tournaments, and big-time professional sport competitions occur worldwide, and each requires effective crowd management. The litigious society in which we live underscores the need of proper crowd management training for facility managers involved in event management.
2. No two events present the same exact crowd management challenges. Therefore each event needs an individualized crowd management strategy.
3. Scores of fans rushing the field or court after a big win present unique challenges to facility managers that in turn demand unique solutions.

4. Crowd management is defined as an organizational tool that assists facility or event administrators to provide a safe and enjoyable environment for their guests through the implementation of the facility/event policies and procedures.

5. The duties of a crowd manager include managing the movement and activities of crowds/guests, assisting in emergencies, and assisting guests with specific concerns related to their enjoyment and/or involvement with the event by communicating with the guests in a polite and professional manner.

6. Crowd management is necessary because of the *legal* duty a facility manager owes to the patrons paying to enter the facility.

7. Lawsuits filed against sport facilities usually revolve around claims of some type of negligent behavior, including negligent hiring of security personnel, negligent supervision, or negligent training.

8. Facility managers are responsible for using *foreseeability* when recognizing potential crowd management problems. If an injury situation occurred in the past at an event, then a facility manager must be prepared as the circumstances may occur again and *due care* needs to be implemented.

9. *Bearman v Notre Dame* is the seminal case pertaining to foreseeability and facility management.

10. Crowd management was developed by two concert promoters as an alternative to using uniformed law enforcement. They employed individuals from similar demographics as those attending the event. These employees are termed *peer-group security*.

11. *Outsourcing* is when crowd management services are provided by an outside agency that provides the necessary staff. This allows the facility manager to concentrate on other priorities.

12. Crowd disasters have occurred for more than 100 years throughout the world, with many taking place at soccer matches.

13. Crowd management strategies changed dramatically in Great Britain after the Hillsborough disaster in 1989. The *Taylor Report* implemented *all-seaters* and eliminated *terraces* and *pens* for all stadiums hosting premiership matches.

14. The United States has witnessed our own share of crowd disasters, such as the Who Concert (Ohio) in 1979, the AC/DC concert (Utah), rap concerts (NYC) in 1991, and the Great White concert (Rhode Island) in 2002.

15. Changes in operational procedures have been implemented to improve crowd management practices. One new procedure is ViSAT, which is a tool that allows venue security managers the opportunity to assess the vulnerabilities of their public assembly facilities.

16. Changes in the search policies at most sport/entertainment venues are a second new procedure. These searches are intended to identify weapons, alcohol, and other prohibited items from being brought into a venue. The searches can be done with a magnetometer, be done visually, or be done through a *pat-down*

search. Pat-down searches allegedly have violated the Fourth Amendment rights of some event goers.

17. A proper crowd management plan may be accomplished through the execution of six fundamental concepts: An effective crowd management plan must: (1) train qualified and knowledgeable staff; (2) implement an emergency or evacuation plan; (3) establish procedures regarding the ejection of disruptive, unruly, or intoxicated patrons; (4) set up an effective communication network; (5) utilize appropriate signage; and (6) implement and evaluate the plan.

Questions

1. Now that you have read both Chapter 9 and this chapter, explain how *crowd* and *risk* management differ. Which is more important?

2. Name some crowd management problems that you have observed either on television or in person. How were they dealt with?

3. Discuss the seating arrangements at any concerts that you have attended. Did any of them utilize "festival seating"? What were your concerns, if any, about the configuration?

4. Discuss several issues that a jury would examine to determine the appropriateness of a crowd management plan.

5. How does a patron's *status* determine the duties a facility manager has to that person?

6. In your opinion what is the most pressing crowd management concern worldwide? In the United States?

7. What was the outcome of the *Seglen* case? What was the outcome of the *Johnston* case? Why do you believe the courts ruled differently in each case?

8. Why do you think Johnston sued the Tampa Sports Authority? Was it really because he felt his Fourth Amendment rights were violated? Why else might he have sued?

9. List and discuss five of the responsibilities that members of the crowd management staff must be trained to undertake.

10. Describe a scenario in which a spectator would need to be ejected. Explain how the crowd management staff should proceed.

11. What are the components of a competent communication network?

12. Explain the difference, through the use of specific examples, between directional and informational signage.

13. Define the following terms:

All-seaters	Festival seating	Peer group
Pens	Duty of care	*Taylor Report*
Terraces	Crush	IAAM
Hooliganism	Stampede	Magnetometer
Invitee	Compression wave	CCTV
ViSAT	Outsourcing	Foreseeability
National Special Security Event		

12

Medical Emergency and Evacuation Plans

Application Exercise

You have been hired as the emergency services manager for an 8-day Women's Professional Tennis (WTA) tournament to be held at the recently completed 5,000-seat Bowden, Georgia Tennis Center. Your objective is to assemble an emergency management team, identify possible emergency/disaster threats, and develop an emergency management plan (EMP) in response to these identifiable threats. You are responsible for developing the basic guidelines and response protocol for all identifiable threats and coordinating responses of all identifiable disaster agencies in the area.

The development of the plan is your responsibility. Include all pertinent information required for a comprehensive emergency management plan. Information may be gleaned from a variety of sources, including your college or university department of public safety, local police or fire departments, or local, state, or federal emergency management

Every venue, large or small, must have an emergency management plan.

agencies (e.g., Department of Homeland Security [DHS] and Federal Emergency Management Agency [FEMA]). Other pertinent sources may include the Internet, this textbook, class notes, and your professors.

Definition of Emergency Management

FEMA defines emergency management as "the process of preparing for, mitigating, responding to and recovering from an emergency" (http://www.fema.gov/). Emergency management is a dynamic process. Developing an emergency management plan is the culmination of a coordinated emergency management planning process and is part of a continual emergency management planning cycle (see Figure 12-1). Training, conducting drills, testing equipment, and coordination with other agencies are all critical emergency management components. However, the steps involved in initial emergency plan development and implementation are the focus of this chapter.

Emergency Management Preplanning

Planning for sport facility/event emergencies is similar to any other type of planning. It involves setting goals and specifying a program to achieve those goals. A sport facility manager involved in emergency management planning will not, in all likelihood, be an expert in emergency management. In addition, while no emergency response or management plan will perfectly address the numerous and varied emergency situations a sport manager might face, basic planning guidelines discussed throughout this textbook provide a solid foundation. Emergency planning, by its very nature, involves planning for the worst, while hoping for the best. However, as the events of September 11, 2001, have shown, the *worst* may be a disaster for which no plan is adequate. The World Trade Center attacks reaffirmed sport facility managers' awareness of the need for comprehensive emergency management planning.

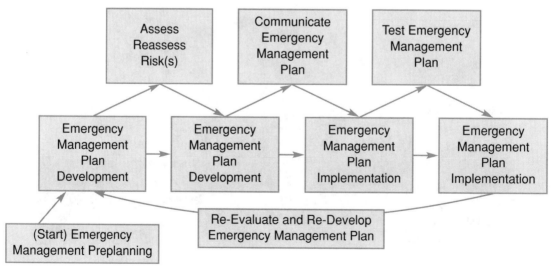

Figure 12-1. Emergency Management Planning Cycle

What can a sport facility manager charged with developing an emergency management plan hope to accomplish? While no amount of planning can completely eliminate the possibility of an emergency occurring, such planning can reduce staff uncertainty and improve a facility's "disaster personality" (Ripley, 2008) by educating employees about the existence of an emergency management plan, presenting basic emergency response principles, clearly delineating staff responsibilities, and implementing ongoing and thorough training programs in which staff members demonstrate their ability to perform assigned tasks in an emergency.

Improving Your Facility's Disaster Profile

People who have never faced an emergency often wonder, "What would I do? How would I respond?" Contemplating an emergency situation—and how you would respond—is a luxury that a person does not have when an actual emergency arises. Unfortunately, "paralysis by analysis" is not an option in an emergency. Neither is relying on luck, fate, or divine intervention. Many people believe surviving an emergency is simply a matter of luck: "I guess it just wasn't their time!" In any emergency, the only individuals who can respond to an emergency are those present. As gonzo-journalist Hunter S. Thompson opined, "Call on God, but row away from the rocks" (Ripley, 2008). However, a few basic concepts are philosophically consistent with more comprehensive emergency management plans. It is worth spending a few paragraphs detailing these guidelines.

Often, the first unsettling human response to an emergency is actually "no response at all." In emergencies people may freeze up, shut down, and become non-responsive. This is vastly different than "breathing, thinking, and then acting." Taking a moment to breathe, gain your composure, and tap into your training to implement a well-conditioned and proper response is not the same as being immobilized and falling into a non-responsive stupor. This response is the "fright" portion of the "fright or flight syndrome." While playing dead may be the appropriate response if attacked by a grizzly bear, such a response is not appropriate during a sport venue emergency, even one at the Memphis Grizzlies' FedEx Forum.

Fortunately, our primal freezing up response is not the only option. People can be trained to respond more appropriately in an emergency. The overriding principle that every sport facility manager tasked with developing and implementing an emergency management plan should remember is: people will more likely overcome their fear through proper training. More training equals less fear; less fear results in less paralysis. Drilling, including mandatory and unexpected "fire drills" (Remember those elementary school drills? They really work!), as well as realistic and well-planned emergency scenarios can dramatically improve staff and patron responses in an actual emergency. Such training provides a response template, which can be utilized in the unlikely event of an emergency.

Sport venue staff leadership is another critical component. People respond to leadership. Just as well-trained athletes can respond quickly and appropriately to loud, succinct, coaching cues, fans can overcome their fright response when well-trained staff members loudly and authoritatively direct them to evacuate the facility. Such leadership comes from knowing what to do and having the confidence to break through the fear-induced paralysis. Once well-trained, sport facility staff members can inhibit groups of fans from succumbing to their paralyzing or panicking fears, such groups most often move as a concerted whole: maintaining hierarchies and looking out for each other (Ripley, 2008).

While many people may be inclined to freeze up from fear, this does not mean they do not want to do the right thing. When you become a sport facility manager tasked with emergency management planning, an important cornerstone of your emergency management plan should be: "Trust my staff." Trust that your fellow sport-industry professionals, whom you have trained, will do their jobs and carry out your emergency response protocol. If you have done your job assessing, developing, implementing, assessing, and reevaluating your emergency management plan, it is very likely your staff will perform admirably in an emergency.

Instilling a proactive, positive attitude in your staff members is one way to improve your organization's disaster profile. Combined with a positive attitude, proper training vastly improves a sport organization's response threshold and increases fans' survivability. "Stop, Breathe, Think, and Act" is a good mantra. Controlling anxiety through controlled, rhythmic breathing not only works underwater in a scuba diving emergency, it works if you have to respond to an emergency at a tennis center in Georgia. It should also be stressed that sport venue staff members who are in better physical condition will be better able to respond in an emergency. If your staff is more physically fit, they will be better able to move. Therefore, an integral part of an emergency management plan

Emergencies can occur in a variety of sport and recreational settings.

should be encouraging staff members to lose some weight (if need be) and exercise consistently. Finally, just reading or talking about emergency management is not enough. The adage, "Perfect practice leads to perfect performance," is sage advice. "Perfect" practice is not spending time planning for any and all possible contingencies. Practice is vital, but prioritizing training is much more effective. Training should be prioritized based on the statistical likelihood of an event's occurrence, as indicated in the risk management risk-threat matrix (see Chapter 9).

With a firm grasp of these guiding principles, let's move on to a more detailed analysis of emergency management components.

Emergency Management Preplanning Components

As we have just discussed, some basic questions guide the development of numerous emergency management plan templates that have been developed for sport facilities. In developing your emergency management plan, never lose sight of the most basic questions, such as "What's being planned for?" and "What needs to be done?" Developing a viable emergency management plan is really all about answering these questions and never losing sight of the basic principles we have previously discussed. Developing an emergency management plan (EMP) is an ongoing process that must become part of the organization's risk management plan. If the EMP becomes part of a sport facility or event's organizational culture ("the way we do things around here"), the plan's successful implementation and long-term acceptance are greatly enhanced (Bolman & Deal, 2001).

Emergency Response Planning

As with most management processes, the first step in emergency response planning is asking, "What's being planned for?" An investigation of emergency response guidelines from various federal, state, and local agencies, including FEMA, the Occupational Safety and Health Administration (OSHA), state emergency management agencies, and the National Safety Council (NSC) (http://www.fema.gov/emanagers/, http://www .osha.gov/, http://www.nsc.org/) clearly demonstrates that answering this question is a critical first step. While an effective emergency response plan may not provide every possible answer to this question, not seeking such answers guarantees that no planning will take place.

An emergency can be defined by its type and scope. The various types of emergency include fire, natural disasters (tornado, hurricane), technical disasters (building or stadium collapse), and medical emergencies (slips and falls, heart attacks, or lacerations). Various types of emergencies are listed in Figure 12-2.

The scope of sport facility emergencies may vary from localized medical emergencies (e.g., a spectator suffers a heart attack, a fan is hit by a foul ball at a baseball game), to a mass casualty situation (e.g., bleacher or stadium section collapse), or an even larger catastrophic event (e.g., an earthquake during a World Series baseball game). Unless the type and scope of emergencies for which the plan is designed are clearly defined, an emergency management plan's effectiveness may be compromised because its scope is too narrow or broad, or because it does not address various types of probable emergencies.

TYPES OF EMERGENCIES			
Fire	Natural Disasters	Earthquakes	Severe Weather
Tornadoes	Thunderstorm	Winter Storms	Floods
Technical Disasters	Structural Accidents	Transportation Accident	Power Failure
Water	Other Emergencies	Bomb Threat	Explosion (might not be from a bomb)
Criminal Activity	Harassing and Disruptive Users	Medical Emergency	Security, Theft, and Vandalism
	Terrorism	Crowd Riot	

Figure 12-2. Types of Emergencies

Scope and Types of Emergencies

In focusing the scope of an emergency management plan, a *local emergency* can be defined as a type of emergency that is confined to a single setting, such as a school gym, athletic contest, or sports event. Managing a local emergency may involve activating a local emergency medical service (EMS) component, such as a 911 system, and providing basic first aid. Local emergencies most often involve relatively few people. In addition to providing first aid and activating a 911 system, managing a localized emergency requires a manager to ensure that calm is maintained among all individuals directly or indirectly involved in the situation. A local emergency may be life threatening, but it is characterized as the lowest in scope of all emergencies. However, a local emergency such as a bomb threat may potentially escalate into a major emergency.

A *major emergency* requires the involvement of several groups outside the organization or event. The scope of a major emergency is dependent on the severity of the threat to people or property. Major emergencies may involve natural or technical disasters. An example of a major emergency might be a building fire, the collapse of bleachers, or a riot during a soccer match. An organization's ability to respond to a major emergency may vary, depending on the number of people involved in the emergency, the severity of injuries, and the extent of any property damage. Providing for protection of persons and property involved in the emergency, while also minimizing additional injuries and damage through proper evacuation and security procedures, are crucial components of a major emergency management plan. If a major emergency is a possibility at an event or location, due to the number of participants or the location of an event, a manager must ensure an increased level of communication and coordination with the EMS system. This may involve various agencies and will be discussed later in this chapter. Out of necessity, a major emergency management plan will be more detailed than a local emergency plan.

A *catastrophic emergency* may involve the entire community in which an event takes place. The local EMS system may not be equipped to handle such an emergency. A catastrophic emergency may, in fact, incapacitate the local EMS authorities. Planning for a catastrophic event may not, in some cases, even be possible for an individual organization or event planning staff. Catastrophic events, by their very nature, often task federal, state, and local agencies or systems. Examples of such emergencies are tornados, earthquakes, and severe storms.

Defining and discussing emergencies often seems overwhelming, especially to a newly hired sport manager whose only previous emergency management experience may have been getting a bag of ice for a sprained ankle as a student-trainer. As you read this chapter, various questions may creep into your mind: "What if I forget to plan for a specific type of emergency? What if the plan isn't perfect? What if I only have a local plan and a catastrophic state-wide emergency occurs?" While these kinds of questions are natural, they aren't necessarily productive. These questions are examples of the *paralysis by overanalysis* that we discussed at the beginning of this chapter. A more productive step in this questioning process is to answer the basic question, "What needs to be done?" while maintaining a delicate balance between planning for emergencies that may never happen and being adequately prepared to respond to the most likely emergencies. The Salt Lake Olympic Committee (SLOC) probably didn't have an emergency response plan for a hurricane, but—in a post-9/11 world—both the Athens and Beijing Olympic Organizing Committees spent a great deal of time, money, and manpower developing emergency management plans focused on thwarting terrorist attacks. However, even though organizing committees spent between $1.5 and $2 billion (USD) on security, they still developed emergency management plans for local and major emergency scenarios. As we have discussed previously, this risk assessment and prioritization process is a critical component of the emergency management planning cycle (see also Chapter 9).

Building fires (major) and tornados (catastrophic) are examples of the differing scopes that emergencies may encompass. (BigStock Photo)

Emergency planning for the 2008 Beijing Olympics involved billions of dollars.

Steps in the Emergency Preplanning Process

No plan can be *everything*. As has been discussed, before emergency planning can take place, an organization must answer two basic questions, "What scope and types of emergencies are most likely to occur? How can we most effectively plan for these emergencies?" After these questions have been at least partially addressed, the next step is answering the question, "How can we get the plan developed and implemented?" Dealing with this question involves a step-by-step process that includes building a preparedness culture, forming an emergency planning team (EPT), developing an emergency management plan (EMP), implementing the emergency management plan, and then continually going through the emergency management plan cycle.

Building a Preparedness Culture

Instead of beginning with a predetermined group of people focusing on a specific plan for a specific emergency, a sport organization, like any organization, must involve everyone within the organization in developing a preparedness culture. While all sport organization staff members don't need to be intimately involved in all phases of the ongoing emergency management planning cycle, everyone must be a member of the organization's preparedness culture. Simply stated, planning for emergencies must not be seen as a negative, but must be looked upon as a proactive process that permeates everything the organization does. Thanks to its preparedness culture, in the frightening aftermath of the World Trade Center attacks, only 13 Morgan Stanley employees (including Rick Rescorla, head of security, and 4 of his security officers) were still inside the towers when they collapsed. The other 2,687 employees were all safely evacuated (Ripley, 2008).

Planning for emergencies must become a part of the organization's mission and organizational culture. Adoption of a formal, written mission statement can help foster this feeling within an organization. However, preparedness must be seen by a sports organization, whether it is planning a local amateur 3-on-3 basketball tournament or hosting a national championship event, as a moral obligation. Everyone in the organization must be committed to protecting staff, participants, clients, and community members through medical emergency and evacuation planning and training. As was discussed in Chapter 2, a sport facility/event manager must take into consideration the needs of the participants, spectators, and sponsors of an event. In the same way, emergency planning must address the safety of everyone attending or participating in an event.

Not only does such planning more likely ensure compliance with legal requirements, but when important stakeholders, sponsors, media, and the general public are aware of an emergency management plan's existence, a sport organization's image and credibility are enhanced. Participants, spectators, and sponsors have a reasonable expectation that an event management team will have a comprehensive emergency management plan in place. They expect an event's organizers to be prepared. The legal principle related to "standard of care" or reasonable prudence (see Chapter 10) also applies to emergency management planning. Your professional level of preparedness will be compared to the standards set by sport-facility/event managers at comparable events. If your facility's preparedness is lacking, you may be judged negligent. In short, developing and implementing an emergency management plan has both marketing and risk management benefits. It is also, clearly, the right thing to do.

Forming an Emergency Planning Team

If your sport organization is committed to truly fostering a preparedness culture, creating an *emergency planning team* (EPT) will be a logical step. However, having an effective EPT does not occur by luck, fate, or divine intervention. There must be a leader committed to developing, implementing, and continually reevaluating and updating the plan. While there must be one overall EPT leader, the team's overall size and composition will be based upon the organization's needs and based upon budgetary considerations. Team members' level of commitment and focused activity is more important than the actual number of team members. However, while there will always be "a few good people" who perform the bulk of the work, input must be obtained from all organizational levels. According to FEMA, other emergency management agencies, and emergency planning consultants, a team approach to emergency planning has numerous advantages. Such identified advantages are outgrowths of basic management and leadership principles (Chelladurai, 2001).

As with any management initiative, if organization members have a sense of ownership because they feel their views are valued, considered, and incorporated when appropriate, then the EMP is more likely to be utilized in an emergency. Most staff members already feel emergency response is part of their job (Ripley, 2008). They tend to feel responsible for the safety and well-being of their co-workers and customers. Building upon this sense of responsibility, it is vital that all employees are properly trained, so they take on leadership roles during emergencies. As has been noted during many emergencies, crowds often wait to be led (Ripley, 2008). Ensuring such training occurs is the EPT's "real" job. Instead of thinking emergency response is someone else's job, all organization members must know and perform their specific jobs.

Utilizing a team approach, more knowledge and expertise can be brought to bear during the planning effort. One person or group doesn't have all the answers. Insights, information, and creative solutions to challenges may come from varied resources. In addition to fostering a more cohesive preparedness culture within an organization, a team approach develops closer professional relationships among local, regional, state, and federal response organizations. Since the U.S. Emergency Management System (EMS) is itself a team approach that involves federal, state, and local emergency management agencies, it only makes sense that a sport organization's EMP makes use of a similar team approach.

In addition to utilizing a team approach, EPT members must understand that while conducting extensive research and making use of templates and outlines from other agencies or organizations as guides are valuable, forming an EPT and developing and implementing an EMP are not simply cookie-cutter, recipe exercises. While most sport facilities have a great deal in common, their unique characteristics cannot be forgotten.

To summarize our discussion, there are several suggestions to keep in mind. First, no matter the scope or type of emergency being planned for, involve all organizational functional levels and units. Make sure this involvement is included in every member's job description. Second, make sure the planning team has real authority within the organization. While it is important to involve members from all organizational levels and functional units, the team must ultimately have actual power and authority within the organization to move beyond just team development. Remember, the ultimate goal is to implement the emergency plan and move consistently through the emergency management cycle, not just form a team. Finally, don't reinvent the wheel. The team needs to realize it doesn't have to develop a plan totally from scratch. Involve outside agency personnel as team members or consultants. Utilize existing plans and resources. FEMA, the American Red Cross (ARC), the Occupation Safety and Health Administration (OSHA), and state and local agencies have numerous plans that the team can utilize as models. In addition, organizations such as International Association of Assembly Managers (IAAM) and journals such as *Journal of Homeland Security and Emergency Management* (http://www.bepress.com/jhsem/) are great resources. Most often, emergency management plans are not closely guarded secrets; colleagues will often share their plan if you simply ask for it.

Emergency Management Plan Development

Now that your EPT has been formed, what is the next step? Answer? Move forward. *Complete tasks.* While not an easy thing to accomplish, developing an emergency managcmcnt plan can often be straightforward and uncomplicated. In order to develop a sound EMP, the planning team must understand and believe that its formation is consistent with the overall organization's mission. The team must also have developed goals. After these two steps, the EPT needs to draft measurable, quantifiable objectives. Once it has been determined what scope and type of emergencies for which to plan, the EPT needs to be able to accurately measure if these objectives have been achieved. To do this, develop checklists of team members' duties and responsibilities, and ensure staff members are trained and can perform identified objectives. Throughout the development phase, always think in terms of what needs to be accomplished before, during, and after an emergency.

As has been stressed over and over, no single emergency plan template applies to all emergencies. However, Figure 12-3 is an example of some fundamental components that might be addressed in an outline for the evacuation of a facility.

EMERGENCY MANAGEMENT PLAN **FACILITY EVACUATION**	
List all emergency phone numbers	Specific duties
Local EMS	Specific individuals
Hospital(s)	Written procedures
Fire Department	Accounting procedures
Local and state police, sheriff	Safe area
Develop communication plan	Roll call procedures
Develop alternate methods of communication	Procedure for reporting missing persons to authorities
Develop written responsibilities and duties	Medical or Rescue Duties
	Specific duties
Develop emergency evacuation procedures	Specific individuals
	Written procedures
Who has responsibility for ordering evacuation	Ensure training
Floor plan	Ensure capabilities of individuals
Designated evacuation routes	Contact information
Who will announce evacuation routes	Designate a specific person for questions
Assembly areas—including disabled individuals	Develop appropriate signage
Assignment of critical duties prior to evacuation	Conspicuously post
	Update signage as appropriate

Figure 12-3. Example of an Emergency Management Plan (EMP) for a Facility Evacuation

Keep in mind that you must constantly *assess and reassess your organization's capabilities*. Determine your organization's internal resources in planning for designated emergencies. If the organization is not capable of dealing with a predetermined emergency, no amount of planning will eliminate that problem. If such internal resources don't exist, the organization must either acquire additional resources or develop an alternative plan that relies on external resources. This basic risk management concept is crucial. Be realistic and honest. Pretending you are prepared is not an option.

After conducting a thorough organizational capabilities analysis, you need to *identify applicable codes and regulations*. Do your research to ensure that your EMP complies with applicable federal, state, and local codes and regulations. Chapter 68 of Title 42 of the United States Code Service (USCS) specifically outlines federal response plans. In addition, Chapter 116 of Title 42 establishes state and local requirements pertaining to emergency planning, including emergency response commissions, emergency planning districts, and local emergency planning committees (United States Code Service [USCS], 2001). Since any individual emergency management plan is part of this established system of emergency preparedness, familiarity with these regulations and guidelines is a good idea.

The next step is to *write the plan*. Assign the task of writing different sections to various members of the planning team. Develop an aggressive timeline for completion. If the plan is not written, you have no plan. Recognize that there can never be a *final* draft without a *first* draft. The process of revision and final distribution must start with a first draft.

The final step in developing an emergency management plan is to *seek final approval*. In actuality any organization's EMP's likely effectiveness is severely diminished unless it has been approved and instituted by the organization and becomes part of the organization's culture. The plan must not only be the *official* plan of the organization or event, it must be "the way we do things around here." This is also called standard operating procedures (SOPs). There is no such thing as a covert emergency management plan.

Emergency Management Plan Implementation

Once an emergency management plan has been developed, it must be implemented. The implementation process involves really making the developed plan part of ongoing organizational facility and event operations. Ensuring that the answers to the following questions are "yes" will contribute to an emergency management plan's integration into a sport facility's organizational culture:

Are all organization levels and functional units aware of and familiar with all elements of the plan? The plan must be distributed to key members of the organization. In addition, the plan must be distributed to outside local agencies through which the plan is to be coordinated.

Are all personnel aware of and trained in their emergency management responsibilities? These two items are inseparable. Personnel must not only know their responsibilities, they must be properly trained and capable of carrying out their responsibilities. An ongo-

All facility personnel must be trained in their responsibilities.

ing training schedule must be developed. Critical parts of a training program must deal with the questions:

- Who will be trained?
- Who will do the training?
- What method of training will be utilized?
- Where and when will the training take place?
- How will the effectiveness of the training be evaluated?
- Have the emergency planning concepts been incorporated into all organization procedures?
- Have all opportunities for distributing the plan been effectively utilized?

Medical Emergencies

In addition to developing an EMP for major or catastrophic emergencies that may involve the evacuation of a sport facility, an emergency medical response plan (EMRP) must be developed for medical emergencies such as heart attacks or "slips and falls"—the number one facility accident category (Occupational Safety and Health Administration, 2007). Slips and falls at sport facilities often occur in conjunction with stairs, steps, or uneven surfaces. Other hazards include deposits of water, food, oil, or other debris (e.g., trash in aisles or section rows). At sport events, fans may be unaware of their surroundings or distracted by the game or event. This often contributes to the likelihood of a slip or fall.

An EMRP increases the likelihood that sport event or facility managers can rapidly and effectively respond to both life-threatening and non-life-threatening medical situations. To ensure a coordinated response, a sport facility or event should have some combination of the following emergency response components: a first aid station, a base medical station (stocked with advanced first aid supplies), roving medical personnel (e.g., emergency medical technicians [EMT] or paramedics), and access to EMS transportation (ambulances or rescue vehicles).

First Aid Station—Any first aid station should have the capability of providing an appropriate level of response. The appropriate level of medical care necessary will be

Even at the Olympics, there may be poorly designed stadium steps.

affected by many factors, including the time and/or distance to more advanced medical facilities, the standard of care normally associated with such an event, and the risks associated with the event or activity (see Chapter 9). Local EMS agencies are invaluable resources in helping sport facility managers and/or sport event organizers determine the appropriate level of first aid care.

Base Medical Station—A base medical station is the focal point that coordinates all emergency medical personnel at a larger sport facility or event. A base station allows for command and control of emergency medical personnel and procedures. A base station's location is critical to response effectiveness. In addition, if a facility or event has more than one base medical station, specific base stations should be assigned specific logistic and/or medical responsibilities. For example, one base station may be responsible for coordination of minor first aid and on-site transportation of minor slip-and-fall incidents. Another base station may be designated for special operations (e.g., heart attacks, more serious injuries) mass casualties, and roving medic coordination. Many times each base station will have its own emergency transportation vehicles, such as a John Deere M-Gator A1 or Polaris Ranger.

Roving Medical Personnel (Medics)—Roving medics provide a primary response mechanism to medical incidents until the patient can be cared for at the first aid location or base station, or transportation to another medical facility can be arranged. At many facilities or events, emergency medical technicians (EMTs) or paramedics provide backup for first responder or basic life support (BLS) medics. EMTs or paramedics act as advanced life support (ALS) personnel and are an important link in a coordinated emergency medical response team.

Emergency transportation is a critical part of any EMRP.

Emergency Transportation—Coordination of transportation of injured or ill patients to an advanced medical facility is another element of a coordinated emergency medical plan. The most desirable situation is to have an ambulance on site for immediate patient transportation. However, in the event of mass casualties, activation of the local EMS system may be necessary. If an on-site ambulance is utilized for transportation, arrangements for a backup ambulance must be in place. Availability of a dedicated vehicle-egress lane should be ensured. If ground transportation is not practical, air ambulance evacuation procedures may be necessary.

Automatic External Defibrillators

A specific medical emergency for which event and facility managers should be prepared is sudden cardiac arrest (SCA) or unexpected cardiac arrest. Sudden death from cardiac arrest occurs when the heart stops abruptly. The American Heart Association (AHA) estimates that somewhere between 250,000 and 350,000 people die each year of coronary heart disease without being hospitalized (American Heart Association, 2008). When a person experiences cardiac arrest, brain death and permanent death begin to occur within four to six minutes.

Automatic external defibrillators (AEDs) are self-contained devices similar in size to a laptop computer. They are designed for use by laypersons with minimal training. Nonphysicians can learn to use an AED in about an hour. The user simply applies the two paddles to the left apex and right base of the chest. The AED reads the victim's heart rhythms and a voice tells the responder whether or not to push the defibrillator button. The AED device literally guides the user through the defibrillation process through audible and/or visual prompts without requiring any discretion or judgment by the user.

According to the American College of Emergency Physicians (2009):

- Having more people who can respond to medical emergencies and trained to use AEDs will greatly increase survival rates for people in sudden cardiac arrest.
- When a person suffers a sudden cardiac arrest, chances of survival decrease by 7 to 10% for each minute that passes without defibrillation. A victim's best chance for survival is when there is revival within four minutes.
- AEDs are most effective when standards are in place for appropriate training, equipment maintenance, and ongoing monitoring of the quality of care (paras. 1–4).

The American Heart Association notes that at least 20,000 lives could be saved annually by prompt use of AEDs (American Heart Association, 2008). Ultimately, with broad deployment of AEDs among trained responders, as many as 50,000 deaths due to sudden cardiac arrest could be prevented each year (American Heart Association, 2008). The American Heart Association (AHA) strongly advocates placing AEDs in targeted public areas, such as sports arenas or stadiums. In addition, when AEDs are placed in a sport facility, the AHA strongly encourages they be part of a defibrillation program, in which organizations take steps to ensure:

- That anyone who acquires (uses) an AED notify the local EMS office,

- That a licensed physician or medical authority provides medical oversight to ensure quality control, and
- That individuals responsible for using the AED are trained in cardiopulmonary resuscitation (CPR) and how to use an AED (American Heart Association, 2008).

Recent technological developments and increased affordability and availability of AEDs allow sport event and facility managers another tool for responding to participants' or spectators' sudden cardiac arrest.

Fears over potential liability in the use of AEDs should not preclude the development of appropriate protocol and training for their use. In a lawsuit involving the use of an AED, the victim (plaintiff) would have to prove that whatever the AED user (defendant) did or did not do was the proximate cause of the plaintiff's injuries (see Chapter 10).

Since a sudden cardiac arrest victim is already dead, if the defendant had not used the AED, the victim would have likely stayed dead (Hodes, 2002). Think of it this way: if a person who has suffered sudden cardiac arrest (SCA) is already *clinically dead* (i.e., is not breathing and has no heartbeat), the use of an AED cannot be seen to have made the victim "deader." In addition, the Cardiac Arrest Survival Act of 2000 provides Good Samaritan protections regarding AED usage. Recently, state legislatures have become much more involved in this issue. In general, state laws have been intended to encourage wider distribution and availability of AED devices, while not creating new regulatory restrictions. Since 1997, when Florida passed the first legislation related to AED usage, which mandated that any person using an AED must have completed a basic AED course and activate EMS services (National Conference on State Legislatures, 2009), a clear change in legislative intent has taken place. By 2001, all 50 states had enacted defibrillator laws or adopted AED regulations (National Conference of State Legislatures, 2009).

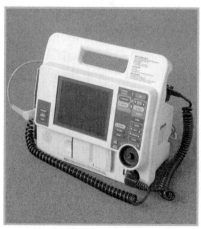

The availability and use of automatic external defibrillators (AEDs) are becoming more common at sports events and facilities. (iStock Photo)

According to the National Conference on State Legislatures (2009), since 1997 subsequent bills have adopted the philosophy that "[an] automatic external defibrillator may be used by any person for the purpose of saving the life of another person in cardiac arrest." In addition, such laws have consistently included provisions, including:

- Requiring AED devices to be maintained and tested to manufacturer's standards
- Creating a registry of the location of all such defibrillators, or notification of a local emergency medical authority
- Allowing a Good Samaritan exemption from liability for any individual who renders emergency treatment with a defibrillator
- Authorizing a state agency to establish more detailed requirements for training and registration (National Conference on State Legislatures, 2009)

As a result of these developments, AEDs are becoming commonplace at sports events and facilities. Most professional and college football, basketball, and baseball teams have AEDs on their sidelines. The use of AEDs in high school sport settings is becoming more common. Airports and other public facilities often strategically place AEDs about one minute apart (American Heart Association, 2008). Such placement has led to dramatically increased survival rates for sudden cardiac victims in such locations. The use of AEDs is a medical development that has been immediately and obviously effective (American Heart Association, 2008; Hodes, 2002). An on-site CPR-AED program should—at a minimum—include strategic placement of AEDs at sports events and facilities and the training of all sport event or facility personnel. A great source for determining whether a sport facility or event should institute an on-site CPR-AED program is the Sudden Cardiac Arrest Foundation website (http://www.sca-aware.org/sca-resources/on-site-aed-programs).

Summary

1. Emergency management may be defined as the process of preparing for, mitigating, responding to, and recovering from an emergency.
2. Training, conducting drills, testing equipment, and coordinating with other agencies are all critical emergency management components.
3. Emergencies may range from localized medical emergencies (slips and falls), to mass casualty situations (bleacher collapse), to large catastrophic events (tornado).
4. Providing for protection of persons and property involved in the emergency, while also minimizing additional injuries and damage through proper evacuation and security procedures, are crucial components of a major emergency management plan.
5. Risk assessment and prioritization are critical elements in emergency planning.
6. Planning for emergencies must be part of any sport organization's mission.
7. A team approach to emergency planning assists in developing a sense of ownership among organization members.
8. A sound EMP includes measurable performance objectives.
9. An effective EMP must be written, approved, and instituted throughout the organization.
10. Implementing an EMP involves making the plan part of ongoing organization operations.
11. Slips and falls are the number one facility accident.
12. An emergency medical response plan (EMRP) must ensure the ability of event or facility management to rapidly respond to both life-threatening and non-life-threatening medical situations.
13. Development of protocol for deployment, training, and use of automatic external defibrillators (AEDs) should be part of any event or facility EMRP.
14. Training in AED use is available from many sources, including the American Heart Association (AHA), the American Red Cross (ARC), and Divers Alert Network (DAN).

Questions

1. Identify and discuss critical emergency management elements.
2. What are some steps that you would take to reduce your staff's uncertainty about your EMP and their responsibilities in the event of various types of emergencies?
3. What is the first step in emergency response planning, and why is it so important?
4. What are some important considerations in the development of a major emergency management plan?
5. Identify and discuss the steps in the emergency planning process.
6. Why is it important to analyze your organization's capabilities when developing an emergency management plan?
7. What are the critical parts of an EMP or EMRP training program?
8. What is an AED?
9. Why should AEDs be part of an event or facility EMRP?
10. What are the American Heart Association recommendations regarding AED usage?

13

Alcohol Management

Application Exercise

On October 25, 2008, Amanda and Travis Muir attended a football game at the Edwards College stadium. They left the game shortly before it ended and began walking through the stadium parking lot toward their vehicle. As they approached their vehicle, the Muirs observed two tailgaters who appeared to be intoxicated. The men were fighting and after one of them was knocked down the other combatant walked away. As the combatant walked past the Muirs, he stumbled and fell into Amanda Muir, knocking her to the ground. Ms. Muir suffered a broken leg from the fall. There were no police or security staff in the parking lot when the incident occurred. Amanda filed an appeal stating that she was a business invitee of Edwards College; therefore, Edwards College owed her a duty to protect from injuries caused by the acts of other persons on the premises. Conversely, the college argued that absent notice or knowledge of any particular danger to a patron, the college could not be held liable for the acts of third persons. The trial court ruled in favor of Edwards College.

Generally, the operator of a place of public entertainment owes a duty to keep the premises safe for its invitees. This includes a duty to provide a safe and suitable means of ingress and egress and a duty to exercise ordinary and reasonable care to protect a patron from injury caused by third parties. However, the landowner is not the insurer of the invitee's safety. Before liability may be imposed on the landowner, the individual must have knowledge of the danger.

The appellate court ruled that a landowner does not have to guarantee a visitor's safety; therefore, the facility owner has no duty of care (see Chapter 10 for explanation) until he or she knows or has reason to know that a third person may cause a problem. The venue owner is responsible to be aware of previous incidents that endangered the safety of a visitor. Therefore there is the possibility that similar acts could occur in the future. If a landowner could reasonably anticipate careless or criminal conduct on the part of third persons, the owner may be under a duty to take precautions against it and to provide a reasonably sufficient number of staff to provide reasonable protection to individuals on the property.

Finally, the appellate court found that Edwards College was aware that alcoholic beverages were consumed on the premises before and during football games. The college was also aware that tailgate parties were held in the parking areas around the stadium. Thus, even though there was no evidence that the college had reason to know of the particular danger posed by the intoxicated tailgater who injured Ms. Muir, the college was aware that some people had become intoxicated and posed a general threat to the safety of other patrons. Therefore, the appellate court ruled that Edwards College had a duty to take reasonable precautions to protect their football fans from injury caused by the acts of third persons.

1. Do you agree with court's decision? Why or why not?
2. Should Edwards College continue to sell alcohol?
3. What can the athletic department do to ensure that similar incidents and litigation do not occur in the future?
4. How could this court decision impact other universities?

Adapted from *Bearman v. Notre Dame*, 453 N.E.2d 1196; 1983 Ind. App. LEXIS 3387.

Introduction

Many sport and entertainment venues have experienced a variety of problems due to the sale of alcoholic beverages. Many venues allow the sale of beer, while others with private restaurants and clubs usually allow liquor and wine to be purchased. In addition, most facilities allow luxury suite owners to serve liquor. Regardless of whether the venue sells alcohol or the attendees drink somewhere else (i.e., tailgate), inebriated fans may become unruly and verbally abusive to other spectators. In addition, spectators who abuse alcohol may become involved in physical confrontations or may injure themselves. These problems are not confined to the interior of a venue. Fans having too much to drink may attempt to drive home, resulting in additional injuries or fatalities. However, drinking and driving is not just a sport-related concern. The National Highway Traffic Safety Administration reported that 12,998 traffic fatalities involving alcohol occurred in 2007 (The Century Council, n.d.). While inebriated fans may become a litigious undertaking, alcohol is sold and managed effectively in many facilities around the world, and an effective alcohol policy will make the difference.

The Price of Serving Alcohol at Intercollegiate Events

Some facilities, especially those at smaller universities with low attendance figures, would find it difficult to generate a profit, if it were not for the sale of alcohol at home games. Many fans want to consume alcohol while enjoying the game or event, and alcohol sales often represent 70 to 75% of all concession revenue (Steinbach, 2004). Therefore a conundrum exists. One contingent in the sports industry believes that revenue generated from beer sales at sport and entertainment events is substantial and worth the risks, while other facilities have determined that alcohol sales are not worth the liabilities associated with this increased revenue.

These liabilities concern both the intoxicated fans and those sitting nearby. Most individuals do not want to spend large sums of money for parking, tickets, and concessions, only to be subjected to a foul-mouthed drunk sitting in the row behind them.

Many venues rely upon alcohol sales to generate a profit.

Some venues have decided these problems elicit enough of a hostile environment to eliminate the sale of alcohol. The University of Southern California began banning the sale of alcohol at their home football games in 2005. It has been estimated the ban has resulted in a $1.8 million loss in alcohol revenue per year. Some administrators believe that amount to be erroneous since the sale of food increased after the ban (Steinbach, 2006). Regardless of the exact monetary figure, the decision regarding the potential sale of alcoholic beverages typically involves a significant amount of money. The willingness of some administrators to eliminate alcohol sales demonstrates the perceived importance of reducing potential facility risks even though revenues will usually be significantly reduced.

The University of Colorado banned alcohol sales inside Folsom Field in 1996 (alcohol was still sold in private suites and club areas). For a year this change in policy resulted in the number of game-day arrests decreasing from 20 to 11 and a decline from 58 to 11 in the number of students referred to the judicial conduct office. However, by 2005 the total game-day arrests rose to 45 and the judicial office had 48 referrals. The number of stadium ejections also doubled to 248 in 2005. The change in numbers has been blamed on tailgating parties before the games. School officials tried to reduce these numbers by limiting alcohol consumption at tailgating activities before the games, but such efforts have been very difficult to enforce (Steinbach, 2006).

Alcohol Problems at Professional Sporting Events

As discussed in Chapter 9, sport and entertainment venue operators must attempt to provide a safe and secure environment for all patrons in order to reduce the possibility of injury and litigation. Undoubtedly, a potential liability exists if a facility allows the sale of alcohol; therefore, a comprehensive alcohol policy, in addition to an effective crowd management strategy, should be an integral part of any facility's risk management plan. Intoxicated patrons may not only create safety concerns for themselves; their disruptive actions may also endanger others around them. Eliminating the dangers posed to innocent spectators from intoxicated third parties must be an important component of any alcohol plan.

Over the years multiple incidents involving alcohol abuse have occurred during professional sporting events. For example, in 1979, Mike Veeck, the son of Chicago White Sox owner Bill Veeck, created a promotion called "Disco Demolition Night." Fans who brought a disco record to the game received a discounted ticket, and the records were to be blown up in between games of a double-header with the Detroit Tigers. The White Sox had hoped the promotion would result in a slight increase in the number of tickets sold, but instead tens of thousands of individuals showed up for the game. The game quickly sold out, resulting in thousands of people milling around the outside the stadium. Many spectators inside the stadium became intoxicated, and when the records were blown up these individuals stormed the field. As a result of damage to the field and the thousands of intoxicated fans on the field, the umpires forfeited the game.

In 2002, an intoxicated father and son rushed onto the field at Comiskey Park and attacked the Kansas City Royals' first base coach. In 2003 another fan who gained access to the field attacked the home plate umpire at U.S. Cellular Field. In 2005, one of the ugliest alcohol-related incidents in professional sport occurred during a Detroit Pistons versus Indiana Pacers game. Ron Artest of the Indiana Pacers had a cup of beer thrown at him by a fan. Bottled beer was not sold at the facility to avoid "harmful" projectiles from being thrown. Artest entered the stands to find the person who threw the beverage. Additional players entered the stands and a small melee ensued with punches and even a chair being thrown. As a result of the incident, the NBA reduced the amount and number of beers patrons could purchase and required teams to announce at each game what is appropriate fan behavior as well as the penalties for misbehavior.

During the past 10 to 12 years the National Football League (NFL) has not been without its share of negative publicity. Some individuals argue the NFL condones the sale of alcohol as a result of corporate sponsorships. For example, in 2005 the NFL signed a $500 million contract with Molson Coors. Many individuals believe that another reason the NFL has alcohol problems is the capacity of NFL stadiums. NFL stadiums are much larger that those of the other professional leagues; more fans equals more alcohol purchases and the possibility of more problems. Perhaps even more daunting, the focus of tailgating has evolved to where alcohol has become an essential component of the fan experience. As a result of a variety of alcohol-related incidents, an NFL directive prohibits alcohol sales after the end of the third quarter for day games and after halftime for night games. However, this directive does not impact those spectators sitting in premium seats (Steinbach, 2004).

In addition, the NFL enacted a Fan Code of Conduct in 2008. The Code requires fans to refrain from any type of behavior that negatively impacts the enjoyment of other fans. The NFL Code specifically mentions penalties for fans entering the field of play ("NFL Teams," 2008). Spectators who violate the Code face various penalties that may include ejection. However, as previously mentioned, the ingestion of alcohol outside the stadium at tailgate activities is also a major concern. Decreasing the number of intoxicated fans entering the stadiums was one of the main focal points for the Code.

The NFL has been concerned about third parties using tickets from season ticketholders and then misbehaving at the game. The NFL plans to use the Code to make season ticket owners responsible for the conduct of anyone using their tickets and occupying their seats.

Drunken fans create a multitude of problems once they enter a facility. They may become involved in verbal and/or physical disputes and in many cases they negatively impact the experience for many other spectators. Therefore, the venue operator's primary concern is preventing intoxicated spectators from entering the stadium. If the number of drunks entering the facility is minimized, then it becomes that much easier to control fans from becoming drunk after they have entered. Some venues utilize roaming pairs of crowd management staff among the spectators entering the stadium in the hopes of identifying and preventing fans under the influence from gaining access to the facility. The

Alcohol consumption creates a large amount of trash. (Photo courtesy of Brian Crow.)

Pittsburgh Steelers, along with other NFL teams, provide fans with a designated phone number, in addition to a 1-800 number, by which concerned fans can send a text message to the command post if they observe an obnoxious or intoxicated third party. An alcohol management team will be sent to assess the situation and eject the culprits if deemed necessary. Each of these initiatives demonstrates the intent of the NFL to curtail alcohol transgressions and to enforce the Code of Conduct.

Legal Issues Surrounding the Sale of Alcohol

The consumption of alcohol at athletic events is often blamed for injuries that result in litigation. Some facility managers lack the ability to foresee these potential dangers. "Foreseeability" is a key term in most court decisions involving alcohol-related incidents. Administrators and managers are expected to take reasonable care to avoid acts they can reasonably foresee causing injuries. If an injurious situation has occurred in the past, then foreseeability dictates the circumstances may occur again. Documenting incidents and reviewing records to determine the problems that occur more often than by random chance is a means of measuring foreseeability. Preventive measures that guarantee these incidents do not reoccur must then be undertaken.

Likewise, the failure to monitor alcohol can generate significant liability. The primary legal theory includes dram shop laws or social host liquor liability laws. Under dram shop laws a *commercial establishment* (restaurant, bar, stadium concessionaire, etc.) can be held liable if an employee sells alcohol to a visibly intoxicated person who later is involved in an accident. The business is responsible to train employees to recognize if someone is already intoxicated; if so, they have an obligation to prevent the person from buying additional alcohol at that venue/establishment.

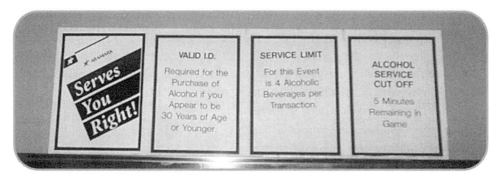

Placing restrictions on alcohol sales will limit concessionaire liability.

An example of dram shop statutes can be seen in *Chalaco v. Munoz* (2002). After two males were drinking at several bars, they were involved in an accident with a truck parked along the side of the road. The plaintiff passenger, who sustained serious injuries, successfully sued the defendant driver and one of the taverns for $1.1 million. The plaintiff stated that the two men were served alcohol even though they were visibly intoxicated and thus did not have the capacity to realize the risks of driving or riding in an automobile ("Jury Awards," 2002)

In contrast, social host liquor liability laws apply to *individuals* who provide alcohol to visibly intoxicated guests. Hosts can be liable for failing to prevent persons from drinking more when they are visibly intoxicated or allowing intoxicated individuals to drive. Liability is predicated on the fact that the host should have known or that it was foreseeable that someone who was drinking could cause injury to others. Under both laws, the proprietor or host will not only be liable for serving alcohol to an intoxicated person, but also for selling/furnishing alcohol to a minor.

Alcohol Training Programs

Training individuals who serve alcohol and/or handle intoxicated patrons is an extremely important facet of a successful alcohol strategy as well as a crowd management plan. Two programs have received national recognition for their effective impact on alcohol-related situations. Training for Intervention ProcedureS (TIPS), and Techniques for Effective Alcohol Management (TEAM Coalition) provide successful training to individuals regarding effective alcohol management. These programs train a variety of individuals who serve alcohol. Several concessionaires and the National Highway Traffic Safety Administration are heavily involved in receiving instruction from TEAM trainers. Most important, TEAM is supported by various professional sport franchises, including many from Major League Soccer (MLS), the National Hockey League (NHL), the National Basketball League (NBA), the National Football League (NFL), and Major League Baseball (MLB). Alcohol training programs educate servers of alcohol regarding how to recognize the effects of intoxication. This will help in reducing the number of drunk drivers. In addition, these programs train individuals to recognize underage consumers, which may help to reduce the problem, which has reached epic proportions.

VERNI v. HARRY M. STEVENS (2006)

The *Verni v. Harry M. Stevens* (2006) case is an excellent example of the liability issues that can be associated with selling alcohol at a sporting event. In 1999 Daniel Lanzaro (the defendant) attended a New York Giants home football game. During the game he consumed around 14 beers and at one point gave a tip to a beer vendor to allow him to circumvent the stadium's 2-beer limit rule. Around the same time as the game concluded the Verni family members (the plaintiffs) were driving home from a pumpkin-picking excursion. Sometime after leaving the stadium Lanzaro crashed head on into the plaintiff's car. Mrs. Verni was seriously injured and two-year old Antonia was paralyzed from the neck down. Antonia is unable to move her arms or legs or breathe on her own and needs around-the-clock care. Antonia will be on a ventilator the rest of her life.

The Vernis filed a lawsuit in October 2003 against Lanzaro, the NFL, the New York Giants, the New Jersey Sport and Exposition Authority (stadium managers), and Aramark (concessionaire). The Vernis' lawsuit stated that Aramark's vendors sold beer to Lanzaro even though he was visibly intoxicated. Following the accident, Lanzaro's blood alcohol level measured 0.266, more than twice the legal limit of .10. On January 18, 2005, Lanzaro and Aramark were equally assessed $60 million in compensatory damages ($30 million each). Lanzaro settled for his insurance limits of $100,000, pled guilty, and was sentenced to 5 years in prison. Aramark remained liable for $30 million. The next day (January 19) the jury ruled Aramark was liable for an additional $75 million in punitive damages ($105 million total).

Although the case was in some ways a simple dram shop case, the fact that it was a stadium vendor who employed hundreds of employees, who sold thousands of beers, rather than a small restaurant or bar, made it more difficult assign guilt. The defense argued that Aramark did nothing wrong. The defense witnesses said that the company had a two-beer limit and trained its employees to spot problems and to refuse to serve those who were intoxicated. However, internal Aramark documents and witnesses demonstrated that more than half the employees on duty that night never had the prescribed alcohol training.

Aramark also claimed that since Lanzaro was a heavy drinker, their employees could not recognize he was intoxicated. The plaintiffs called a toxicologist to testify that, with a blood alcohol level that was twice the legal limit at the time of the accident, there was little doubt Lanzaro would have showed signs of intoxication when he bought the beers at halftime. Lanzaro testified that he was slurring his speech by halftime. In addition, Lanzaro's own brother and sister-in-law testified that they noticed he was showing signs of being intoxicated at halftime.

In August 2006 the New Jersey Appellate Court overturned the trial court decision and ordered a new trial. In October 2007 a New Jersey Superior Court judge approved a settlement between the two parties. Public documents revealed that Aramark paid $23.5 million to Antonia and $1.5 million to her mother in the settlement (Hackney, 2008). The Vernis had already reached a settlement of more than $700,000 with the NFL, the New Jersey Sports Authority, the New York Giants, and NFL Commissioner Paul Tagliabue (*Verni v Harry M Stevens*, 2006).

The Verni case is not an isolated incident. A 2002 case involved an intoxicated fan who, while driving home from a Minnesota Wild hockey game, rolled his vehicle, rendering him a paraplegic. The plaintiff's blood alcohol content (BAC) was measured between .27 and .37. Minnesota law prohibits a person from recovering medical costs for their own DUI. However, the plaintiff's wife attempted to recover household costs due to her husband's disability by using a Minnesota law that prohibits the sale of alcohol to someone who is obviously intoxicated (Steinbach, 2004).

BEARMAN v. UNIVERSITY OF NOTRE DAME (1983)

The *Bearman* case described in Chapter 10 (and used as the example for this chapter's "Application Exercise") was the seminal case pertaining to foreseeability and its relation to alcohol policies. The Indiana State Supreme Court determined that Notre Dame had a "duty" to its paid fans. In addition, the facts of the case demonstrated that the university was aware of the tailgating activities taking place on university property. During ensuing litigation the facts of the Bearman case demonstrated that intoxicated individuals might pose a general danger to university patrons. Previous court decisions have determined that a "duty of care" is considered the responsibility of an individual or group to conform to the standards that have been established as the minimum allowable conduct for a profession. Thus, "foreseeability" dictated that Notre Dame had a "duty" to protect its fans from the potentially dangerous actions of intoxicated third parties.

Components for an Effective Alcohol Plan

The first decision a facility manager needs to make is whether alcohol should be served at the venue. While some venues do not actually serve alcohol inside the facility, they do allow tailgating to occur in their parking lots. In addition, there are numerous commercial products sold, such as the "beer belly" that spectators will hide under their garments to smuggle alcohol into the facility. Some of these containers are actually designed to look like binoculars and cell phones.

Regardless of whether alcohol is served, a comprehensive alcohol management plan needs to be developed. An effective alcohol management plan will become a component of the facility's larger risk management plan. Similar to the other components of a successful risk management plan, a commitment from the venue's upper management will provide the financial and operational assets necessary for the facility manager to implement an effective plan. In addition, such a commitment emphasizes the alcohol policy's value.

While alcohol strategies must treat spectators humanely, the plan exists to ensure a safe environment. The following elements are effective when executing an alcohol management plan.

1. Facility management must require alcohol management training such as TIPS or TEAM to those employees involved in alcohol sales. This training will help to limit the number of intoxicated fans while providing minimal protection to the facility from litigation. Non-serving employees should also undergo training in this area, as they may be able to spot an intoxicated person.
2. Every individual attempting to purchase alcohol should have his or her identification checked. If the patron meets the 21-year age restriction, a plastic wristband is then placed around her or his wrist. It is extremely difficult to remove the wristband without breaking it. The wristband will eliminate having to recheck the person's ID before future purchases.
3. The number of beers sold per transaction should be restricted. In addition, facilities should determine a proper container size for alcohol sales. Industry

Alcohol Management   207

standards usually enforce a 2-beer limit per transaction, and the size of each serving is normally no larger than 12 to 14 ounces.

4. Beer sales must be eliminated at a specific point prior to the completion of the event. This provides some time for attendees to digest any consumed alcohol before they leave the facility. MLB recommends facilities stop selling alcohol at the end of the seventh inning. The NFL and NBA recommend the end of the third quarter. Finally, the NHL recommends the end of the second period. It is important to realize that a venue may utilize a different cut-off time than what is recommended.

5. Tailgating should be permitted only in parking lots under the supervision of outsourced security and/or law enforcement officials. Controlling the abuse of alcohol in the parking lots will assist in limiting the number of intoxicated spectators entering the venue.

6. The deployment of trained crowd management personnel at the facility entrances will prohibit intoxicated individuals from entering the facility. This will decrease the potential for these individuals to injure themselves or other spectators. In addition, the trained crowd management employees can prevent patrons from entering the facility with alcoholic beverages. These two procedures assist in controlling alcohol consumption, thus protecting the facility from the previously discussed dram shop liability suits.

7. The incorporation of a designated driver program will provide a service by building rapport with event patrons and increase individual awareness of the need to drink responsibly. Designated driver programs have been utilized at a variety of sport facilities since the 1990s. A designated driver signs a pledge card not to drink and oftentimes is rewarded by being provided with free soft drinks during the game.

8. An effective and stringent ejection policy needs to be implemented. An alcohol management plan is useless if transgressors are allowed to remain in the facility. These individuals pose a risk to themselves and to innocent third parties. It is wise to take a photo of the person being ejected or even videotape the ejection. This documentation may prove valuable if at a later date the ejected fan tries to sue for excessive force. One novel idea involving ejections occurred during the late 1990s. The city of Philadelphia established a courtroom in the basement of Philadelphia Veterans Stadium where a judge presided over incidents involving intoxicated fans ejected from the stadium. The courtroom was established as a result of a nationally televised football game that witnessed multiple fights and fans running onto the field.

9. Venue security must be aware that ejecting an intoxicated fan from the facility only shifts the problem to the outside of the facility. Depending on the gender of the person being ejected from the venue, sexual or physical assaults outside of the facility become a potential liability. The facility must provide an area where those under the influence have an opportunity to sober up. Another technique that some venues employ is to establish an agreement with a local taxi company

Restricting the location of alcohol consumption will limit potential problems.

to drive the ejected fan home. However, this option creates its own set of potential liabilities.

10. Non-alcohol or family sections should be made available to those patrons not wishing to drink. This option will provide a seating location for fans wanting to enjoy the event free from loud, obnoxious, intoxicated fans.

Summary

1. Some facilities would find it difficult to generate a profit if it were not for home game beer sales. Other facilities believe that the liabilities associated with alcohol sales are not worth the increased revenue.

2. Obviously, if a facility allows the sale of alcohol, a potential liability exists. Thus, it should become paramount for a facility risk management plan to include a comprehensive alcohol policy. Even if a facility does not serve alcohol, it may still need to deal with alcohol-related problems in the parking lots or from attendees attempting to bring alcohol into the facility.

3. Since "foreseeability" is a key determinant in most court decisions involving alcohol-related incidents, a facility manager's ability to foresee harmful alcohol risks is an important way to potentially reduce liability.

4. *Verni v. Harry M. Stevens* (2006) is an excellent case study of the potential liabilities for the team, facility, concessionaire, and organizing league that exist due to the sale of alcohol. The mistakes made by the concessionaire provide good examples of how an alcohol policy can be improved.

5. *Bearman v. University of Notre Dame* (1983) was the seminal case pertaining to foreseeability and its relation to alcohol policies. Due to the concept of foreseeability, Notre Dame had a "duty" to protect their fans from the potential dangerous actions of intoxicated third parties.

6. *Dram shop* laws and *social host liability* are two state statutes that make it essential for facility managers to implement alcohol management strategies in order to prevent their patrons from drinking too much.

7. Training for Intervention ProcedureS (TIPS) and Techniques for Effective Alcohol Management (TEAM) are the two main alcohol-training programs implemented in most sport facilities.

8. An effective alcohol policy should include the following elements: require alcohol management training for those employees involved in both the sale of alcohol and

those dealing with spectators as they enter the facility; check the ID of anyone purchasing alcohol; serve only two beers per transaction in cups no larger than 12 to 14 ounces; eliminate beer sales at a specific point during the event; permit tail-gating only if supervised; deploy trained crowd management personnel at the facility entrances; incorporate designated driver programs; implement an effective and stringent ejection policy; recognize that ejecting an intoxicated fan from the facility does not end the problem; and provide non-alcohol or family sections for every event.

Questions

1. Should facilities serve alcohol at athletic events? Support your argument with specific examples.
2. Foreseeability is a key determinant in cases regarding alcohol. Discuss the concept of foreseeability and explain why it is important in crowd and alcohol management.
3. What is the difference between dram shop laws and social host liability? As a student, which will impact you the most before graduation? How?
4. Using the Internet, conduct some basic research into the TIPS and TEAM alcohol training programs. What seems to be the main differences between the two?
5. Why is the *Verni v. Harry M. Stevens* case important? If you had been the concessionaire, what would you have done differently? If you had been the team or the league, what would you have done differently?

14

Food Service Management

Application Exercise

Mike Riley was an assistant athletic director at Casablanca University (CU), a medium-sized National Collegiate Athletic Association (NCAA) Division I institution located in the Pacific Northwest. CU did not have a football team, but their basketball team was very successful, resulting in sold-out games throughout the season. Riley was responsible for all athletic department facility operations, and his duties included supervising and staffing the arena's concession stands. There were four main stands and three portable carts that provided food and beverages for every event taking place at the arena. The concession stands were staffed by a variety of community members, including those from service organizations, local high school booster clubs, and church groups. The groups worked the concession stands as fundraisers. Before each season Mike conducted various preliminary planning meetings with other athletic department staff, campus police, and representatives from the various community organizations. By the beginning of the season he was confident that most of the logistics were in place and the concession operations would be successful during the next two months.

The basketball season was to begin with a two-day, four-team tournament, including two teams from the previous season's Sweet 16. The 14,000-seat CU Center sold out two months before the event. On Wednesday, two days before the opening tip-off, Mike received a disturbing phone call. The local high school band, scheduled to work the four main concession stands, had just returned from a tour of several Latin American countries. Five members of the band had exhibited flu-like symptoms upon their return. A local doctor diagnosed the problem as a contagious viral infection and quarantined the entire 36-member marching band. After several frantic calls, Mike was able to convince the local junior college's football booster club to work the four concession stands during the tournament.

On the Monday after the tournament, Mike was calculating the cost of goods sold (COGS) for the event. Mike had estimated a COGS percentage should have been around 12% for the draft beer sold during the tournament. However, he was shocked to find out that the *actual* COGS percentage was *much* higher. After checking his records, he determined the concession stands had supposedly sold 10 kegs of beer. The local distributor provided the kegs to the university for $75 each. Mike knew from experience that each keg held 16 gallons, which translated to 2,048 ounces per keg. The concession stands limited all beer sales to 16-ounce cups. The records showed the concession stands had sold a total of 1,050 cups of beer at $5 per cup, grossing $5,250.

1. How many cups should they have sold per keg?
2. How many total cups should they have sold?
3. What should their total revenue have been?
4. What was the *actual* COGS percentage for the beer sold (round to nearest %)?
5. What *should* have been the profit margin for the beer sold (round to nearest %)?

See if you can determine the correct responses. The answers, as well as how they are determined, can be found at the end of this chapter.

Introduction

Nationally, costs associated with attending a typical athletic event have gradually increased. With costs rising, more spectators desire an entertainment experience that provides *value* for their money. Therefore, in order for sport facility operators to generate revenues and realize a profit they must provide an entertaining and enjoyable experience that not only attracts fans but encourages repeat purchases. Venue *amenities* include facility offerings that entice fans to visit once and then return again Potential amenities include benefits such as proximity of parking, width of seats, size of scoreboard, number of restrooms, and politeness of staff. One of the most important of these outcomes is the food and beverages sold at the event, as in most venues food service is the second largest source of revenue after ticket sales. More than 30% of sporting fans buy food

Concession stands come in many shapes and sizes.

and beverages while attending an event (Morroll, 2005), making it a critical component of the overall customer experience. While fans have always expected their food to be hot and their beer to be cold, many are now expecting a varied menu that offers traditional ballpark fare and numerous other potential choices.

Food Service Management

Food service management can be defined as the business operation that sells and delivers food and beverages to facility guests. While more individuals are now calling the industry "food service management," terms such as "concessions" and "concession operations" are interchangeable. An efficiently managed concession operation plays a vital role in the financial success of any sport or entertainment facility. Depending on the size of the venue, game-day revenue at major college football games can amount to hundreds of thousands of dollars. Generally, concession companies keep 55 to 60% of the revenue generated from concession sales at major league venues. However, before the opening of Washington Nationals Park, Centerplate—one of the better-known concession companies—agreed to a 20-year food and merchandise contract that guaranteed the Nationals 45% of concession sales (Muret, 2009a). This contract made it extremely difficult for Centerplate to show a profit due to the close margins it had to maintain on each sale. Despite the generous split of the concession revenues, the Nationals were not satisfied and switched to Levy Restaurants as their concession provider beginning in 2009.

If a facility's concession operation is to increase its productivity and profitability, management must be concerned with more than just serving quality food at appropriate prices. Concession managers needs to possess extensive knowledge about marketing, financial management, purchasing, inventory management, legal aspects, insurance, and personnel issues.

Obviously, long lines, cold food, warm beer, or dirty conditions will cause customers to refrain from making initial or repeat purchases, but other issues such as customer service and employee appearance also impact overall sales. Therefore, a positive guest experience is of paramount importance. Concession stands should be brightly lit, conveniently located, and ergonomically designed. If possible, digital menu boards with attractive and appealing pictures of the food being served should be utilized. Signage should be clearly marked, colorful, and neon lit rather than hand painted. The organization of the stands is not only important to promote fast service, but it will help to eliminate many crowd management problems. Research studies have demonstrated that many fans become restless after waiting three to four minutes for a transaction to be completed (Morroll, 2005).

Utilizing trained staff that employs effective sales techniques will speed up the transaction process, helping to ensure satisfied customers while also increasing the facility's financial bottom line. For many years facilities resisted accepting any payment system besides cash. Credit cards and other cashless payment systems are now utilized in most facilities and generally speed up the purchasing process. In addition, research has indicated that consumers who pay with a credit card or other cashless mechanism are likely to purchase more items than if they paid with cash. Facilities are experimenting with

Table 14-1. Facts Concerning Food Service Operations

1. Beer and other alcohol sales account for the highest percentage of concession profits.	2. Most fans prefer using credit and debit cards to make their purchases. Credit card operations pay for themselves with the increased revenue that they generate.	3. Green buildings have begun to impact the food service industry. Environmentally friendly tactics such as energy-efficient appliances, recycling grease from food and cooking oil, eating utensils made from recycled materials, and filtering waste water are being utilized by most concessionaires.

Some venues, such as Cleveland's Progressive Field, provide picnic areas beyond the outfield fences.

newer methods to continue to decrease the amount of time spent in line. Despite the facilities' best efforts, customers will sometimes end up waiting in line. Most fans do not want to miss any of the game while standing in line, so television monitors should be conveniently located within eyesight of each concession line.

Concession Operations

Concession operations may be *outsourced* (contracted to an outside organization) or provided by the facility, which is known as doing it *in-house*.

Outsourcing

This option involves a facility manager negotiating with an outside organization to provide the entire food service operation for a specific number of years. These contracts are typically commission fee-based with the food service company realizing a commission of between 25 and 75%. A major reason to outsource the concessions is that the liability for the food service operations is transferred from the facility to the concessionaire. Obviously, this would help to reduce potential financial losses from litigation. However, this type of contractual relationship will usually result in a lower profit potential for the facility, and may prove disastrous if the outsourced company drives away spectators by providing poor customer service, improperly preparing food, or maintaining dirty conditions.

Since most of the popular outside vendors are national organizations, they are employed at a variety of venues. This allows the companies to purchase food, materials, and equipment in bulk and usually at lower prices. *Volume purchasing* enables the vendor to often provide quality products at reduced prices. Concession companies normally assist with the purchase of any equipment, and the management staff is usually experienced, which generates a higher profit margin. Maintenance issues, inventory, storage, and purchasing concerns become the food service management company's sole responsibility when an outsourcing agreement is signed. In addition, employing an outside concessionaire diminishes the venue's role in dealing with hiring, scheduling, worker's compensation, and equal opportunity issues.

In-house

If a facility does not outsource its concessions, then the facility manager and staff are responsible for all aspects of the operation. Higher profits are certainly a possible since revenues will not be shared, but higher financial losses may also occur if significant mistakes are made. Keeping the concessions in-house absolves the facility manager from having to formally complain about poor service from its concession partner or potentially seek termination of an agreement if dissatisfied with its service. The facility manages everything, including buying supplies, hiring, training, and scheduling. An in-house operation gives facility management control regarding the types of employees hired, the product offered, the price charged for the product, and the way the product will be marketed. Unfortunately, this option also means the facility managers are responsible for all employee and administrative problems. In addition, it is tough to get national pricing since one facility does not have volume purchasing power.

Organizing a concession stand may even include the condiments!

Facility Design and Concessions

The design of the food service operation is extremely important and, since the late 1990s, architects of many of the newer facilities have included representatives from the food industry to assist in the design. Unfortunately, despite the importance of food service and the involvement of food service staff in facility planning, inadequate square footage for the food service area is a major concern that some architects do not properly address. Additional elements to proper food service such as trash removal, recycling stations, and elevators also need to be carefully planned (Emmons, 2004).

Providing high-quality food is not the only requirement for a facility's concession operations to be successful. Concessions will not be an effective source of revenue if the stands are not conveniently located. If the facility design does not allow for sufficient purchase points, vendors or "hawkers" (concession employees who walk among the crowds selling food and beverages) should be utilized to bring the product to the fans. In most facilities there should be sufficient numbers of concession stands to serve the total number of seats, with each patron being able to reach the nearest the point of sale (concession stand) from his or her seat within 60 to 90 seconds. Ideally, there should be a ratio of one point of purchase per 175 spectators, depending on the size of the facility and the type of event (Emmons, 2004). However, some industry experts believe that the number of stands will depend on their location in the facility. For example, there should be a ratio of one stand per 200 spectators (1:200) on the upper levels; 1:175 on the lower levels, and 1:150 on the club level (Cameron, 2001).

Installing wide concourses will assist with concession stand accessibility and will help prevent congested concession lines. Line congestion can not only reduce the volume of potential customers, but it could also incite a crowd management problem. A general rule of thumb mandates one foot of concourse for every row in the stadium bowl. For example, Invesco Field at Mile High Stadium has 38 rows of seats in the stadium bowl, but the concourse is 44 feet wide, more than 8 feet wider than necessary (Cameron, 2001).

Examples of wide concourses at Invesco Field at Mile High Stadium in Denver.

Projecting Operational Costs

Projecting sales is a crucial but sometimes difficult task to undertake because the potential revenue generated from event to event is often difficult to determine. Variables such as weather, temperature, crowd size, and customer demographics will influence spectator-buying habits. The operational costs need to be recorded for any facility concession operation. The majority of the time these costs will decrease as the food service operations become more streamlined.

Cost of goods sold (COGS) is used to determine the profit a concession company receives from a product. Simply put, COGS profit equals: *the cost of the product to the concessionaire ÷ the price for which the concessionaire sold the product.* One of the problems with the costs incurred with food and beverages is the perception of the food service industry. Depending on the type, beverages are typically viewed as a profit generator, while food operations are likely to break even or generate a financial loss. However, not all beverages have the same profit margins. In most cases alcoholic drinks have one profit margin, fountain drinks a second, and bottled soft drinks and juices a third. Usually liquor has a lower COGS than does beer while wine has the highest COGS in the alcohol category. A soft drink example may help explain the concept. Let's say the wholesale expense to purchase a 20-ounce drink, including ice, cup, straw, and lid, typically is approximately 25 cents. If a concession stand sells the 20-ounce drink for $1.50, the facility nets $1.25 in profit with a 17% *pour cost* (.25/1.50). A pour cost is what the product costs the facilities for the product container and any associated labor. Beverage distributors, however, charge concession providers 50 cents per 20-ounce soft drink *bottle*. Everything else being equal, the facility captures $1.00 in gross profit while assuming a 33% (.50/1.50) pour cost. For *specialty* drinks and some juices, beverage distributors typically charge concessionaires up to $2 per bottle, which obviously negates any profit margin for the concession operator.

Food Service Management Companies

While there are literally tens of thousands of concession organizations, most are very small. In fact, the largest 50 companies arguably do 90% of the business.

Aramark

The largest sport concessionaire is based in Philadelphia, Pennsylvania. Since 1998, Aramark has been consistently ranked as one of the top three most admired companies in its industry (as evaluated by peers and industry analysts). Aramark has continued to expand its food service operations. For example, in 2000 Aramark bought Harry M. Stevens and the Ogden venue concession businesses. In 2007 the company signed a 30-year contract for Citi Field, home of the New York Mets, to provide food service and merchandise stands at the new facility. Aramark is one of the food service management companies with an international presence, as it has existing contracts ranging from Belgium to Chile and it was the concessionaire for the 2006 World Cup in Germany. Recently (2008) Aramark signed a 10-year deal with the 50,000-seat Rogers Centre in Toronto.

Centerplate

Centerplate provides catering, concessions, management, and merchandise services for a variety of North American venues. Headquartered in Spartanburg, South Carolina, it was originally known as the Automatic Canteen Company of America. By 1998 it was known as Volume Services Inc. and in 1998 it merged with Service America to form Volume Services America. The company changed its name to Centerplate in 2003. In 2009 Centerplate was taken private by Kohlberg & Company. Centerplate was the New York Yankees food service company for 43 years until the team decided to go in-house for their new stadium that opened in 2009. Two of Centerplate largest contracts are with FedEx Field and Lucas Oil Stadium.

Delaware North Sportservice

Delaware North Sportservice (Sportservice), one of the oldest and most established food service management companies, is headquartered in Buffalo, New York. It is a privately owned company that for many years focused on concession services to only North American venues. In 2002, it was awarded a 25-year contract to manage England's Wembley National Stadium. That was followed in 2005 by earning the contract for Emirates Stadium, the home of Arsenal F. C. The company also has an existing contract to provide the food services at Melbourne & Olympic Park, home to the Australian Open tennis tournament; Sportservice has certainly made a large international impact (Cameron, 2006). In addition to its international presence Sportservice also has concession contracts at a variety of sport venues, including the Great American Ballpark (Cincinnati Reds) in Major League Baseball (MLB) and the St. Pete Times Forum (Tampa Bay Lightning) in hockey.

Levy

The Levy brothers were involved in the restaurant business in Chicago when they recognized the untapped market of providing premium food services to premium seat-holders. In 1982 the brothers convinced the owners of the Chicago White Sox to grant their

Premium food services are provided at a variety of locations, including glassed-in restaurants at Progressive Field and Toronto's Rogers Centre.

restaurant, Levy Restaurants, the opportunity to serve premium food to fans sitting in the Comiskey Park skyboxes. The idea was revolutionary and unbelievably successful. The niche market identified by the Levy brothers was lucrative enough that most other concession companies now have a premium food section as part of their operations. In September 2000, Compass Group, the largest concession company in the world, acquired a 49% interest in Levy Restaurants. Five years later, Compass Group acquired the remaining 51% interest. Levy Restaurants provide services to numerous sport venues across the United States. In 2009 the company was awarded the concession contract for Washington Nationals Park. Levy Restaurants has also developed an international presence, as it signed concession contracts at Old Traford, home to Manchester United F. C., as well as the O2 Arena in London and the O2 World Arena in Berlin.

Ovations Food Services

Ovations Food Services, originally called Leisure Food Services, has provided food and beverage services to a number of minor league baseball facilities in the mid-Atlantic region. In 2000 the company was bought by Comcast Spectacor and now provides services to a number of additional sport facilities. Some of their most well-known contracts are with Jacksonville Municipal Stadium (Jacksonville Jaguars), the Rose Garden (Portland Trailblazers), and the Nashville Superspeedway. In 2009 they were awarded a 10-year contract for the Greensboro, North Carolina Coliseum.

Legends Hospitality Management

One of the newest concession companies has also generated a huge amount of discussion. In the fall of 2008 executives from the New York Yankees and the Dallas Cowboys joined forces to launch their own concession company known as Legends Hospitality Management. It is headquartered in Newark, New Jersey, and will provide food services to both teams at their new stadiums. Only time will tell how successful Legends Hospitality will be in brokering deals with additional facilities.

Employee Training

Due to the litigious nature of our society, the importance of customer service, and the intense competition in the concession industry, staff training is vitally important to most food service providers. Aramark, Levy, Centerplate, Delaware North Sportservice, Legends Hospitality, and Ovations Food Services all have staff training programs (Muret, 2009b). For example, Centerplate has a "job task" training program taught by an expert from the resort industry (Traiman, 2007). "Fan Focus" training allows Aramark to combine customer service and hospitality into a program for all employees. GuestPath is a training program for the employees of Sportservice. It teaches employees how to provide effective customer service, emphasizing more than 1,200 fan "touch points" (Muret, 2009b).

Concession Trends

The food service industry has changed dramatically in the past decade. The use of brand names and regional favorites, multiple beer options, the introduction of cashless payments, "all-you-can-eat seats," and value menus have assisted in the modification of the traditional concession model.

Brand Names and Regional Favorites

As mentioned earlier in this chapter, the revenue from the sale of food and beverages is second only to ticket revenue for many facilities. Therefore, the ticket-buying patron needs to be motivated to visit the concession stands during the game. Failure to entice spectators to buy popcorn, peanuts, Cracker Jack, and other products will impose a huge financial challenge for the facility manager to overcome.

Utilizing known name brands assists consumers in making decisions about the type of food and beverage to purchase. McDonalds, TCBY Yogurt, Ballpark Franks, Taco Bell, Dippin' Dots, and Coors beer are recognized by the majority of fans attending sport events. The quality of the food assures the patrons and perpetuates their buying habits. In addition, some ballparks contain well-known chain restaurants. Miller Park, home to the Milwaukee Brewers, contains a TGI Friday's. The Rogers Centre, home to the Toronto Blue, has had a Hard Rock Café located in center field since 1989 and PNC Park, home to the Pittsburgh Pirates, had an Outback Steakhouse in center field from 2001 to 2007. These popular restaurants not only attract day-of-game traffic but also are local favorites on non-game days.

Regional favorites are popular in many ballparks. Fish tacos in San Diego, cheese steaks in Philadelphia, shrimp Po'boys in New Orleans, barbeque in Memphis, and Primanti Brothers sandwiches in Pittsburgh are all examples of desired fare in various geographical locations across the United States. Some locations have rather strange offerings as well. Not only do teams in Denver offer burgers made from buffalo meat, but Rocky Mountain oysters (fried bull testicles) are also a local favorite. Similar parts of

Brand name recognition helps customers choose quality products they can trust.

turkeys are a popular option in Sioux Falls, Iowa. The Sioux Falls Canaries, a minor league baseball team, are the first to offer deep-fried turkey testicles. The "Fowl Balls" are sold along with the fan's choice of dipping sauce.

Beer Options

Many ballparks now offer a selection of micro-brewed beers to their fans. Several ballparks, including Coors Field in Denver, Colorado, actually have a micro-brewery located inside the ballpark. Many patrons believe these types of beers provide a better taste. In most cases, the micro-brewed beers are sold at a higher price than more established national brands.

The switch to plastic bottles instead of draft beer has occurred at several venues. The Gwinnett Center in Atlanta, Georgia, was the first venue built without draft beer lines. The facility owners saved $1.5 million by not having to install a draft beer system. Many fans prefer beer out of a plastic bottle due to its taste. Some individuals question the cleanliness of the draft beer lines, others are unhappy with the quality of cups used for draft beer, while still others are unsure if the name of the beer on the tap handle is actually the beer that is being poured. While eliminating draft beer lines may become more accepted in the future, industry experts still recommend central beer lines being installed in facilities with more than 250 events per year (Emmons, 2004).

Cashless Purchasing

As previously mentioned, the ability to use debit and credit cards to purchase concessions has become a preferred choice for most people attending sport and entertainment events. The ArenA Card, developed in 1996 by the management of the Amsterdam Arena, was the first cashless payment system used by sport venues. The card had a small microchip embedded in it and could be used for all food, beverage, and merchandise purchases. The card itself could be purchased using a credit card, a debit card, or cash from a vendor or vending machine. Similar types of cards have been developed since then, but they all share some of the same characteristics. Due to the lack of actual cash being exchanged, the reduction of transaction time can increase the sales volume up to 15%. In addition, since no currency changes hands the purchasing process becomes more hygienic and the chance of employee theft is virtually eliminated. Finally, consumer purchasing patterns can be tracked for future promotional efforts. The cost to manufacture a card is around 60 cents and potential sponsors (willing to pay for the process) can add their logo to the card for another 20 cents. Studies have shown that an average of 18% of the card's value is never used, which increases the profit margin of the food service provider (Blin, 2004). The unused portion of these cashless cards is known as breakage and is also found in loaded tickets.

Loaded Tickets

Around 2004, a number of professional teams in the United States began offering stored-value tickets similar to the ArenA Card. These have become known as loaded tickets and in various forms can be used to purchase tickets, pay for parking, procure food and beverages, and buy merchandise. Various dollar amounts are loaded into a barcode and the credit may last for a single game or for multiple games, depending on the customer's preference. In 2004, at Citizens Bank Park, home to the Philadelphia Phillies, Aramark was the first food services management company to test loaded tickets.

All-You-Can-Eat Seats

Including all-inclusive food packages in the price of ticket is nothing new. The St. Louis Cardinals introduced the concept in 1996, but it had usually been confined to suites and club seats. Beginning in 2006, several MLB teams began using the concept to sell to the regular ticket buyer and use it to sell less popular seats. Depending on the team and the seat location in the venue, the all-you-can-eat option added $10 to $30 to the cost of the ticket. As the idea became more popular, food service companies began to sell all-you-can-eat packages to their season ticket-holders as well. For example, during the 2007 MLB season the Atlanta Braves sold a "ballpark favorites" all-you-can-eat package for $30 and a "barbecue and more" package for $60. The "barbecue and more" package included all-you-can-drink beer. Previously, the tickets had been sold as individual game offerings, but they will begin offering them as season-ticket packages (Monasso, 2007). Obviously, liability issues abound if a facility were to include alcohol with the package. In addition, some teams believe it could take away from the image that the team is trying to adopt.

National Basketball Association (NBA) and National Hockey League (NHL) teams began introducing the all-you-can-eat ticket in 2007. For example, during the 2007 NHL season, the Scottrade Center, home to the St. Louis Blues, provided an all-you-can-eat alternative for more than 1,000 club seat buyers. The $100 per seat option included hot dogs, chicken fingers, popcorn, pretzels, beer, and soda. The team saw a 66% increase in club seat ticket sales from 2006 when food was not available (Muret, 2007).

Value Menus

The U.S. mortgage scandal, corporate greed, and the October 2008 Wall Street meltdown resulted in a severe economic recession in the United States. The impact on the sport industry was a decrease in season ticket sales, non-renewal of sponsorship packages, and thousands of fans staying at home instead of attending athletic events. Sports were no longer seen as recession proof. Facility managers and food service providers realized that traditional pricing strategies and sales techniques were no longer adequate. A paradigm shift was needed in order to entice those fans who continued to buy tickets to also purchase food and beverages. Some food service providers believed that discounting their concessions was a viable solution. The Colorado Rockies established "Diamond Deal" stands where all items sold for $2.50. The San Diego Padres began a Five for $5 promotion. For $5 fans received an all-beef hotdog, a bag of peanuts, a 22-ounce soda, a bag of popcorn, and a cookie. At Fenway Park, Aramark established the "Fenway Family Hour." For one hour after the gates opened nine items were sold at half-price. Other facility operators and food service providers did not believe offering food and beverages at discounted rates was the correct option. These groups believed that the additional volume in sales would be negated by the reduced price.

Merchandise

Merchandise includes a variety of products such as hats, T-shirts, CD screen-savers, sweatshirts, posters, and authentic jerseys. The distribution and organization of merchandise stands are similar to concession operations and utilize many of the same techniques. Interestingly enough, many of the larger food service management companies, such as Aramark, manage and staff their own merchandise operations.

Virtually every sport facility has a team store of some kind located on-site. These stores have a variety of catchy names, such as Colts Pro Shop at Lucas Oil Stadium (Indianapolis), CAVS Town at Quicken Loan Arena (Cleveland), and The Dugout at Coors Field (Denver). These stores have the potential to be major sources of revenue if managed properly. Whoever manages the store needs to decide if they want to operate the shop as a customer service or as a profit center.

Merchandise sales occur in a variety of settings.

The sale of unlicensed merchandise is known as "bootlegging." It is common practice for most major events, with merchandise for sale, to obtain a federal injunction dealing with copyright law infringement. This provides police with the authority to arrest bootleggers and/or confiscate unauthorized merchandise. Local city ordinances governing the sale of items on the street can be most beneficial in dealing with and eliminating bootleggers.

Application Exercise Solution

As stated at the beginning of the chapter, Mike had estimated a COGS of 12% for draft beer sold during the tournament. How did he determine this? Read the following and you will recognize the answer.

Here is the information you will need to know to answer the five questions. The concession stands supposedly sold 10 kegs of beer. The kegs cost the university $75 each. Each keg held 16 gallons, which translates to 2,048 ounces per keg. Beers were sold in 16-ounce cups. The records showed the concession stands sold a total of 1,050 cups of beer at $5 per cup, grossing $5,250.

1. How many cups should they have sold per keg?
   This is an easy one. Each keg held 2,048 ounces. The beers were sold in 16-ounce cups, so simple division (2,048/16) gives us 128 cups (should have been sold per keg).
2. How many total cups should they have sold?
   Simple multiplication this time . . . 128 (cups per keg) × 10 (kegs) = 1,280 cups.
3. What should their total revenue have been?
   Simple multiplication again . . . 1,280 (cups) × $5 (per cup) = $6,400.
4. What was the *actual* COGS percentage for the beer sold (round to nearest %)?
   This is a little more difficult, but not all that hard. Remember COGS is determined by:

   > *The cost of the product to the concessionaire ÷ the price the concessionaire sold the product for*

   So the cost of the beer to the university was:
   10 (kegs) × $75 = $750 ÷ $5,250 = 14%. This translates to an 86% profit.
5. What *should* have been the profit margin for the beer sold (round to nearest %)?
   This is easy . . . just substitute the numbers:
   $750 (cost of kegs) ÷ $6,400 (derived from #3) = 12%. This is the percentage that Mike originally had estimated. This translates to a profit of 88%. So the sales practices of the junior college football booster club cost the university 2% in profit.

Your final question: What could have caused the 2% difference? That one you will have to answer for yourself!

Summary

1. Concessions include food service management (food and beverage sales) as well as the sale of merchandise.
2. Concessions may be outsourced to an outside company or they may be conducted in-house, where the facility controls everything. When outsourced, the facility management must maintain a certain degree of control to ensure product quality.
3. The majority of the volume in the food service industry is conducted by fewer than 50 companies. Some of the most well-known concessionaires include Aramark, Centerplate, Delaware North Sportservice, Levy, Ovations, and Legends Hospitality.
4. Recent trends in concession management include brand names and regional favorites, multiple-beer options, cashless payments, all-you-can-eat seats, and value menus.
5. Merchandise stores are often operated by concession companies and may be oriented as a profit center or for customer service.

Questions

1. Explain the following terms: outsource, hawkers, cost of goods, breakage, premium service foods, and bootlegging.
2. Describe the circumstances that would require you to outsource the food service operations at your facility.
3. Describe how cost of goods can be estimated.
4. If you were a food service provider, would you offer all-you-can-eat seats or value menus? Explain your reasoning.

15

Ticketing and Box Office Management

Application Exercise

Jim Cervik has just been hired as the box office manager at a Division I athletic department. The athletic department sponsors 16 varsity sports (7 male and 9 female) and has recently seen its men's and women's basketball teams and women's volleyball team qualify for the National Collegiate Athletic Association's (NCAA) postseason tournament. Currently, the 40-year-old Memorial Gym can seat 7,200 spectators for athletic events, but much of the seating is bleachers, and the locker rooms and athletic department offices have not been significantly remodeled since the facility was opened. The university has recently announced plans to construct an 11,500-seat state-of-the-art arena that will not only provide one of the best environments to host intercollegiate athletic contests, but, unlike the current arena, will also be an attractive venue for concerts and other entertainment events.

Cervik faces some important challenges as he begins his tenure as box office manager. First, he must review current ticketing practices at Memorial Gym. The recent success of the men's and women's basketball team has generated a significant following—particularly when the teams play league games. Five years ago when the teams were struggling, students who wanted to attend a game could show up 20 minutes prior to the event and usually receive a ticket. Currently, all men's basketball games are sold out weeks in advance and most women's games attract thousands of attendees. For some highly desirable men's and women's games, tickets are resold on the open market at a significant markup from the original price. In addition, numerous alums, sponsors, and members of the local community have expressed an interest in purchasing additional season tickets for all athletic events. Currently, the athletic department allocates 3,000 free student tickets for men's and women's basketball games, but for many games the student demand has been two-to-three times that amount. The strong student support has generated media attention, as the student section is typically loud and boisterous during games. However, many students who have had to wait in long lines only to eventually be denied a ticket have complained that as students they should be given the opportunity to go to any sporting event because they not only attend the university, but they also pay continually escalating athletic fees. There have also been some safety issues with ticket distribution, as students have often misbehaved while waiting in long lines for the tickets to be sold.

The athletic department currently offers 3,000 season tickets to members of the athletic department alumni association and to various sponsors. It also sells 1,000 seats for individual games at the beginning of the season. For men's basketball games, these seats are typically purchased within a day or two after they are initially offered. The athletic department has also sold 200 seats in upper sections of the facility for $10 each. Fans are only able to purchase these seats the day of the game and they are limited to two tickets per person.

The new facility will open in two years and some athletic department employees feel that no additional tickets, beyond the current 3,000 seats, should be allocated for student use. In addition, many athletic department officials in the development and fundraising areas have wondered why the school has not ever charged students for tickets to sporting events. Most students would probably pay money to purchase their game tickets that they are currently receiving for free. Though students would likely pay money for their tickets, there is no doubt that members of the community would pay much more money to have greater access to games—particularly if they could purchase some of the courtside sections currently reserved for students. There are now thousands of people on the season-ticket waiting list, and the athletic department will be able to accommodate some, but not all, of their requests when the new facility is opened.

Cervik needs to review ticketing protocols for the remaining two years in the current facility and then must determine what types of tickets to offer in the new facility. In addition, since the facility is currently in its design stage, Cervik must provide insights regarding the location and space allocated to the box office in the new facility. Since the new facility will attract concerts and other entertainment events, he must ensure that the box office staff is able to effectively service not only existing customers, but also those who have never previously been to the facility. The added entertainment events will likely attract customers who are not familiar with the university's campus and the facility's ticketing procedures.

Introduction

Fifty years ago the vast majority of *tickets* to athletic contests, concerts, the circus, and other live entertainment events were sold at a facility's *box office*. The main responsibility of the *box office manager* or *director of ticket operations* was to ensure that employees were organized and able to sell tickets to patrons on-site. The manager was concerned primarily with the location of the box office within the facility, available physical space, visibility for arriving patrons, and potential hours of operation. Though these issues are still certainly important and will be discussed in this chapter, the box office manager's responsibilities include many others beyond just processing and selling tickets to on-site customers. Present-day box office management involves organizing and staffing the box office, establishing financial controls, determining if a ticketing partner will be utilized, selecting the types of tickets to be offered for each event, determining when and how to distribute tickets, marketing and initiating sales, and gathering data to develop better relationships with customers.

Since sport and entertainment events are perishable, it is critical that box office managers undertake activities that maximize their sales opportunities. Once the event has concluded, there is not another opportunity to sell unused tickets. In addition, facilities that are not filled to capacity fail to maximize ancillary revenues from parking, concessions, and licensed merchandise (see Chapter 5). Athletes and entertainers prefer to perform in front of capacity crowds, which can only happen if the director of ticket operations and the staff work in conjunction with other departments to not only maximize ticket sales but also to provide an enjoyable event experience.

Box Office Design and Administration

The box office is a critical component of a sport or entertainment facility. The box office should be located in a visible and accessible location. Adequate signage indicating the location of the box office should be strategically placed throughout the facility's footprint and surrounding parking areas so that every arriving patron can immediately recognize the box office location. In addition, signage should clearly denote which lines are to be utilized for various customer transactions, such as day-of-event purchases, will call, and future event sales.

Historically, many facilities were not designed and built with the box office as a primary concern. Too often, inadequate space and signage made it difficult for customers to know exactly where to go and what line to enter. That difficulty often led to employee and customer frustration and potentially fewer ticket sales. The majority of recently constructed facilities have incorporated large box office areas and extensive

Cramped box offices restrict potential sales.

signage to assist patrons. Numerous older facilities have cramped box offices that cannot accommodate many employees and, therefore, cannot quickly sell and distribute
tickets to potential patrons. In some cases, older facilities utilize additional temporary
external box offices when a highly anticipated event occurs. Fortunately, since tickets
are now usually distributed through a computer system that can print tickets in multiple locations, any of the box office windows that are linked to the main box office can
print tickets for customers. In situations where a previously printed hard ticket is the
only option available, the box office manager may need to investigate methods to increase the flow of purchasers through the main box office area.

The importance of an adequately functioning box office cannot be overstated. The
worst possible outcome in any marketing venture is when a business is unable to execute a sale to an interested customer. The time, effort, and money necessary to attract
customers to an event are often considerable; therefore, the box office must function effectively and efficiently at all times.

The size of the box office area will certainly vary by facility. At the least, the box office should be able to handle multiple lines and should have adequate room for patrons
to move away from the box office window after completing their transactions. The box
office areas where employees work and customers purchase tickets need to comply with
the Americans with Disabilities Act (ADA) of 1990. Ideally, the box office will be designed and strategically positioned so that lines for patrons entering the facility will not
become intermingled with customers waiting to use the box office. In addition, the box
office area should be covered so that patrons are not exposed to the elements. Waiting
in line is certainly more difficult if the sun is hot or there is rain or snow falling.

One of the most important aspects of operating any distribution outlet, including a
box office, is managing the potential lines that customers form while they wait. *Queue
management* involves the study of customer lines and development of strategies to increase efficiency. The speed of customer lines can be increased by a variety of methods.
Ticket managers should first investigate the box office's *servicescape*—the design, layout,
available signage, and ambiance in the box office area (Zeithaml, Bitner, & Gremler,
2006). The physical environment may limit the types of lines that can be formed at the
box office. For instance, typically the most efficient lines are the ones where a single line
is formed (often with a serpentine configuration) and customers reaching the front of
the line are served by the next available customer service representative (Barbaro, 2007).
This type of single line enables the better customer service employees to cover for the
slower-performing employees. In addition, if a situation arises in which a patron has an
issue that requires an extensive period of time to resolve, that patron's line will not stop
moving. However, this type of line may be impossible to implement if the box office
servicescape does not offer sufficient space.

Each box office must have signage that is visible from a distance so customers can
quickly recognize where they should go to complete their desired type of transaction. In
addition, signage should clearly note ticket prices and availability. Ideally, visible signage
will enable customers waiting in line to ascertain what types of tickets they would like
to buy before they arrive at the ticket window. Any potential questions that can be

Box offices should have sufficient room for multiple lines to form.

answered prior to a customer's interaction with the customer service employee can increase efficiency, resulting in more tickets being sold and customers rapidly entering the facility.

Regardless of the type of line employed and the availability of visible signage, every facility should ensure that employees are providing a high level of customer service. Nagel (2008) discovered that in a typical sport and entertainment facility there is a large discrepancy between the performances of various service employees. The box office manager should develop training protocols for every newly hired employee. Proper training ensures that each employee has a basic understanding of his or her job responsibilities and how to interact with customers in a pleasant manner. Box office managers must also develop methods to evaluate the performance of employees and to then assist the poorly performing employee to improve. Poorly performing employees cause lines to move at a slower pace, which potentially slows sales and certainly causes other employees and the waiting customer to become agitated. If a facility is providing consistent employee performance, lines are likely to move efficiently and customer complaints will be minimized. When customers progress through lines quickly, not only will they have a more favorable attitude regarding their experience, but they will also have more time once they enter the facility to purchase concessions and licensed merchandise.

The main box office will typically operate during normal business hours on non-event days. However, on days when there is an event, the box office may open early and it is likely to remain open until at least half-time or intermission. To increase repeat sales, many facilities now operate day-of-event ancillary box offices inside the facility so that customers who are leaving an event can purchase tickets to upcoming events without having to go outside the facility.

The box office is the primary source of information for arriving spectators, so personnel should be trained to provide information regarding the facility and specific policies in a pleasant manner—even when some customers become agitated or overly assertive. Customers typically ask questions regarding seat location; bringing in personal items such as cameras, food, and beverages; and potential ticket exchanges. For outdoor events—such as baseball games—that may be postponed or cancelled due to bad weather, the box office should know the customer's potential options, which may vary depending on the specific situation.

Patrons who forget or lose their tickets prior to arriving at the facility present an interesting challenge for the box office manager and employees. In most cases, the concerned patron did actually lose or forget the tickets, but in some cases patrons attempt to defraud the facility by selling the ticket and then trying to get an additional one. Since most tickets are now printed with a barcode for identification, if the patron is a season ticket-holder, it is fairly easy to void the original ticket and replace it with a new ticket. The season ticket-holder can be told that if the original ticket is used by a different patron, then the facility could revoke that season ticket-holder from purchasing tickets again in the future due to attempted fraud (if the ticket was sold rather than stolen). Non-season ticket-holders who purchased their ticket from the facility can be traced by the purchasing credit card. In these cases a replacement ticket can be provided. Of course, there have been situations where tickets have been stolen from mailboxes and then either used or resold on the *secondary market*. In these cases, the box office manager may need to exercise caution. Certainly, the theft of tickets is a serious matter and should be reported to the police. However, most thieves who steal tickets will simply resell them to unsuspecting patrons. Though the facility does not have to provide entry to someone who purchased a stolen ticket, in some cases in which the event is not sold out the facility may provide a replacement ticket. The facility can not only generate revenue from concessions and licensed merchandise sales from that particular patron, but it can also direct the patron to utilize the primary and secondary ticketing services of the facility in the future. Further, providing assistance when it is not required can build positive rapport with the patron.

Although the box office is important for an efficiently managed facility, it normally employs a minimal number of full-time staff. Usually, a manager will be responsible for all box office personnel. Typically, only a few assistants will constitute the full-time employees. Interns and hourly employees will also work in the box office—particularly on event days. The primary role of the ticket staff is to distribute tickets, but most box office personnel retain additional responsibilities regarding ticket policy development, season-ticket sales, group sales, and suite sales.

Though there will always be potential customers who stop by to solicit information in person from the ticketing staff, the vast majority of potential customers will seek information regarding the facility and upcoming events through the Internet. It is critical that the facility's web site, as well as the web site of any ticketing vendor, be organized in an efficient manner. Customers visiting pertinent web sites should be able to easily determine upcoming events, ticket availability, pricing, and potential payment options. When the box office is closed, the answering machine should clearly detail pertinent information, such as the box office's hours, upcoming events, ticket availability, and directions to the facility. Every potential interaction with customers—whether in person, on the phone, or via the Internet—should be effectively organized to create a helpful and convenient environment for the customer to solicit information that can lead to a potential sale.

Types of Tickets

The type of tickets offered to customers varies by event. When determining the type of ticket to offer customers, the director of ticket sales, in consultation with the facility operations department, should analyze the potential event. Every event has a unique audience and every audience will have event-specific expectations related to the event and the facility. For instance, during a two-week period a facility may host an intercollegiate basketball game, a *Disney-on-Ice* show, and a Widespread Panic concert. Each of these events will attract a different crowd. Though there may be spectators who attend all three of these events, they will likely have different expectations of appropriate behavior for each event. The facility set-up and ticketing plan should be tailored to the needs of the potential audience.

Tickets are normally classified as either *general admission* or *reserved*. General admission tickets allow individuals to sit virtually anywhere they want on a first-come, first-served basis. The ticket is not for a specific seat, but for a seat somewhere in the facility. General admission seating is popular for certain sections of seats at many intercollegiate athletic events. Most student sections at college football and basketball games are general admission, which enables early-arriving students to claim the closest seats. For example, the boisterous behavior of Duke University's student section has caused commentators to dub the students the "Cameron Crazies." Though Duke's student section is in a prime location near the basketball court, other schools have elected to seat their students farther away from the action so that those seating areas can be sold for higher prices.

For some concerts, general admission seating is called *festival seating*. This general-admission designation is somewhat misleading because the concertgoer does not have an actual seat. At many outdoor amphitheaters there is a lawn area in the back of the facility, and instead of allocating a seat, the general admission ticket permits a patron to watch the event from anywhere within the designated lawn area. However, at many venues, festival seating is utilized directly in the front of the performance area. With the floor area in front of the stage void of seats, more tickets can potentially be sold, generating higher revenues. Many performers enjoy the tightly packed crowds close to the stage, as it creates a lively environment. However, festival seating increases the risks of physical injury, as patrons may be smashed against each other or the stage area. Facility managers must determine if the extra revenue is worth the increased risks and liability due to fainting and other potential bodily injuries.

When ticket buyers purchase a specific seat for an event, they have bought a reserved ticket. This ensures that the ticket buyer has a specific section, row, and seat for the event. The majority of sporting events in North America utilize reserved seats. In fact, after a series of deadly crowd crushes, many of the stadiums in England have resorted to using reserved seats. These stadiums are termed *all-seaters* by the British.

Events that utilize reserved seating may create an unusual concern for facility managers. When general admission seating is utilized, most patrons will select the best seats as they arrive. However, when using reserved seating there is the chance that some of the best seats may go unsold while other, less desirable seats are purchased. In some cases, purchased tickets may not be utilized by patrons. When prime reserved seats are not utilized, it presents the facility with a potential dilemma. The facility certainly does not want to diminish the value of the sold reserved seats by letting patrons who purchased less desirable seats move into the prime locations. However, the events' performers usually like to have many customers in close proximity. Customers who see open seats may attempt to move once the event has commenced. For this reason, every facility should develop and enforce a consistent policy regarding unused seats. Facility employees should know the policy and make every effort to enforce the wishes of the facility's management, whether that is to restrict access to seats under all circumstances or to permit patron movement after a certain point in the event.

Pricing

Although the sport and entertainment industries are now multibillion-dollar enterprises, pricing tickets for events is not nearly as sophisticated as in many other industries. Tickets to sporting events have traditionally been priced with the previous year as a baseline. In most cases ticket prices usually increase each season with the rate of increase being impacted by the team's recent performance or anticipated upcoming performance. Tickets to concerts typically were priced to attract a wide array of fans, who would then—hopefully—purchase the performers' CD. Irving Azoff radically changed the concert industry's pricing structure in 1994 when, as manager of The Eagles, he offered the first-ever concert tickets for more than $100. Azoff has continued to dramatically increase the price of concert tickets for The Eagles and his numerous other bands (Wyman, 2009). Though ticket prices for sport and entertainment events have been consistently and, in some cases, dramatically increasing, there is still a tremendous opportunity to study ticket pricing in the future (Christenson, Nagel, & Taylor, 2008).

One of the most important factors in ticket pricing is who sets the price. If the main tenant or the facility itself establishes the price, the strategy is known as *house scale*. This often occurs with professional sport teams that establish the pricing strategy each year when they play multiple games at the facility. If an outside promoter or event establishes the price for a one-time or once-a-year event, a *performance scale* is used. The box office manager and staff are often in an uncomfortable position because they usually will not have input regarding the ticket pricing. Customers may complain to the box office about the ticket prices—particularly when they escalate rapidly from year to year. Of course customers who complain and still purchase tickets are not nearly as much of a problem as people who complain and then do not purchase or people who simply decide the price for the event is too high. Though the general manager and the director of marketing will be primarily responsible for setting ticket prices, a well-run facility may involve the box office manager in this decision. Establishing the proper price is critical for maximizing revenues.

The price of any good or service will have an impact upon demand. This relationship is called *elasticity of demand*. Most people assume that the elasticity of demand for any product or service has a 1-1 relationship (also known as *unitary demand*) (see Figure 15-1). They think that if the price is cut in half then demand will double or that if price is doubled then demand will be cut in half. Though this type of corresponding relationship can exist, in most cases demand is either elastic (varies tremendously by price) or inelastic (varies little by price). Figure 15-2 depicts an elastic demand curve, while Figure 15-3 demonstrates an inelastic demand curve. Facility managers must study how demand for their tickets will be affected by price changes. If ticket demand for a sporting event or concert will likely remain unchanged if the price is increased, then the facility should increase prices to maximize revenue. Conversely, if demand can be increased dramatically with a small decrease in ticket prices, then ticket price should be decreased. Setting the price where demand yields the greatest revenue should be the primary goal.

One of the most important aspects of elasticity of demand is the understanding of *every* facility revenue source. Most facilities will generate revenues through the sale of tickets, parking, concessions, licensed merchandise, and other sources (see Chapter 5). In some cases the facility's tenant will negotiate to control one of these revenue sources entirely. For instance, Ringling Brothers and Barnum and Bailey's Circus has typically negotiated to receive all souvenir (though not the concessions) revenue during their per-

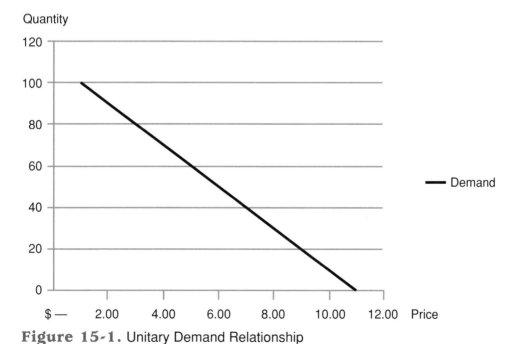

Figure 15-1. Unitary Demand Relationship

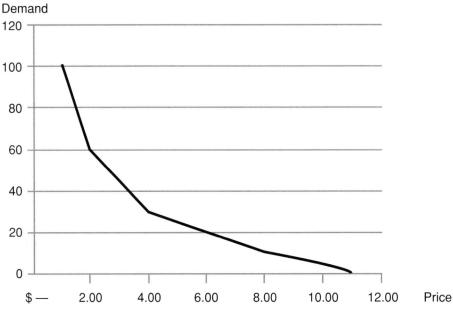

Figure 15-2. Elastic Demand Curve

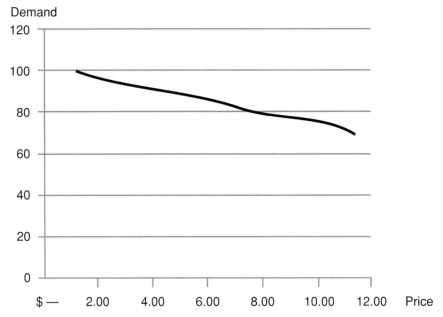

Figure 15-3. Inelastic Demand Curve

formances. Additionally, they sell cotton candy, snow cones, and other items not traditionally sold by venue concessionaires for other events. In some situations, such as some of the recent large-scale rock'n'roll performances, the tenant and the facility will *split* a portion of revenue generated from different sources entirely. When certain revenue sources are shared, then the facility and the tenant must often negotiate the prices that will be charged for various services. Most facilities will want to control every potential revenue source so that they not only generate revenue but so that they can also control the pricing and actions of service providers. The facility staff members typically field customer complaints about pricing and service, even if they were not directly responsible.

If the facility controls every revenue source, then the box office manager, in consultation with the director of finance, director of marketing, and other pertinent employees, should research the elasticity of demand for *every* revenue source. In most cases, different revenue sources have different elasticities of demand. For instance, most patrons have greater price sensitivities for tickets and parking than for concessions—particularly alcohol purchases. If the tickets are perceived as too expensive, the patron may elect to stay home. If the parking is deemed to be too expensive, then public transportation, car pooling, or parking great distances from the facility and then walking may become more likely options. However, alcohol consumption is usually less likely to be affected by price increases. If the general manager and the director of marketing have determined the prices that will affect potential demand, then an overall revenue plan can be developed. One typical marketing method to maximize revenue through an understanding of elasticity of demand is to utilize *loss leaders*—pricing a product or service at a level where money is lost (cost and expenses to create and provide product or service > generated revenue) on each sale. A loss leader is utilized to attract potential customers. Once the customer has arrived to purchase the loss leader, he or she hopefully will then decide to purchase other items that have much higher pricing markups, which not only recoups the lost money from the sale of the loss leader but generates much higher profits than if the loss leader had been set at its normal price. Major League Baseball franchises often utilize special "dollar days" or other similar lower-price promotions to attract fans. Though the ticket price is much lower than normal, the team is anticipating that the sale price on tickets will attract new customers who would not have attended but for the special ticket price. Though the ticket prices are drastically reduced, the facility will likely see an increase in the sale of licensed merchandise and concessions—causing the overall revenues to be higher than if ticket price reduction had not occurred.

For most of the 20th century, sport and entertainment events offered different prices for various seating locations. Typically, the closer the seat to the field, court, or stage, the higher the ticket price. However, teams or performers playing multiple games or events over the course of a season or tour did not typically alter the price of their tickets based upon factors such as day of the week, month of the year, opening act, opposing player or team, or many other factors. The airline and hotel industries have traditionally utilized variable ticket pricing (VTP) to maximize their revenues by pricing the same location (airline ticket, hotel room) differently based upon various factors. For instance, most airlines will charge higher prices for seats on planes that fly on Mondays than on Saturdays since business travelers who must attend weekday meetings are not as likely to be as price sensitive as vacation travelers who have more flexible schedules. Similarly, the same Las Vegas hotel room may cost more for a Friday- or Saturday-night stay than for one during the week because more people tend to visit Las Vegas during the weekend. Many sports' franchises have recently begun pricing games based upon various factors that may contribute to demand. Many Major League Baseball teams now have weekday prices that are different than those charged on the weekend. Similarly, if a

YANKEES' HIGH-PRICED TICKETS

The recent facility building boom has been primarily fueled by a desire to offer more club seats and luxury suites for high-end customers (see Chapter 5). The new Yankee Stadium that opened in 2009 certainly received tremendous media attention for its high prices and empty seats. Despite opening during an economic downturn, the Yankees initially priced many tickets in the new stadium as high as $2,500 per game. Unfortunately for the Yankees, many of the highest-priced seats did not sell, which left television viewers to watch some games with many of the best seats behind home plate empty (Sandomir, 2009). To avoid further embarrassment, the Yankees eventually had to lower some prices and offer season ticket-holders special opportunities to purchase many of the empty seats at a significant discount. Despite the Yankees' efforts, pundit Jason Kottke (2009) noted that New York residents who desired to watch a New York Yankee–Seattle Mariners' game from the "best seats in the house" would spend much less money by purchasing plane tickets to Seattle, a luxury hotel room for two nights, a rental car, meals, and two front-row seats in Seattle's Safeco Field than by purchasing two tickets in the front row at Yankee Stadium.

prominent player from an opposing team may be playing in a particular game or series then the facility may charge higher prices. Though most think of VTP as being implemented primarily to increase prices and revenues for prominent games or events, it can also be utilized to lower the price of less-desirable games to attract patrons who might not be able to afford typical event pricing.

Variable ticket pricing is much easier to utilize now than it was 15 years ago because most facilities do not have the *menu costs* that they did in the past. Since signage is now often operated by computers, it is much easier to change posted prices than in the past when there was a hard sign that had to be re-painted. In addition, since tickets are typically printed at time of purchase, it is much easier to alter the price by simply changing the information on the computer. Nagel (2000) speculated that eventually prices for sporting events would be set in a manner similar to that of the price of companies on a stock exchange. The various stock markets set prices for available company shares based upon the number of shares being purchased. If more people offer to purchase a specific stock, the computer reacts by increasing the posted stock price. Traditionally, tickets have been offered at a set number of price points (typically 4 to 10 for a large sport or entertainment facility), but if computer systems are programmed to react to market demand, the price of tickets could be changed instantly after each ticket is purchased. Though ticket sales have not yet been based entirely upon the stock market model, the San Francisco Giants recently implemented a new ticketing software system that incorporates ticket demand, pitching match-ups, weather, and other factors into its pricing structure. During the 2009 season, the Giants realized a 20% increase in ticket sales for the seats that were offered with the new dynamic pricing model (Belson, 2009).

Ticket Distribution

Thirty-five years ago the vast majority of tickets were sold at the facility's box office. Tickets to highly sought-after events were typically purchased by customers who waited in lines—sometimes overnight—in the hopes that they could have the opportunity to see their favorite team play a big game or watch a popular performer. Since sponsorship and corporate relationships with the sport and entertainment industries were not as common, there was a feeling among most fans that if they were willing to wait in line long enough, they could have potential access to the best seats.

Since the box office was the primary or sole distribution point for tickets, the opportunity for anyone to purchase tickets theoretically existed. However, many box office managers recognized the power they retained since they controlled the only point of sale. Unfortunately, this led to many underhanded practices. Box office managers and their staffs often withheld prime tickets from the marketplace so that they could sell them to their contacts—often at a significant personal markup. It was also not uncommon for will-call tickets to be lost by the ticketing staff and then resold to other patrons. In some cases, facility managers encouraged this type of behavior by refusing to pay box office staff members anything more than minimal salaries. In other cases, facility managers worked with the box office staff to turn potential facility profits into personal profits. Though this type of behavior unfortunately still exists, the ticketing industry has certainly evolved into a more professional environment. Today, most facilities will not tolerate the misappropriation of tickets by any staff member. In addition, box office managers are usually paid a salary that is commensurate with their responsibilities.

The initial distribution of tickets in remote locations often occurred at supermarkets or other local outlets. Many teams allowed sponsors to sell tickets as part of their promotions. During the 1970s most facilities began to take an increasing number of ticket orders over the telephone. The rise in phone orders corresponded with an increased understanding by facilities that making ticket purchases convenient would increase sales. In addition, a heightened customer understanding that credit card information could be provided somewhat securely over the telephone increased ticket sales.

During the 1990s, the proliferation of the Internet dramatically impacted ticket distribution. Most fans research potential sport and entertainment events through the Internet. Having a functional and attractive Internet location is critical for every facility. Potential customers must have the ability to determine available seats and prices when they visit a web page. This is especially important when highly sought-after tickets are offered for sale. Unfortunately, web sites that are not easy to understand or that contain insufficient information can diminish potential sales. Even if customers purchase tickets for highly sought-after events through a faulty web site, the substandard experience may negatively impact their future purchases of other events through that site.

Though many fans cherish the torn ticket stub from a special game or entertainment event they attended in the past, the use of the Internet has often changed the physical description of the ticket. Many facilities now utilize barcode technology to admit patrons to events. This serves a variety of purposes. In most cases, scanning tickets with an electronic device is much more efficient than having the ticket-taker inspect and then tear a patron's ticket. Barcode technology also enables the facility to more easily replace lost or stolen tickets. In addition, customers can often print their tickets at home after purchasing them via the Internet. This is especially useful when last-minute purchases are executed with insufficient time available to mail the patron a hard ticket. Though the customer could pick up a purchased ticket at the will-call booth, this would lengthen the potential line and potentially require additional box office staff to work at the event. Ironically, the convenience of print-at-home tickets has caused some fans to be disappointed that they did not receive a hard ticket with a colorful depiction of the event (Lister, 2006). Some facilities have begun to mail tickets with pictures of the facility/team/player and sponsor as souvenirs to customers even though the ticket would not permit the patron to enter the facility.

Ticketing Companies

During the 1970s many teams and facilities began to outsource their ticketing operations to save money and increase ticket distribution. In most cases, Ticketron was the likely choice. Founded in 1969, Ticketron had developed technology that allowed kiosks to be deployed in malls and other public places. The kiosks allowed potential customers to purchase tickets for concerts and sporting events without phoning or visiting the facility's box office. Though Ticketron was the dominant ticketing company throughout the 1970s and early 1980s, it did not continue to develop its technology ("Ticketmaster Group, Inc.," n.d.). Eventually, Ticketron lost its standing as the top ticketing company and was purchased by Ticketmaster in 1991.

In 1976, two Arizona State University students, Albert Leffler and Peter Gadwa, noticed that most of the external ticketing outlets had a specific allotment of tickets and once that allotment was gone, waiting customers would have to visit another outlet to find remaining available seats. These students worked to design a computer system whereby all the ticketing outlets could access the remaining tickets. This eliminated a customer's need to potentially travel to various distribution points to purchase available tickets. It also enabled teams and concert promoters to more efficiently meet demand. Leffler and Gadwa, along with Gordon Gunn, founded Ticketmaster and in 1977 Electric Light Orchestra became their first client ("Company History," n.d.).

Though Ticketmaster experienced early financial troubles before becoming profitable, its continual advances in ticket technology enabled it to become the industry leader by the late 1980s. Ticketmaster streamlined ticketing operations for its clients and enabled facilities to focus upon generating revenues through other operations, such as parking and concessions. In the 1980s, Ticketmaster employed a large number of call centers that could provide longer hours of service more effectively than most facilities. Ticketmaster was especially helpful to concert promoters planning and promoting nationwide tours. Promoters were confident that no matter the size or type of show, Ticketmaster could efficiently handle the sale and distribution of tickets around the country. In the 1990s, Ticketmaster was effective at moving much of its operations to the Internet. Though the Internet diminished the need for Ticketmaster to retain as many call centers, it enabled the company to establish and expand its presence in international markets. By 1991, Ticketmaster had become successful enough to acquire Ticketron, effectively eliminating most of its ticketing competition.

Ticketmaster generates most of its revenue from ticketing service fees charged to customers when tickets are purchased. When Ticketmaster purchased Ticketron, many sport and entertainment industry executives were concerned that Ticketmaster would

LIVE NATION–TICKETMASTER BATTLE YIELDS A NEW COMPANY

For many years Ticketmaster has been the dominant company in the live event ticket business. Live Nation, Inc., the most powerful concert promoter in the United States, was formed in 2005 as a spin-off of Clear Channel Communications. In addition to promoting concerts, Live Nation owns a variety of entertainment venues in North America. In 2008, despite a long-standing relationship with Ticketmaster, Live Nation announced plans to create its own ticketing company. Live Nation believed it could retain a significant amount of money from ticketing revenues it was currently outsourcing to Ticketmaster for its concert productions. In addition, the new Live Nation venture would compete with Ticketmaster for other events that were not under Live Nation's control (Pethokoukis, 2008). Since 17% of its $1.2 billion in yearly revenue was generated from its relationship with Live Nation's venues and events, Ticketmaster was forced to react to the new ticketing venture (Smith, 2008).

To counter Live Nation's activities, Ticketmaster elected to merge its operations with Irving Azoff's Front Line Management, Inc. For many years, Front Line Management has managed dozens of the highest-grossing musical acts in the world. The merger would have dramatically hurt Live Nation's ability to promote many high-revenue producing shows, because Azoff (who would have become the CEO of the merged company) and his staff would have certainly either refused to permit any of their musical acts to perform in Live Nation venues or would have negotiated highly favorable terms for any access to its clients.

The Ticketmaster–Front Line Management merger generated significant headlines, but it eventually became a moot point. In early 2009, Ticketmaster and Live Nation elected to merge their operations into a new $2.5 billion company called Live Nation Entertainment (Rooney, 2009). The combined company would control 80% of the venues where live events are staged (Chmielewski, 2009). Since the new company would become such a dominant company in the live-entertainment industry, the merger elicited government scrutiny in both the United States and the United Kingdom (Swash, 2009). During congressional hearings in the United States, Peter Luukko, president of Comcast-Spectacor, testified that the merger should be permitted:

> Even though we compete with Ticketmaster we're not against the merger . . . I think the more opportunity they have to be involved in the process, from the band's rights through the ticketing experience and all the merchandising capabilities, it gives them the opportunity to control more revenue streams which will give them the ability to do more tours and take more risks. I believe it [the merger] will have the ability to create more content and more touring acts. (Crockford, 2009, para. 4)

The proposed merger will likely be approved or terminated by the government in late 2010.

retain a virtual monopoly. Though some smaller ticketing companies existed and many facilities retained their ticketing operations in-house, Ticketmaster's acquisition of Ticketron resulted in government scrutiny. Though the U.S. Department of Justice approved the merger, numerous individuals complained about Ticketmaster's potential control of the marketplace. Every time Ticketmaster raised its fees, customers, promoters, facilities, and performers became concerned that Ticketmaster was improperly wielding monopolistic power. Its most notable critic was the band Pearl Jam. In 1994 Pearl Jam argued before the U.S. Department of Justice that Ticketmaster operated as an unfair monopoly due to its apparent control of most of the prominent venues in the United States. Pearl Jam had attempted to keep individual concert ticket prices below $20, which was not possible given the band's expenses and Ticketmaster's ticketing service fees. The Department of Justice ruled in Ticketmaster's favor and four years later Pearl Jam resumed its relationship with Ticketmaster.

The Secondary Ticket Market

Since tickets were first sold for sporting events, there have been entrepreneurs who have resold purchased tickets for a profit. For many years, ticket brokers, sometimes derisively known as *scalpers*, usually bought and sold tickets in person. Reselling tickets was often viewed as a frowned-upon activity and numerous states and local governments passed strict anti-scalping laws to attempt to curtail resale activity. Despite these laws, ticket reselling continued in most cities across the United States. Though most patrons who purchased resold tickets did not worry about breaking the law, there was a constant concern that scalped tickets were not legitimate. Many patrons who purchased resold tickets could not be sure that the individual they were meeting (often for the first time) in person was going to provide a valid ticket to the sport or entertainment event.

As the marketing and distribution of selling tickets became more sophisticated, so did the efforts of ticket resellers. During the 1990s, numerous ticket resellers began operating brick and mortar businesses that guaranteed their ticket sales. Patrons could have some faith that a ticket purchased through a ticket-reselling business would permit access to the desired event. Many of these businesses purchased and resold tickets before they were actually released for sale. Ticket resellers always have to monitor what tickets they have purchased and what tickets they have sold. Ticket resellers who misjudge an event's popularity can be forced to overpay for tickets to meet their obligations or can be stuck with unused tickets if demand decreases below their expectations. Perhaps the most tragic story concerning a mistake by a ticket reseller occurred in 1997, when Allen Caldwell III committed suicide after he was unable to meet his obligations to provide badges to The Masters Golf Tournament in Augusta, Georgia (Clayton, 1998).

Ticket brokers will utilize a variety of methods to acquire tickets. In some cases, they have predetermined season ticket-holders who have agreed to supply tickets. Brokers may also utilize computerized-telephone technology that repeatedly calls ticket outlets when tickets are first released. In other cases, brokers may pay people to stand in line at the facility box office or other ticket distribution points prior to tickets being sold. Since tickets have been distributed extensively on the Internet, ticket brokers have had to utilize creative methods to maximize their ticket allotment for the most popular events. Most ticket sale web sites will ask ticket purchasers to retype a distorted set of letters and numbers prior to purchasing their allotted number of tickets (typically two or four tickets for most shows). This is requested in an effort to prevent ticket brokers from using computer programs that purchase newly released tickets. Some savvy ticket brokers have hired human employees in India who type in the distorted information so that the ticket broker can maximize their ticket allotment.

Since ticket brokers will seek nearly any means to resell tickets, many teams, facilities, and ticketing companies have begun to offer their own ticket reselling services. In 2000, Major League Baseball's San Francisco Giants were the first professional sport team to began such a program for their season ticket-holders ("San Francisco Giants Launch," 2000). The "Double Play Ticket Window" provided each season-ticket-holder a password that allowed access to the system to post his or her ticket information. Potential buyers would access the web site and, if interested, contact the Giants box office by email with a credit card number. The box office would deactivate the barcode on the ticket, and a new barcode would be issued. The buyer picked up the ticket at the Giant will-call window or printed the ticket at home. The Giants realized a profit from each transaction by receiving 10% of the resale value from the ticket seller as well as 10% from the ticket buyer. The season ticket-holder was able to recapture revenue from tickets that may have gone completely unused, and the ticket buyer had access to seats that would normally not have been available for purchase.

The system utilized by the Giants generated enough positive publicity and revenue that most of the other North American professional sports franchises began to offer ticket resale options for their customers. However, each of these potential options was not without controversy. In 2002, the Chicago Cubs established Wrigley Field Premium Ticket Services (WFPTS) as a separate ticket resale agency. The Cubs, who typically sell out almost all of their games, received tremendous negative publicity when it was revealed that the Cubs sold tickets to WFPTS at face value and then WFPTS resold the tickets with a significant markup. Some fans attempted to sue the Cubs for fraud and deceptive practices, but lost in court ("Scurrilous or Savvy," 2005). Despite their victory in court, the Cubs' separate ticket brokerage attracted the attention of the other Major League Baseball (MLB) owners and the MLB Players Association. Since MLB teams share some revenues and player compensation is partially negotiated based upon potential team revenues, if a team could generate revenue outside its core organization, potential financial problems could occur.

Recognizing the proliferation of the secondary ticket market and the potential problems associated with team-operated secondary ticket services, Major League Baseball elected to utilize StubHub as its official ticket resale partner (for all teams but the Boston Red Sox) in 2008. Since being founded in 2000, StubHub has become a leader in the secondary ticket marketplace. StubHub provides a secure location where customers can buy and sell tickets to sport and entertainment events. The company usually charges a ticket seller a 15% fee and buyers a 10% fee of the ticket resale price. StubHub, acquired by EBay in 2007, has been one of the leading companies that have successfully lobbied to have many anti-scalping laws repealed. The growth of StubHub and other secondary ticket companies was certainly recognized by MLB. Kenny Gersh, senior vice president of business development for MLB Advanced Media, noted, "The secondary market is going to happen anyway, so we wanted to give fans the best experience we could" (Lee & Mohl, 2007, para. 8).

Though some sport franchises have recognized and attempted to maximize their revenues through the secondary ticket market, numerous performing artists have utilized different methods to react to potential ticket scalping. Many musicians do not want to be perceived as "gouging" the consumer, so they often instruct their managers and promoters to not price their concert tickets to meet demand. Since the demand for popular musicians can greatly exceed the supply of "underpriced" tickets, many ticket brokers will reap the profit on the ticket resale. Though the performer was trying to offer lower ticket prices to its fans, the rapidly escalating ticket prices on the secondary market still results in many fans becoming disappointed with the performer. Recently, some performers have begun to offer ticketless entry. When a ticket is purchased, a receipt is sent to a consumer's cell phone. The cell phone becomes the ticket to gain entry to an event, which (if set by the promoter to be non-transferable to another phone) restricts ticket re-sales and insures more initial ticket purchasers attend the event.

Ticketless entry was first utilized by Guns N' Roses in 2006 in London (Lister, 2006). In 2009 Miley Cyrus utilized ticketless entry after her 2008 tour resulted in numerous complaints regarding the high prices charged by ticket resellers. Though the system did help to curtail scalping since those who purchased the tickets needed to appear at the box office to show their cell phones, the Cyrus concert presented some interesting logistical issues. Though most concert attendees purchase their own tickets, the Cyrus tour attracted numerous adolescent attendees who did not have the ability to purchase their own tickets. Parents purchased tickets for their children to attend, but for the children to gain access, the parents had to appear with their cell phones at the box office ("Miley Cyrus Performs," 2009).   Since many of the parents did not attend the concert, an interesting dynamic occurred in which ticket purchasers admitted their children to the event and then left to do something else until the concert was completed. Since much of the seating was reserved, attendees who did not use a cell phone to purchase seats had to find out where their seats were located after entering the facility.

Customer Loyalty Programs

In addition to determining how and when to sell tickets, box office managers must work with the marketing department to maximize customer loyalty. It is much more difficult to sell tickets to someone who has never purchased before than it is to retain current customers. Fan loyalty programs have been in existence for several years and were originally associated with fan cards. AIM Technologies, Inc., based in Austin, Texas, claims to be the first company to create and implement the fan-card program (Schaffer, 1999). Interested fans signed up for the program by completing a short questionnaire upon entering the ballpark. On each subsequent visit the fan answered a question or two at an interactive kiosk. In return, the fan received credits toward concessions or merchandise similar to airline mileage bonuses. The responses were placed in a database where club officials might glean ticketing or marketing information, whenever necessary. The program began with two minor league baseball teams and has grown to include teams in a variety of other sports.

Fan loyalty programs have been developed to now incorporate more advanced technologies. In some cases, fan cards have been replaced with customers' cell phones. Certain teams, such as the Atlanta Hawks, have utilized cell phone technology to provide better customer service while also tracking their customers' purchasing habits. The Hawks cell phone plan enables enrolled customers to swipe their phone for access to the facility and for any concessions purchases. Transactions within the facility can be executed more quickly than if the customer utilized cash or a credit card. This helps concession lines move more efficiently, potentially leading to more sales during halftime and other breaks in the action. In addition, the Hawks can monitor the purchase behavior of their customers and note any potential changes. In addition, since the phone is utilized for every transaction, as more customers utilize the technology, the Hawks can better position personnel at specific entry points or concession areas.

Fan loyalty programs are an important component of customer relations management (CRM). The goal of any organization should be to know and understand the unique needs of each individual customer. Marketers desire to send specific messages that will elicit a favorable response. Every facility should strive to know its customers' purchase habits. Fortunately, technological advances are enabling facilities to better understand the needs of their customers. Ticketing software can now not only track purchases but also utilize analytical tools to determine what types of marketing messages would likely elicit a favorable purchase response. For example, if a customer made ticket purchases for events only on Saturdays and Sundays, the CRM ticketing software would begin to generate a profile of this person as a weekend consumer. Future weekend events could be marketed to this customer, while the marketing of future weekday events may be deemphasized or eliminated. The software may also incorporate the type of events into its analysis. A customer who purchased tickets for hockey and basketball games involving visiting teams from New York may be identified as a transplanted New York resident. The computer would not only attempt to market future sporting events involving New York teams, but other entertainment events with a New York connection or theme.

As CRM activities have become more important, a battle regarding the ownership of ticket purchase information has developed. In the case of a concert, the promoter of the band, the ticketing company, and the venue will likely desire to have access to the database that contains customer information. Certainly, each party would make an argument regarding why they should have access to the data. It is likely that ownership or access to customer data will become an even more important component of facility rental agreements in the future.

Summary

The role of the box office manager has greatly expanded in the past 30 years. In addition to staffing and supervising the box office employees, box office managers now determine potential ticketing partners, formulate pricing strategies, and investigate opportunities to increase sales through various marketing activities. Technology improvements have dramatically altered the selling and reselling of sport and entertainment tickets. Though the importance of building relationships with customers has been and always will be important, the mechanisms available to box office managers now have changed many of their approaches. Anticipating future changes will be an important skill all box office managers will need to have as they advance their careers.

Questions

1. What are the main roles of a box office manager?
2. What are some of the important considerations when designing a box office?
3. How has the Internet influenced box office operations? What changes might occur in the future?
4. What are the main types of tickets and the potential positives and negatives of each type?
5. How have barcodes on tickets changed the distribution of tickets?
6. Explain the concept and importance of elasticity of demand.
7. What is variable ticket pricing and how does it impact sport and entertainment ticketing?
8. How have teams changed their attitudes regarding scalping since 2000? What trends in this area do you see developing in the future?
9. What is CRM and why is it important for box office managers?

References

Abernethy, B. (2004, November) Worst-case scenarios. *Stadia*. Retrieved November 27, 2004, from http://www.stadia.tv/archive/user/news_article.tpl?id=20041124173315.

About us. (n.d.). Retrieved July 1, 2009, from http://www.aegworldwide.com/08_corporate/about_us.html.

Allen, L. M. (2008, June 20). The latest on plaintiff suing NASCAR for discrimination. *Sports Litigation Alert*, *5*(11), 15–16.

American College of Emergency Physicians. (2009, June). *News room: Automatic external defibrillators*. [Fact Sheet]. Retrieved from http://www.acep.org/pressroom.aspx?LinkIdentifier=id&id=26022&fid=3496&Mo=No&acepTitle=Automatic+External+Defibrillators.

American College of Sports Medicine. (1992). ACSM's *health/fitness facility standards and guidelines*. Champaign, IL: Human Kinetics.

American Heart Association. (2004). Sudden deaths from cardiac arrests—statistics. Retrieved August 1, 2008, from http://www.steelonfire.com/ems/cardiacarrest.pdf.

American Heart Association. (2008, May 28). "AED program Q & A." Retrieved August 16, 2008, from http://www.americanheart.org/presenter.jhtml?identifier=3011859.

Ammon, R., Jr. (1993). Risk and game management practices in selected municipal football facilities. (Doctoral dissertation, University of Northern Colorado, 1993). *Dissertation Abstracts International*, *54*, 3366A–3367A.

Ammon, R., Jr., & Brown, M. (2007). Risk management process. In D. J. Cotten & J. Wolohan (Eds.), *Law for recreation and sport managers* (4th ed., pp. 299–300). Dubuque, IA: Kendall/Hunt Publishing Co.

Ammon, R., Jr., & Fried, G. (1998). Assessing stadium crowd management practices and liability issues. *Journal of Convention & Exhibition Management*, *1*(2–3), 119–150.

Ammon, R., Jr., Miller, J., & Seidler, T. (2008, May). Pat-down searches: Reduction technique for terrorist threat or litigation waiting to happen? Paper presented at the North American Society of Sport Management annual conference, Toronto, Canada.

Ammon, R., Jr., Southall, R., & Blair, D. (2004). *Sport facility management: Organizing events and mitigating risks*. Morgantown, WV: Fitness Information Technology, Inc.

Ammon, R., Jr., & Unruh, N. (2007). Crowd management. In D. J. Cotten & J. Wolohan (Eds.), *Law for recreation and sport managers* (4th ed., pp. 334–344). Dubuque, IA: Kendall/Hunt Publishing Co.

Associated Press. (2005, February 2). SEC fines South Carolina for fans on court. *FindLaw*. Retrieved February 19, 2005, from http://news.findlaw.com/scripts/printer_friendly.pl?page=/ap/s/2060/2-18-2005/200502181.

Baade, R. A., & Matheson, V. (2002, September). Full of promises: Economic impacts of mega events. *Stadia*, *18*, 62–64.

Barbaro, M. (2007, June 23). A long line for a shorter wait at a supermarket. *The New York Times*. Retrieved April 28, 2009, from http://www.nytimes.com/2007/06/23/business/23checkout.html.

Barbieri, K. (2001, November 12). Aftershocks of terrorist attack still being felt in touring industry. *Amusement Business*, *113*(45), 6.

Baugus, R. V. (2003, January/February). Insurance escalates in wake of attacks. *Facility Manager*, *19*(1), 28–30.

Bearman v. University of Notre Dame, 453 N.E.2d 1196; 1983 Ind. App. LEXIS 3387

Beauchamp, N., Newman, R., Graney, M. J., & Barrett, K. (2005). Facility management. In L. P. Masteralexis, C. A. Barr, & M. A. Hums (Eds.), *Principles and practice of sport management* (2nd ed., pp. 253–271). Sudbury, MA: Jones & Bartlett.

Beer, M., Spector, B., Lawrence, P., Quinn-Mills, D., & Walton, R. (1984). *Managing human assets: The groundbreaking Harvard business school program*. New York: The Free Press.

Belson, K. (2009, May 17). Baseball tickets too much? Check back tomorrow. *The New York Times*. Retrieved May 18, 2009, from http://www.nytimes.com/2009/05/18/sports/baseball/18pricing.html.

Billing, J. (2000). Staff recruitment, selection, retention, and termination. In H. Appenzeller & G. Lewis (Eds.), *Successful sport management* (2nd ed., pp. 5–21). Durham, NC: Carolina Academic Press.

Bissonnette, Z. (2008, August 27). Alabama county mulls bankruptcy; could be largest failure in history. Retrieved September 1, 2008, from http://www.bloggingstocks.com/2008/08/27/alabama-county-mulls-bankruptcy-could-be-largest-failure-in-his/.

Blin, J. (2004, June). No money, no problem. *Venues Today*, 3(5), 18–19.

Boardman, L. (2007, November). Let's hear it for the band. *Venues Today*, 6(11), 34–35.

Bolman, L. G., & Deal, T. E. (1997). *Reframing organizations: Artistry, choice, and leadership* (2nd ed.). San Francisco: Jossey-Bass Publishers.

Brenneman, R. (2008, July 22). Judge rules for UC Berkeley in oak grove case. *The Berkeley Daily Planet*. Retrieved August 2, 2008, from http://www.berkeleydailyplanet.com/issue/2008-07-17/article/30643?headline=Judge-Rules-for-UC-Berkeley-in-Oak-Grove-Case.

Cameron, S. (2001, July 30–August 5). Traffic flow inside venue as important as outside. *Street & Smith's SportsBusiness Journal*, 4(15), 22.

Cameron, S. (2006, January). Food for thought. *Stadia*, 38, 28–30.

Carlson, R. (2008, June). Harnessing the sun. *Venues Today*, 7(6), 14–16.

Carpenter, L. J. (2000). *Legal concepts in sport: A primer* (2nd ed.). Champaign, IL: Sagamore Publishers in conjunction with AAALF.

Chelladurai, P. (2001). *Managing organizations for sport and physical activity: A systems perspective.* Scottsdale, AZ: Holcomb Hathaway, Publishers.

Chmielewski, D. C. (2009, February 11). Ticketmaster, Live Nation announce merger plan. *Los Angeles Times*. Retrieved June 14, 2009, from http://articles.latimes.com/2009/feb/11/business/fi-live-nation11.

Christenson, P., Nagel, M. S., & Taylor, K. (2008, November). *The customer experience.* Presentation at the Sport, Entertainment, and Venues Tomorrow Conference, Columbia, SC.

Clayton, W. (1998, April 7). It didn't used to be this way. Retrieved June 19, 2009, from http://sportsillustrated.cnn.com/augusta/stories/040698/tic_history.shtml.

Company history. (n.d.). Retrieved July 1, 2009, from http://www.ticketmaster.com/history/index.html.

Contemporary Services Corporation (n.d). About us. Retrieved January 11, 2006, from http://www.contemporaryservices.com/pages/about.html.

Cooking the books: Congress projects soda tax revenues to increase every year. (2009, June 4). Retrieved June 28, 2009, from http://www.kxmc.com/getArticle.asp?ArticleId=385620.

Cotten, D. J. (2007a). Defenses against liability. In D. J. Cotten & J. T. Wolohan (Eds.), *Law for recreation and sport managers* (4th ed., pp. 58–70). Dubuque, IA: Kendall/Hunt Publishing Company.

Cotten, D. J. (2007b). Immunity. In D. J. Cotten & J. T. Wolohan (Eds.), *Law for recreation and sport managers* (4th ed., pp. 71–84). Dubuque, IA: Kendall/Hunt Publishing Company.

Cotten, D. J. (2007c). Waivers and releases. In D. J. Cotten & J. T. Wolohan (Eds.), *Law for recreation and sport managers* (4th ed., pp. 85–94). Dubuque, IA: Kendall/Hunt Publishing Company.

Cotten, D. J. (2007d). Which parties are liable? In D. J. Cotten & J. T. Wolohan (Eds.), *Law for recreation and sport managers* (4th ed., pp. 46–57). Dubuque, IA: Kendall/Hunt Publishing Company.

Crockford, P. (2009, May 22). Ticketmaster/Live Nation merger: Ticketmaster's market influence extends too far. Retrieved June 13, 2009, from http://www.ticketnews.com/Ticketmaster-Live-Nation-merger-Ticketmaster-market-influence-extends-far-and-wide5092256.

Crompton, J. L. (1999). *Financing and acquiring park and recreation resources.* Champaign, IL: Human Kinetics.

Crowd disasters. (2008, June 18). *Crowd dynamics.* Retrieved July 5, 2008, from http://crowddynamics.com/.

D'Antonio, M. (2009). *Forever blue.* New York: Riverhead Books.

Deckard, L. (2005, June). Promoting good sportsmanship is an operational issue at most colleges. *Venues Today*, 4(18), 6–7.

Deckard, L. (2007, September). Green and egalitarian. *Venues Today*, 6(9), 16–19.

Dejardin, Y. (2007, March). Putting on a show: The Stade de France has become an expert organizer of specialist events. *Stadia*, 41, 66.

Dick, G. (2007, November). Green building basics. *California Integrated Waste Management Board.* Retrieved June 9, 2008, from http://www.ciwmb.ca.gov/GreenBuilding/Basics.htm.

Drucker, P. F. (1954). *The practice of management.* New York: Harper & Row.

Drucker, P. F. (1989). *The new realities: In government and politics, in economics and business, in society and world view.* New York: Harper & Row.

Durham, A. (2006, Winter). In a perfect world. The Vulnerability Self-Assessment Tool. *Facility Manager Safety: Security*, 9–10.

Emmons, N. (2004, September 22). Concession experts talk operations. *Venues Today*, 3(30), 17–19.

Equal Employment Opportunity Commission (1997). *Facts About Disability-Related Tax Provisions* [Fact sheet]. Retrieved from http://www.eeoc.gov/facts/fs-disab.html.

espn.com. (2007, October 2). Jury rules Thomas

harassed ex-executive; MSG owes her $11.6M. Retrieved August 8, 2008, from http://sports .espn.go.com/nba/news/story?id=3046010.

Estrella, C. (2005, December 16). NFL's pat-down policy challenged 49'ers season-ticket holders, ACLU sue to stop searches. *SFGate.com*. Retrieved January 20, 2006, from http://www.sf gate.com/cgi-bin/article.cgi?f=/c/a/2005/12/16/PAT.TMP.

Euro 2004 security plan unveiled. (2004, May 26). *BBC News*. Retrieved June 12, 2004, from http ://news.bbc.co.uk/go/pr/fr/-/2/hi/uk_news/374 8267.stm.

Fall, S. (2007, September/October). Going green. *Stadia*, *43*, 36–42.

Farmer, P., Mulrooney, A., & Ammon, R., Jr. (1996). *Sport facility planning and management*. Morgantown, WV: Fitness Information Technology, Inc.

Federal Emergency Management Agency (FEMA). 2002. Retrieved from http://www.fema.gov/.

Fombrun, C., Tichy, N. M., & Devanna, M. A. (1984). *Strategic human resource management*. New York: John Wiley and Sons, Inc.

Fox, D. (2007, March). Back to the future. *Stadia*, *41*, 48–52.

Garner, B. (Ed.). (2004). *Black's law dictionary* (8th ed.). St. Paul, MN: West Group.

Gaskin, L. P., & Batista, P. J. (2007). Supervision. In D. J. Cotten & J. T. Wolohan (Eds.), *Law for recreation and sport managers* (4th ed., pp. 119–132). Dubuque, IA: Kendall/Hunt Publishing Company.

Georgia Tech becomes first university to outsource ticket operations at Bobby Dodd Stadium. (2009, May 29). Retrieved June 30, 2009, from http://www.stadiatech.com/3793.

Gietschier, S. (1995, January 23). Go west, young Rams. *The Sporting News*. Retrieved June 14, 2009, from http://findarticles.com/p/articles/mi_m1208/is_n4_v219/ai_16218447.

Gokhale, J. (2008, January 11). Cato scholar comments on Moody's U.S. bond rating warning. Retrieved December 27, 2008, from http://www.cato.org/pressroom.php?display=comments &id=806.

Gordon, J. (2004, May 14). In San Francisco, the Giants went private for their stadium. Retrieved June 28, 2009, from http://news.minnesota .publicradio.org/features/2004/05/14_gordonj_ sanfranpark/.

Gotsch, N. (2004, November). Basketball brawl prompts reassessment. *Venues Today*, *3*(37), 3.

Graham, S., Neirotti, L. D., & Goldblatt, J. J. (2001). *The ultimate guide to sports marketing* (2nd ed.). New York: McGraw-Hill.

Hackney, H. (2008, December 8). Appeals court reveals $25M settlement in Aramark case. *Sport Litigation Alert*, *5*(23), 21.

Hayden v. Notre Dame 716 N.E.2d 603: 1999 Ind.App.

Henricks, M. (2007, October/November). A blueprint for building success. *Facility Manager*, *23*(5), 37–39.

Hodes, J. (2002, March 29). Buying automatic defibrillator may save financial, legal headaches. *The Business Review*. Retrieved June 28, 2002, from http://albany.bizjournals.com/albany/sto ries/2002/04/01/focus3.html.

IAAM. (n.d.). About IAAM. Retrieved June 29, 2008, from http://iaam.org/aboutiaamhistory .htm.

Iacono v. MSG Holdings, 801 N.Y.S.2d 778; 2005 N.Y. Misc.

iLogos Research. (2003). *Global 500 Website Recruiting 2003 Survey* [Dataset]. Available from iLogos Web site http://www.ilogos.com.

In Atlanta, unrest over secret school deals. (2007, October 18). Retrieved July 28, 2008, from http://foiadvocate.blogspot.com/2007/10/in-atlanta-unrest-over-secret-school.html.

Investor Words. (2009). Risk management. Retrieved June 20, 2009, from http://www.inves torwords.com/4304/risk_management.html.

James, A. (2007, March). Ice stage. *Stadia*, *41*, 55–56.

Johnston v Tampa Sports Authority, 490 F.3d 820; 2007 U.S. App. Lexis 15190.

Jones, G. R., & Wright, P. M. (1992). An economic approach to conceptualizing the utility of human resource management practices. In K. Rowland & G. Ferris (Eds.), *Research in personnel and human resource management*. Vol. 10. Greenwich, CT: JAI Press.

Judge ends Enron's stadium naming rights. (2002, April 26). Retrieved June 30, 2009, from http://www.click2houston.com/news/1420283/detail .html.

Jury awards $1.1 million to victim of car crash. (2002, March 11). *National Law Journal*, *24*(27), B2.

Katz, C. (2009, February 22). End Madison Square Garden tax breaks, sez city pol. *New York Daily News*. Retrieved June 28, 2009, from http://www .nydailynews.com/ny_local/2009/02/22/2009-02-22_end_madison_square_garden_tax_breaks_sez .html.

Kelo v. City of New London. (2005). 545 U.S. 469.

Kottke, J. (2009, May 12). The economics of the new Yankee Stadium. Retrieved May 13, 2009, from http://www.nytimes.com/2009/04/29/sports/baseball/29tickets.html.

Lamberth, C. (2008, April/May). The green game: Achieving sustainable design. *Facility Manager, 24*(2), 53.

Lee, S. Y., & Mohl, B. (2007, August 2). MLB, StubHub ink resale deal. Retrieved June 15, 2009, from http://www.boston.com/business/globe/articles/2007/08/02/mlb_stubhub_ink_resale_deal.

Legislative effort to ensure on-field safety. (2004, April). *Sport Lawyers Association Update, 4*(4), 7.

Li, M., Ammon, R., Jr., & Kanters, M. (2002, Summer). Internationalization of sport management curricula in the United States: A National Survey. *International Sports Journal, 6*(2), 178–194.

Lister, D. (2006, June 10). The week in arts. The Independent. Retrieved December 15, 2009 from http://www.independent.co.uk/opinion/columnists/david-lister/david-lister-the-week-in-arts-481753.html

Lucas, F. (2006, March 16). Eminent domain outcry pierces statehouses. Retrieved July 28, 2008. from http://www.stateline.org/live/ViewPage.action?siteNodeId=136&languageId=1&contentId=96421.

Lucas, J., Davila, A., Waninger, K., & Heller, M. (2005). Cardiac arrest on the links: Are we up to par? Availability of Automated External Defibrillators on golf courses in southeastern Pennsylvania. *Prehospital and Disaster Medicine 21*(2). 112–114. Retrieved August 1, 2008, from http://pdm.medicine.wisc.edu/21-2%20PDFs/waninger.pdf .

MacAloon J. (1984). Olympic games and the theory of spectacle in modern societies. In J. MacAloon (Ed.), *Rite, drama, festival, spectacle: Rehearsals toward a theory of cultural performance* (pp. 241–280). Philadelphia: Institute for the Study of Human Issues.

Manica, D. (2008, March/April). Whole new ball game. *Stadia, 45*, 50–54.

Marcus, M. (2009, May 26). The best way to find (and fill) a job online [Online exclusive]. Forbes.com. Retrieved June 17, 2009, from http://www.beyond.com/i/md425/media/in-the-news/the-best-way-to-find-and-fill-a-job-online.htm.

Martens, T. (2009, June 27). Report: Refunding Michael Jackson tickets to be "messy," "expensive" process. *Los Angeles Times*. Retrieved June 30, 2009, from http://latimesblogs.latimes.com/music_blog/2009/06/report-aeg-stands-to-lose-fortunes-on-michael-jackson-concerts.html.

McMillen, J. D. (2007). Game, event and sponsorship contracts. In D. J. Cotten & J. T. Wolohan (Eds.), *Law for recreation and sport managers* (4th ed., pp. 398–408). Dubuque, IA: Kendall/Hunt.

Mickle, T. (2007, September 3–9). Real Madrid, using TV tours to continue growth. *Street & Smith's SportsBusiness Journal, 10*(19), 11.

Miley Cyrus performs "ticketless" concert at Conseco. (2009, November 17). Retrieved December 15, 2009 from http://www.msnbc.msn.com/id/33981668/ns/local_news-indianapolis_in/

Miller, L. K., Stoldt, G .C., & Ayres, T. D. (2002, January). Search me: Recent events make surveillance efforts even more likely to pass judicial muster. *Athletic Business, 26*(1), 18, 20–21.

Monasso, (2007, December 17–23). Braves adding more seats for "all-you-can-eat." *Street & Smith's SportsBusiness Journal, 10*(34), 15.

Morroll, A. (2005). Refreshing solutions. *Stadia Showcase*, 72–74.

Mosier, J. (2008, February 12). Arlington increases settlement in eminent domain cases. Retrieved July 28, 2008, from http://www.dallasnews.com/sharedcontent/dws/news/localnews/cowboys stadium/stories/021308dnmetarldomain.3775641.html.

Muret, D. (2007, September 14). Nationals sign lucrative deal with Centerplate. *Washington Business Journal*. Retrieved December 30, 2007, from http://bizjournals.com/washington/stories/2007/09/17/story16.html.

Muret, D. (2008, January 21–27). Opening in '08. *Street & Smith's SportsBusiness Journal, 10*(38), 15, 18.

Muret, D. (2009a, January 19–25). Change comes to Washington as Nats switch from Centerplate. *Street & Smith's SportsBusiness Journal, 11*(37), 12.

Muret, D. (2009b, June 8–14). Serving notice. *Street & Smith's SportsBusiness Journal, 12*(8), 12–14, 17.

Nagel, M. (2000, July 31–August 6). Pac Bell technology rewrites the rules. *SportsBusiness Journal, 3*(15), 45.

Nagel, M. S. (1999). Recognition of corporate-named professional sports facilities and the implications for future sponsorship agreements. Doctoral dissertation, University of Northern Colorado.

Nagel, M. S. (2008). Standardizing customer service: A problem with concessions? *Proceedings of the Sport Marketing Association Conference*. Gold Coast, Brisbane, Australia.

Nagel, M. S., & Southall, R. M. (2007). A stadium in your front yard? Eminent domain and the potential sport marketing implications of *Kelo v City of New London*. *Sport Marketing Quarterly, 16*(3), 171–173.

National Collegiate Athletic Association. (2009). *NCAA licensing program: Frequently asked questions*. Retrieved June 26, 2009, from http://

www.ncaa.org/wps/ncaa?key=/ncaa/NCAA/Abo ut The NCAA/Corporate Relationships/Licens ing/faqs.html.

National Conference on State Legislatures. (2009, January). State laws on cardiac arrest & defibrillators. Retrieved June 30, 2009, from http://www.ncsl.org/IssuesResearch/Health/LawsonCardiacArrestandDefibrillatorsAEDs/tabid/14506/Default.aspx (Author).

National Safety Council 2002. Retrieved from http://www.nsc.org/.

NFL teams implement fan code of conduct. (2008). NFL.com. Retrieved March 25, 2009, from http://www.nfl.com/news/story?id=09000d5d809c28f9&template=without-video&confirm=true.

Nuttall, I. (2001, July). Secure all areas. *Stadia, 10,* 83–84.

NYC Council: Enough with the MSG tax break already. (2009, February 24). *Field of Schemes*. Retrieved June 28, 2009, from http://www.fieldof schemes.com/news/archives/2009/02/3549_nyc _council_eno.html.

Occupational Safety and Health Administration, Department of Labor (2007). Retrieved from http://www.osha-slc.gov/index.html.

Parks, J., Quarterman, J., & Thibault, L. (2007). Managing sport in the 21st century. In J. B. Parks, J. Quarterman, & L. Thibault (Eds.), *Contemporary sport management* (3rd ed., pp. 5–25). Champaign, IL: Human Kinetics.

Peiser, B., & Minten, J. (2003). Soccer violence. In T. Reilly & A. M. Williams (Eds.), *Science and Soccer* (pp. 230–242). New York: Routledge.

Pethokoukis, J. (2008, January 11). Live Nation to launch ticket business in '09. Retrieved June 15, 2009, from http://www.reuters.com/article/technology-media-telco-SP/idUSN1129751020080114.

Phillips, D. (2006). *An analysis of security outsourcing at NCAA D1 A and D1 AA collegiate football games*. Unpublished manuscript. The Center for Spectator Sports Security Management, Hattiesburg, MS.

Powers, R. (2006, August/September). No skidding around. *Facility Manager,* 22–26.

Red Sox fans can get logo on coffins. (2008, December 1). Retrieved June 30, 2009, from http://www.redorbit.com/news/oddities/1603491/red_sox_fans_can_get_logo_on_coffins/.

Regan, T. H. (1997). Financing facilities. In M. L. Walker & D. K. Stotlar (Eds.), *Sport facility management* (pp. 43–50). Sudbury, MA: Jones and Bartlett Publishers.

Ripley, A. (2008). *The unthinkable: Who survives when disaster strikes—and why*. New York:

Crown Publishers.

Rooney, B. (2009, February 10). Ticketmaster, Live Nation join forces. Retrieved June 14, 2009, from http://money.cnn.com/2009/02/10/news/companies/ticketmaster_live_nation/index.htm.

Saints agree to new Superdome lease. (2009, April 30). Retrieved June 28, 2009, from http://sports.espn.go.com/nfl/news/story?id=4114297.

San Francisco Giants launch Double Play Ticket Window; First-of-its-kind services enables charter seat holders to resell tickets. Retrieved June 30, 2009, from http://www.allbusiness.com/technology/software-services-applications-electronic/6460234-1.html.

Sandomir, R. (2009, April 28). Yankees slash the price of top tickets. *The New York Times*. Retrieved April 29, 2009, from http://www.nytimes.com/2009/04/29/sports/baseball/29tickets.html.

Schaffer, A. (1999, June 14). Tracking fans goes hi-tech. *Amusement Business, 111*(24), 23–24.

Scurrilous or savvy? Free market and the practice of ticket reselling. (2005, July 6). Retrieved June 15, 2009, from http://knowledge.wpcarey.asu.edu/article.cfm?articleid=1062.

Selzer, T. (2001, July/August). Safety at events: Disaster strikes again and again at football stadiums around the world, when will we learn? *Facility Manager, 17*(4), 36–44.

Sharp, L. (2007). Premises liability. In D. J. Cotten & J. T. Wolohan (Eds.), *Law for recreation and sport managers* (4th ed., pp. 193–204). Dubuque, IA: Kendall/Hunt Publishing Company.

Sharp, L. A. (1990). *Sport law*. National Organization on Legal Problems of Education. USA: Pace-Setter Graphics, Inc.

Sharp, L., Moorman, A., & Claussen, C. (2007). *Sport law: A managerial approach, Achieving a competitive advantage*. Phoenix, AZ: Holcomb-Hathaway Publishers.

Shaw, A. (2003, March). *Staff planning model*. Paper presented to Sport-Event Management (SPMG 3663), University of West Georgia, Carrollton, GA.

Sherborne, P. (2005, April 27). Crowd control legislation considered in Ohio. *Venues Today, 4*(14), 4–5.

Slack, T., & Parent, M. M. (2005). *Understanding sport organizations: The application of organization theory* (2nd ed.). Champaign, IL: Human Kinetics.

SMG at a glance. (n.d.). Retrieved July 1, 2009, from http://www.smgworld.com/worldwide_venues.aspx.

Smith, E. (2008, October 23). Ticketmaster to acquire

star power in Azoff deal. *Wall Street Journal*. Retrieved June 15, 2009, from http://online.wsj.com/article/SB122473027565161583.html.

Sparrow, P. R., & Hiltrop, J. M. (1994), *European human resource management in transition*. London: Prentice-Hall.

Staff Pro (n.d.). History. Retrieved June 21, 2008, from http://www.staffpro.com/.

State of North Dakota v. Seglen, 700 N.W.2d 702; 2005 N.D.

Stavropoulos, P. (July 23, 1999). Rush to complete new stadium blamed for deaths of three US construction workers. Retrieved February 6, 2008, from http://www.wsws.org/articles/1999/jul1999/milw-j23.shtml.

Steinbach, P. (2004, September). Drinking games. *Athletic Business 28*(9), 60–68.

Steinbach, P. (2006, January). Last call? *Athletic Business 30*(1). Retrieved June 5, 2009, from http://athleticbusiness.com/articles/article.aspx?articleid=1136&zoneid=28.

Steinbach, P. (2008, April). Ambiguous boundaries. *Athletic Business 32*(4), 94–100.

Swash, R. (2009, June 11). Ticketmaster and Live Nation merger investigated. *The Guardian*. Retrieved June 15, 2009, from http://www.guardian.co.uk/music/2009/jun/11/ticketmaster-live-nation-merger.

Talk is cheap: Latest steward communication system sets standards in crowd safety. *Stadia*, 70.

Telega v. Security Bureau, Inc., 719 A.2d 372; 1998 Pa. Super.

The Century Council. (n.d.). Drunk driving. Retrieved June 5, 2009, from http://www.centurycouncil.org/learn-the-facts/drunk-driving-research.

The Palace of Auburn Hills. (n.d.). Retrieved June 30, 2009, from http://www.checkersedan.com/resources/detroit_pistons/the_palace_of_auburn_hills.

Ticketmaster Group, Inc. (n.d.). Retrieved April 26, 2009, from http://www.fundinguniverse.com/company-histories/Ticketmaster-Group-Inc-Company-History.html.

Tierney, R. (2001, September 24). Zumwalt examines the new threat. *Amusement Business*, *113*(38), 1, 4.

Tokito, M. (2008, February 13). USC's all-cash arena. *The Oregonian*. Retrieved July 28, 2008, from Oregonlive.com.

Traiman, S. (2007, November/December). Catering. *Stadia*, 59–62.

Tucker, E. (2006, February 1). Band's tour manager strikes plea deal in fire. *USA TODAY*, p. 3A.

U.S. Department of Justice. (n.d.). *Accessible Stadiums* [fact sheet]. Retrieved from http://www.ada.gov/stadium.pdf.

United States Access Board (n.d.). *Americans with Disabilities Act Accessibility Guidelines (ADAAG) Checklist for Buildings and Facilities* [Fact sheet]. Retrieved from http://www.access-board.gov/adaag/checklist/a16.html#What%20Are%20%22Places%20of%20Public%20Accommodation.

United States Code Service. (2001). *Title 42. The public health and welfare Chapter 68. Disaster relief emergency preparedness power and duties* (42 USCS §5196, 2001). Retrieved December 27, 2001, from Lexis-Nexis Academic Universe: http://web.lexis-nexis.com/universe.

University of Texas at El Paso v. Moreno, 172 S.W.3d 281; 2005 Tex. App.

van der Smissen, B. (1990). *Legal liability and risk management for public and private entities*. Cincinnati, OH: Anderson Publishing Co.

van der Smissen, B. (2007a). Elements of negligence. In D. J. Cotten & J. T. Wolohan (Eds.), *Law for recreation and sport managers* (4th ed., pp. 36–45). Dubuque, IA: Kendall/Hunt Publishing Company.

van der Smissen, B. (2007b). Human resource law. In D. J. Cotten & J. T. Wolohan (Eds.), *Law for recreation and sport managers* (4th ed., pp. 156–168). Dubuque, IA: Kendall/Hunt Publishing Company.

Venue list. (n.d.). Retrieved July 1, 2009, from http://media.eventbooking.com/57957_st.pdf.

Verni v. Harry M Stevens, 903 A.2d 475; 2006 N.J. Super. LEXIS 229.

Welcome to Global Spectrum. (n.d.). Retrieved July 1, 2009, from http://www.global-spectrum.com/default.asp?lnopt=-1&sn1opt=1&sn2opt=1&month=7&year=2009&newsID=0.

Wong, G. M. (2002). *Essentials of sports law* (3rd ed.). Westport, CT: Praeger.

Wong, G. M., & Masteralexis, L. P. (1999). Legal principles applied to sport management. In L. P. Masteralexis, C. A. Barr, & M. A. Hums (Eds.), *Principles and practice of sport management* (pp. 97–116). Gaithersburg, MD: Aspen Publishers.

Wyman, B. (2009, February 10). Azoff kicks it old school. Retrieved April 12, 2009, from http://www.hitsville.org/2009/02/10/irving-azoff-kicks-it-old-school/.

Zeithaml, V. A., Bitner, M. J., & Gremler, D. D. (2006). *Services marketing* (4th ed.). Boston: McGraw-Hill.

About the Authors

Robin Ammon, Jr., EdD, is a full professor and Chair of the Sport Management Department at Slippery Rock University in Slippery Rock, Pennsylvania. He recieved his doctorate in sport administration from the University of Northern Colorado and his areas of research include: legal liabilities in sport, risk management in sport and athletics, and premises liability. At SRU, he teaches undergraduate and graduate courses in risk management in sport facilities and events, sport law, event and facility management, and senior seminar. Dr. Ammon has written extensively with over a dozen articles in refereed journals, nine chapters in sport management books, and two textbooks. He has presented over 50 times at local, regional, national, and international conferences on a variety of topics including facility, legal, crowd management, and security issues. The past nine years have seen Dr. Ammon accompany sport management students to Spain, Italy, Ireland, Costa Rica, England, France, and Germany to visit sport facilities. Before entering the academic arena, he was involved in intercollegiate athletics for 10 years as a coach and administrator. In addition he has been associated with special events as a practitioner since 1976. Dr. Ammon has worked for himself and for two national crowd management companies (Contemporary Services Corporation & Landmark Event Staff Services) as a supervisor, manager, and consultant. This experience has included various Super Bowls, collegiate athletic events, and hundreds of concerts all across North America. Recently, Dr. Ammon has served as an "expert witness" in various court cases regarding several of these issues. In 2002, Dr. Ammon was elected as the 17th President of the North American Society for Sport Management (NASSM). In 2009 he was selected as a highly skilled trainer for the delivery of the Department of Homeland Security (DHS) Risk Management Training for Sports Event Security Management. This entails developing highly effective security management systems for sport events held at national intercollegiate football stadiums.

Richard M. Southall, EdD, is an assistant professor of sport administration and coordinator of the Graduate Sport Administration Program at the University of North Carolina at Chapel Hill. He is also director of the College Sport Research Institute (CSRI) at the University of North Carolina at Chapel Hill.

He received his doctorate in sport administration from the University of Northern Colorado in 2001. His undergraduate degree (B.A., summa cum laude) from Western State College of Colorado included concentrated coursework in English, history, and philosophy. Dr. Southall's areas of professional expertise include sport marketing, legal, social, political, and ethical issues in college sport, and sport facility and event management. He is a former president of the *Sport and Recreation Law Association* (2004–2005).

Dr. Southall has authored/co-authored 24 peer-reviewed articles dealing with such issues as NCAA's institutional logics, university policy responses to criminal behavior by college athletes, legal and marketing implications of National Football League ticket transfer policies, academic fraud scandals in college sport, and organizational culture dynamics in college athletic departments. He has authored/co-authored seven chapters in edited books and contributed to more than 30 technical/research reports. In addition, he has given over 80 presentations (both refereed and invited) at national and international academic conferences.

Mark S. Nagel, EdD, is an associate professor in the Department of Sport and Entertainment Management at the University of South Carolina. He received his BA from the University of San Francisco (1995), his MA from St. Mary's College (1997), and his doctorate from the University of Northern Colorado (1999). Prior to his work at USC, he was the director of the graduate sport management program at Georgia State University. At Georgia State he was responsible for all aspects of the sport management program including recruiting and advising students, developing and scheduling courses, identifying and supervising adjunct faculty, and maintaining alumni and sport business relationships. Dr. Nagel has also previously worked as a sport management professor at the University of West Georgia and San Jose State University. He currently serves as an adjunct faculty member at the University of San Francisco and St. Mary's College, where he teaches summer courses in sport administration. Before pursuing a career in academe, Dr. Nagel worked in a variety of areas of sport management—primarily in athletic coaching and administration as well as campus recreation. During his years as an assistant coach of the women's basketball team at the University of San Francisco, he helped lead the team to three NCAA Tournament appearances and a spot in the 1996 Sweet 16.

Dr. Nagel has authored or co-authored numerous articles in refereed journals such as the *Journal of Sport Management, Sport Marketing Quarterly, Entertainment and Sport Law Journal, International Journal of Sport Finance*, and *Sport Management Review*. He has published extensively in professional journals as well as written numerous academic book chapters and given dozens of research presentations. He has also served as treasurer for the North American Society for Sport Management and the Sport and Recreation Law Association.

Index

unilateral contract, 112
unitary demand, 235
University of Phoenix Stadium, 7
University of Texas at El Paso v. Moreno, 159
user agreements, 114–119
  examples of, 115–118
  key elements of, 114
user fees, 73
ushers, 173
utilities, 75

V
value menus, 222–223
variable ticket pricing (VTP), 237–238
Verni v. Harry M. Stevens, 205
Veterans Stadium, 168
violence in sport, 5–6
volume purchasing, 215
volunteer immunity statutes, 144
Vulnerability Self-Assessment Tool (ViSAT),
  169

W
Wachovia Center, 71
waivers, 130, 145–146
  elements necessary to be enforceable, 146
Washington Nationals Park, 4, 213
Wembley Stadium, 8, 218
Wilcox, Mary Rose, 62
Wrigley Field, 7, 168
Wrigley Field Premium Ticket Services
  (WFPTS), 243

Z
zoning, 57
Zumwalt, Damon, 164